AAT

Technician

NVQ Level 4

Unit 14

Cash Management and Credit Control

TEXTBOOK

0955/J99

British Library Cataloguing-in-Publication Data

A catalogue record for this book is available from the British Library.

Published by AT Foulks Lynch Ltd
Number 4
The Griffin Centre
Staines Road
Feltham
Middlesex
TW14 0HS

ISBN 0 7483 4095 5

Acknowledgements

We are grateful to the Association of Accounting Technicians, the Association of Chartered Certified Accountants, the Chartered Institute of Management Accountants and the Institute of Chartered Accountants in England and Wales for permission to reproduce past examination questions. The answers have been prepared by AT Foulks Lynch Ltd. The copyright to the questions remains with the examining body.

CONTENTS

PREFACE - USING THIS TEXTBOOK

This is the 1999 edition of the AAT NVQ textbook for Unit 14.

The text has been written to cover the syllabus in great detail and adopts a brick-building style, building up the knowledge or practical skills required in a carefully constructed manner. Thus at the start of each chapter we identify the underpinning knowledge and understanding or performance criteria covered in that chapter and then list the main topics covered to show how the subject matter is built up.

Our texts are, however, very different from a more traditional style text book. The texts are written in a way that will help you assimilate the information easily and give you plenty of practice at the various techniques involved. The Units require a very practical approach to the various topics and these texts use many simulations and practical examples to illustrate precisely how the various techniques work.

Particular attention has been paid to producing an interactive text that will maintain your interest with a series of carefully designed features.

- **Activities**. The text involves you in the learning process with a series of activities designed to arrest your attention and make you concentrate and respond.

- **Definitions**. The text clearly defines key words or concepts. The purpose of including these definitions is **not** that you should learn them - rote learning is not required and is positively harmful. The definitions are included to focus your attention on the point being covered.

- **Conclusions**. Where helpful, the text includes conclusions that summarise important points as you read through the chapter rather than leaving the conclusion to the chapter end. The purpose of this is to summarise concisely the key material that has just been covered so that you can constantly monitor your understanding of the material as you read it.

- **Step-by-step illustrations.** Where appropriate, we illustrate topics using a step-by-step technique that explains how each part of an operation or answer is performed in a logical way.

Complementary workbook

There is a complementary workbook that is designed to be used with this textbook which contains numerous practice questions and simulations which reflect and simulate the workplace environment. These workbooks also contain practice devolved assessments which will prepare you for the assessment procedures that are part of your course.

College Kits

In addition to the Textbooks and Workbooks for each Unit, AT Foulks Lynch offers colleges adopting our material the very popular 'College Kits'.

The College Kits for units with a Central Assessment contain much more additional Devolved and Central Assessment material in looseleaf form which can be photocopied to provide practice classwork for students, and much of this additional Central Assessment material is taken from the AAT's own Central Assessments. The Kits also contain the looseleaf answers to the class examples from the Workbooks.

These Kits are supplied at no extra cost and may be photocopied under the limited licence which is granted to adopting colleges.

SYLLABUS

UNIT 14 OPERATING A CASH MANAGEMENT AND CREDIT CONTROL SYSTEM

UNIT COMMENTARY

What is the unit about?

This unit is concerned with the management of cash and credit. The unit involves the management of cash balances as well as the granting of credit and the collection of outstanding debts.

Elements contained within this unit are:

ELEMENT: 14.1 MONITOR AND CONTROL CASH RECEIPTS AND PAYMENTS
ELEMENT: 14.2 MANAGE CASH BALANCES
ELEMENT: 14.3 GRANT CREDIT
ELEMENT: 14.4 MONITOR AND CONTROL THE COLLECTION OF DEBTS

Content	*Chapter where covered in this text*
KNOWLEDGE AND UNDERSTANDING	
The Business Environment	
• A clear understanding of the main types of cash receipts and payments; capital receipts and payments; drawings/dividends and disbursements; exceptional receipts and payments (Element 14.1)	2
• The basic structure of the banking system and the money market in the UK. The relationships between financial institutions (Element 14.2)	4, 6
• An understanding of bank overdrafts and loans; terms and conditions; legal relationship between bank and customer (Element 14.2)	5, 7
• Types of marketable security (Bills of exchange, certificates of deposit, government securities, local authority short term loans); terms and conditions; risks (element 14.2)	7, 8
• A basic understanding of Government monetary policies (Element 14.2)	4
• Legal issues: basic contract; terms and conditions of contracts relating to the granting of credit; Data Protection Act and credit control information (Element 14.3)	9, 10
• Sources of credit status information (Element 14.3)	10
• External sources of information: banks, credit agencies and official publications (Element 14.3)	10
• Legal issues: remedies for breach of contract (Element 14.4)	9
• Legal and administrative procedures for the collection of debts (Element 14.4)	11
• The effect of bankruptcy and insolvency on organisations (Element 14.4)	11
Accounting Techniques:	
• Form and structure of cash budgets (Element 14.1)	2
• Lagged receipts and payments (Element 14.1)	2
• Basic statistical techniques for estimating future trends: moving averages, allowance for inflation (Element 14.1)	3
• Computer models to assess the sensitivity of elements in the cash budget to change (eg, price, wage rate changes) (Element 14.1)	2
• Managing risk and exposure (Element 14.2)	8
• Discounts for prompt payment (Element 14.3)	7
• Interpretation and use of credit control information (Element 14.3 & 14.4)	10, 11
• Methods of collection (Element 14.4)	11
• Factoring arrangements (Element 14.4)	7
• Debt insurance (Element 14.4)	11
• Methods of analysing information on debtors: age analysis of debtors; average periods of credit given and received; incidence of bad and doubtful debts (Element 14.4)	11
• Evaluation of different collection methods (Element 14.4)	11

Content	*Chapter where covered in this text*
Accounting Principles and Theory:	
• Cash flow accounting and its relationship to accounting for income and expenditure (Element 14.1)	1, 2
• Liquidity management (Elements 14.2, 14.3 & 14.4)	1, 2, 6, 7, 8
The Organisation:	
• Understanding that the accounting systems of an organisation are affected by its organisational structure, its administrative systems and procedures and the nature of its business transactions (Elements 14.1, 14.2, 14.3 & 14.4)	Throughout
• Understanding that recording and accounting practices may vary in different parts of the organisation (Elements 14.1 & 14.4)	Throughout
• An understanding that practice in this area will be determined by an organisation's specific financial regulations, guidelines and security procedures (Element 14.2)	Throughout
• An understanding that in public sector organisations there are statutory and other regulations relating to the management of cash balances (Element 14.2)	Throughout
• Understanding that practice in this area will be determined by an organisation's credit control policies and procedures (Element 14.3)	10
• An understanding of the organisation's relevant policies and procedures (Elements 14.1, 14.3 & 14.4)	Throughout

UNIT 14: OPERATING A CASH MANAGEMENT AND CREDIT CONTROL SYSTEM

Element 14.1: **Monitor and control cash receipts and payments**

Performance criteria

Content		*Chapter where covered in this text*
i	Cash receipts and payments are monitored and controlled against budgeted cash flow	1, 2
ii	Appropriate staff are consulted to determine the likely pattern of cash flows over the accounting period and to anticipate any exceptional receipts or payments	2
iii	Forecasts of future cash payments and receipts are in accord with known income and expenditure trends	2, 3
iv	Cash budgets are prepared in the approved format and clearly indicate net cash requirements	2
v	Significant deviations from the cash budget are identified and corrective action is taken within defined organisational policies	2

Range Statement

1 **Cash flows to be monitored:** regular revenue receipts and payments; capital receipts and payments; drawings or dividends and disbursements; exceptional receipts and payments

Evidence Requirements

- Competence must be demonstrated consistently, over an appropriate timescale with evidence of performance being provided of different types of cash flow being monitored and controlled

Sources of Evidence (these are examples of sources of evidence, but candidates and assessors may be able to identify other, appropriate sources)

- ***Observed performance,*** eg,
  - Action taken when cash budget reveals problem
  - Meetings relating to the cash budget control
  - Phone calls relating to the cash budget control
- ***Work produced by candidate,*** eg,
  - Cash budget documentation
  - Cash flow statements
  - Variance reports
  - Correspondence relating to the monitoring and control cash budgets
  - Fixed asset registers
  - Investment registers
- ***Authenticated testimonies from relevant witnesses***
- ***Personal accounts of competence,*** eg,
  - Report of performance
- ***Other sources of evidence to prove competence or knowledge and understanding where it is not apparent from performance eg,***
  - Reports and working papers
  - Performance in independent assessment
  - Performance in simulation
  - Responses to verbal questioning

UNIT 14: OPERATING A CASH MANAGEMENT AND CREDIT CONTROL SYSTEM

Element 14.2: Manage cash balances

Performance criteria

	Content	*Chapter where covered in this text*
i	Overdraft and loan facilities are arranged in anticipation of requirements and on the most favourable terms available	6, 7
ii	Surplus funds are invested in marketable securities within defined financial authorisation limits	6, 8
iii	The organisation's financial regulations and security procedures are observed	6, 7
iv	Account is taken of trends in the economic and financial environment in managing cash balances	4, 8
v	An adequate level of liquidity is maintained in line with cash forecasts	1, 8

Range Statement

1 **Marketable securities:** bills of exchange; certificates of deposit; government securities; local authority short term loans

Evidence Requirements

- Competence must be demonstrated consistently, over an appropriate timescale with evidence of performance being provided of overdraft and loan facilities being arranged

Sources of Evidence (these are examples of sources of evidence, but candidates and assessors may be able to identify other, appropriate sources)

- ***Observed performance eg,***
  - Presentations made to colleagues relating to the management of cash balances
  - Discussions and meetings with colleagues relating to the management of cash balances
  - Action taken when cash budget reveals problem

- ***Work produced by candidate eg,***
  - Reports containing investment recommendations
  - Correspondence relating to the management of cash flow balances

- ***Authenticated testimonies from relevant witnesses***

- ***Personal accounts of competence eg,***
  - Report of performance

- ***Other sources of evidence to prove competence or knowledge and understanding where it is not apparent from performance eg,***
  - Reports and working papers
  - Performance in independent assessment
  - Performance in simulation
  - Responses to verbal questioning

UNIT 14: OPERATING A CASH MANAGEMENT AND CREDIT CONTROL SYSTEM

Element 14.3: Grant credit

Performance criteria

Content		*Chapter where covered in this text*
i	Credit terms are agreed with customers in accordance with the organisation's policies	10
ii	Internal and external sources of information are identified and used to evaluate the current credit status of customers and potential customers	10
iii	New accounts are opened for those customers with an established credit status	10
iv	The reasons for refusing credit are discussed with customers in a tactful manner	10

Range Statement

1 **Internal information derived from:** analysis of the accounts; colleagues in regular contact with current or potential customers or clients

2 **External information derived from:** credit rating agencies; supplier references; bank references

Evidence Requirements

- Competence must be demonstrated consistently, over an appropriate timescale with evidence of performance being provided of credit being discussed and granted to customers

Sources of Evidence (these are examples of sources of evidence, but candidates and assessors may be able to identify other, appropriate sources)

- ***Observed performance eg,***
  - Meetings with customers relating to the granting of credit
  - Phone calls relating to the granting of credit
  - Meetings with Banks and other agencies relating to the granting of customer credit

- ***Work produced by candidate eg,***
  - Correspondence relating to the granting of customer credit
  - Research into potential customer credit history
  - Aged debtors lists
  - Minutes of internal and external meetings relating to the granting of credit
  - Correspondence relating to the evaluation of customer credit status and granting/rejection of customer credit

- ***Authenticated testimonies from relevant witnesses***

- ***Personal accounts of competence eg,***
  - Report of performance

- ***Other sources of evidence to prove competence or knowledge and understanding where it is not apparent from performance eg,***
  - Performance in simulation
  - Responses to verbal questioning

UNIT 14: OPERATING A CASH MANAGEMENT AND CREDIT CONTROL SYSTEM

Element 14.4: Monitor and control the collection of debts

Performance criteria

	Content	*Chapter where covered in this text*
i	Information relating to the current state of debtors' accounts is regularly monitored and appropriate action taken	11
ii	Information regarding significant outstanding accounts and potential bad debts is promptly sent to relevant individuals within the organisation	11
iii	Discussions and negotiations with debtors are conducted courteously and achieve the desired outcome	10, 11
iv	Debt recovery methods used are appropriate to the circumstances of individual cases and are in accordance with the organisation's procedures	11
v	Recommendations to write off bad and doubtful debts are based on a realistic analysis of all known factors	11

Range Statement

1 **Information on debtors:** age analysis of debtors; average periods of credit given and received; incidence of bad and doubtful debts

2 **Appropriate Action:** information and recommendations for action passed to appropriate individual within own organisation; debtor contacted and arrangements made for the recovery of the debt

---

Evidence Requirements

- Competence must be demonstrated consistently, over an appropriate timescale with evidence of performance being provided of discussions and negotiations being undertaken with debtors and recommendations for action being made to own organisation

---

Sources of Evidence (these are examples of sources of evidence, but candidates and assessors may be able to identify other, appropriate sources)

- ***Observed performance eg,***
  - Discussions/meetings with debtors
  - Discussions/meetings with internal departments relating to debt recovery strategies
  - Discussions/ meetings with outside agencies
- ***Work produced by candidate eg,***
  - Inter company memos
  - Reports relating to debts and debtors
  - Minutes of meetings relating to debts and debtors
  - Correspondence relating to debts and debtors
  - Bad debt w/o transfer journals
  - Preparation of court proceedings
- ***Authenticated testimonies from relevant witnesses***
- ***Personal accounts of competence eg,***
  - Report of performance
- ***Other sources of evidence to prove competence or knowledge and understanding where it is not apparent from performance eg,***
  - Performance in independent assessment
  - Performance in simulation
  - Responses to verbal questioning

1 CASH AND CASHFLOW

PATHFINDER INTRODUCTION

This chapter covers the following performance criteria and knowledge and understanding.

- Cash flow accounting and its relationship to accounting for income and expenditure (Element 14.1)
- Liquidity management (Elements 14.2, 14.3, 14.4)
- Cash receipts and payments are monitored and controlled against budgeted cash flow (Element 14.1)
- Appropriate staff are consulted to determine the likely patterns of cash flows over the accounting period and to anticipate any exceptional receipts or payments. (Element 14.1)
- An adequate level of liquidity is maintained in line with cash forecasts (Element 14.1)

Putting the chapter in context – learning objectives.

In this chapter we will consider the role of cash in a business and the importance of cash control to the success of a business. Much of this material is dealt with in more detail later in this text, so this chapter's objective is to provide a background for studying these items in more detail later.

At the end of this chapter you should have learned (in overview) the following topics.

- Definitions of cash, cashflow and funds
- The importance of cash flow management in company survival
- The importance of cash flow management for sustainable growth
- Cashflow patterns for different organisations
- The cashflow information provided by the operating cycle
- The relationships between cash and accruals accounting, and between cashflow and profit
- Cash handling procedures
- Centralised cash control
- The role of the treasury in cash management
- Sources and applications of funds
- Investment management principles

1 DEFINE CASH, CASHFLOW AND FUNDS

1.1 Cash

Definition Cash obviously comprises coins and bank notes, but it also includes balances on current accounts held with banks, building societies and similar institutions. The inclusion of current account balances as cash is because of the availability of immediate access to such funds.

1.2 Cashflow

Definition Cashflow is the continuous movement of cash in the organisation as a result of receipts and payments occurring due to transactions of the business. Receipts are described as cash inflows whereas payments are described as cash outflows.

1.3 Funds

Definition Funds is used to refer to monetary resources in a wider context than cash described above. Funds includes cash, but also includes other items readily convertible into cash such as notice accounts held with banks and building societies.

2 CASHFLOW MANAGEMENT, LIQUIDITY AND COMPANY SURVIVAL

2.1 Cashflow management

The management of an organisation's cashflow may be analysed into the control of its inflows (receipts) and outflows (payments).

Cash inflows are received from customers to whom goods or services have been supplied. These supplies may have been paid for immediately (cash transactions) or they may be paid for some weeks or months after the supplies were provided (credit transactions). It is these credit transactions which require control by management.

Cash outflows are payments made to suppliers for goods or services supplied to the business, and payments made to employees in the form of wages. There are also payments made to the government in the form of taxes and to the owners of the business. Some of these payments are made immediately whereas others are made after a period of credit.

Cashflow management is concerned with balancing the timing of receipts and payments and ensuring that receipts and payments in respect of credit transactions are made in accordance with the terms agreed.

2.2 Liquidity

Liquidity is a wider term than cash or funds. It is usually used to refer to the organisation's working capital.

Definition Working capital is the difference between an organisation's current assets and current liabilities (amounts due to be paid to creditors within one year).

Definition Current assets are assets which are expected to be converted into cash within twelve months. Current assets include stocks, debtors, bank balances and cash in hand.

It is important for an organisation to have sufficient liquidity to be able to meet its debts as they fall due. Careful management of cashflow should ensure that such liquidity is achieved.

2.3 Activity

Exe Ltd has the following assets and liabilities at 31 December 1997:

	£
Stocks	4,200
Motor vehicle	5,800
Debtors	1,200
Bank	3,900
Cash in hand	1,250
Creditors due within 30 days	2,150
Creditor due April 1998	600

Calculate the value of Exe Ltd's working capital at 31 December 1997.

2.4 Activity solution

The motor vehicle is not a current asset and should be ignored, all other items are relevant to the calculation:

	£	£
Current assets:		
Stocks	4,200	
Debtors	1,200	
Bank	3,900	
Cash in hand	1,250	10,550
Current liabilities:		
Creditors due within 30 days	2,150	
Creditor due April 1998	600	(2,750)
Working capital		7,800

2.5 Company survival

The survival of a company over the longer term requires that it is profitable, but in the short-term cashflow is more important than profit. In the short-term a lack of cash which results in non-payment of a supplier could result in legal action by the supplier which closes down the company. As the following example shows, a lack of cash does not also mean a lack of profit.

2.6 Example

In September 1997 Peter entered into a contract whereby he would repair electrical equipment which failed within a warranty period. He would invoice the manufacturer as follows:

Labour	-	£25 per hour
Materials	-	cost + 40%

Peter would receive payment against an invoice, payment to be made by the manufacturer 60 days after the invoice date.

Peter pays wages of £10 per hour, paying his employees at the end of each week. Materials are paid for one month after receipt from the supplier.

The following details relate to October, November and December 1997:

	October £	*November* £	*December* £
Wages cost	400	500	700
Material cost	600	800	1,000
Sales invoiced	1,840	2,370	3,150

As we can see the contract is obviously profitable, the sales invoice values are much more than the costs; but let's consider the cashflow:

	October £	*November* £	*December* £
Receipts:			
Sales invoiced	Nil	Nil	1,840
Payments:			
Wages cost	400	500	700
Material cost	Nil	600	800
	400	1,100	1,500
Surplus/(Deficit) c/f	(400)	(1,500)	(1,160)

As you can see Peter has to be able to fund the wage costs and material costs for the first two months before any money is received from the manufacturer for the work done.

3 THE IMPORTANCE OF CASHFLOW FOR SUSTAINABLE GROWTH

3.1 Introduction

A business grows by increasing the amount of equipment, number of employees, sales outlets and other similar items. Each of these requires an investment of funds in the business.

Cashflow is essential to provide funds which can be invested in the business to provide for its growth in the longer term.

The sources of funds which are appropriate for long-term growth are considered later.

Conclusion

- Liquidity describes items other than simply cash
- Working capital is the difference between current assets and current liabilities
- Short-term survival requires a positive cashflow
- Cashflow and profits are not the same
- Cashflow management should ensure survival and promote growth

4 CASHFLOW PATTERNS FOR DIFFERENT ORGANISATIONS

4.1 Introduction

The flow of cash within organisations can be very different due to the nature of their activities. Three different organisations will now be compared to illustrate the differences in cash flow which might occur.

4.2 Retail shops

A retailer will normally buy items for resale on credit terms which may vary from 30-60 days, however most of its sales (sometimes all of its sales) will be paid in cash or by using credit cards (for which funds are received within 3-4 days).

This means that goods will often be sold and the money received from the customer before the supplier is paid for the goods.

4.3 Hat manufacturer

The business of a hat manufacturer is seasonal, with most of their sales occurring in the springtime. However production will occur throughout the year, and thus costs arise at a fairly constant rate throughout the year. Most sales will be on 60 days credit, whereas purchases will often be on 30 days credit.

4.4 Training college

Most training colleges receive their income in full at the commencement of the course, with costs being incurred as the course is provided.

4.5 Example

The following example profit and cashflow statements illustrate the situations described above for each of these organisations:

Profit statement
6 months to 31 March 1998

	Retail shop £	*Hat manufacturer* £	*Training college* £
Sales	500,000	200,000	70,000
Purchases	440,000	200,000	5,000
Stock adjustment	(5,000)	(50,000)	-
Wage costs	25,000	10,000	30,000
Overhead costs	15,000	15,000	10,000
Profit/loss	25,000	25,000	25,000

Cashflow statement
6 months to 31 March 1998

	Retail shop £	*Hat manufacturer* £	*Training college* £
Receipts from customers	500,000	160,000	140,000
Payments for:			
Wages	23,000	9,000	28,000
Purchases	375,000	180,000	4,500
Overhead costs	14,000	14,000	9,500
Surplus/(Deficit)	88,000	(43,000)	98,000

As can be seen from the above example although all three types of business have the same profit of £25,000 they have different cashflow.

5 CASHFLOW INFORMATION

5.1 Cashflow and the operating cycle

Earlier in this chapter cashflow was described as the effects of cash inflows and cash outflows, but the control of cashflow requires information concerning the working capital of the business.

Definition The operating cycle is the term used to describe the link between working capital and the flow of cash into and out from a business.

A diagram can be used to illustrate the operating cycle:

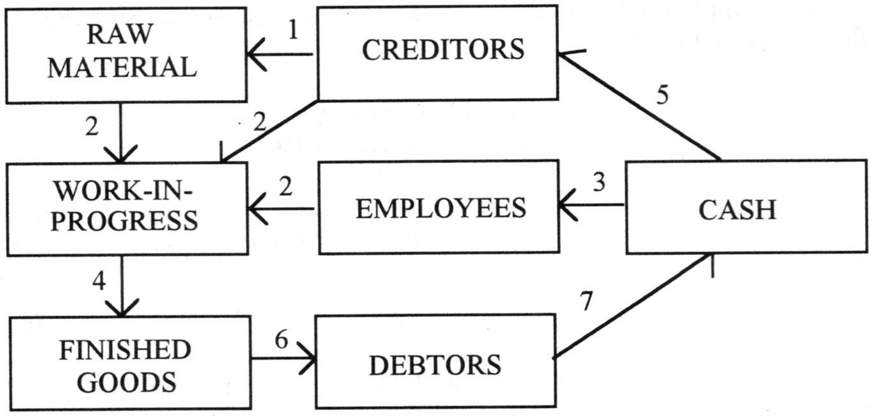

1 Raw materials are bought on credit from suppliers, who are creditors of the business until they are paid.

2 Raw materials are issued to production and the process of converting them into the finished product begins by the actions of employees using equipment which incurs overhead costs (incurred on credit).

3 Employees are paid wages, usually on a weekly or monthly basis.

4 The production process is complete, the goods are finished and ready for sale.

5 The suppliers of the raw materials and overhead costs are paid.

6 The finished goods are sold to customers (often on credit). Customers become debtors until they have paid for the goods.

7 Payment is received from customers for their goods.

5.2 The length of the operating cycle

The length of the operating cycle is usually measured in days, though it could be measured in weeks or months.

The length of the operating cycle will vary between businesses depending on the period of credit received from suppliers and given to customers.

5.3 Example

Suppose an organisation buys its raw materials on credit from suppliers who give 30 days credit. Materials are held in stock for an average of 5 days before being issued to production.

The production process takes 12 days to convert the raw materials into finished goods, which are sold to customers on average 3 days after completion.

Customers take an average of 45 days to pay for the goods.

The length of the cash cycle is 35 days, calculated as follows:

	Days
Raw material stocks held	5
Production process	12
Finished goods stock held	3
Customer payment period	45
	65
Supplier credit period	(30)
Operating cycle	35

5.4 Cashflow reporting

The reporting of cashflow on a regular basis is an essential control mechanism. As has already been stated earlier in this text the survival of the business depends on its ability to generate cashflow rather than profit, especially in the short-term.

By measuring the cash inflows and outflows and managing each element of working capital (stocks, debtors and creditors as well as cash and bank balances), managers can ensure that action is taken to control cashflow as appropriate.

Conclusion

- Different businesses have different cashflow cycles
- The cashflow cycle shows the relationship between the elements of working capital and cash inflows and outflows
- The length of the cashflow cycle can be measured taking account of the stockholding periods and credit periods applicable to creditors and debtors
- Cashflow reporting is an essential part of management reporting to ensure short-term survival.

6 CASH ACCOUNTING AND ACCRUALS ACCOUNTING

6.1 Cash accounting

This is a system of accounting for costs and income on the basis of payments and receipts. This is not generally accepted as good accounting practice because businesses enter into transactions which are legally enforceable prior to the exchange of cash. Thus the use of cash accounting does not reflect the transactions which have taken place. Instead a system of accruals accounting is used.

6.2 Accruals accounting

This is the system of accounting which reports each transaction in the period in which it takes place, even if the cashflow of the transaction occurs in a different period.

Definition The accruals concept is defined in SSAP 2 as follows:

'Revenues and costs are accrued (that is, recognised as they are earned or incurred, not as money is received or paid), matched with one another so far as their relationship can be established or justifiably assumed, and dealt with in the profit and loss account of the period to which they relate'.

Accruals accounting is recognised in company legislation, and is the form of accounting required for external financial reporting.

6.3 Cashflow management

The management of cashflow considers cash inflows and outflows. It is not concerned with when the transaction took place, only with the timing of the cashflow it creates. For cashflow management and control, cash accounting is appropriate.

7 CASHFLOW AND PROFIT

7.1 Introduction

Earlier in this chapter we considered three different organisations and showed how the profit/loss was different from the cashflow of the businesses. This is because of the cashflow cycle and because the accruals principle is used when preparing profit statements.

7.2 Reconciling profits and cashflow

The profit statements and cashflow statements of the retail shop, hat manufacturer and training college shown earlier in this text are reproduced below:

Profit statement
6 months to 31 March 1998

	Retail shop £	*Hat manufacturer* £	*Training college* £
Sales	500,000	200,000	70,000
Purchases	440,000	200,000	5,000
Stock adjustment	(5,000)	(50,000)	-
Wage costs	25,000	10,000	30,000
Overhead costs	15,000	15,000	10,000
Profit/loss	25,000	25,000	25,000

Cashflow statement
6 months to 31 March 1998

	Retail shop	*Hat manufacturer*	*Training college*
	£	£	£
Receipts from customers	500,000	160,000	140,000
Payments for:			
Wages	23,000	9,000	28,000
Purchases	375,000	180,000	4,500
Overhead costs	14,000	14,000	9,500
Surplus/(Deficit)	88,000	(43,000)	98,000

We will now show (by reconciliation) why the profit/loss and cashflow values differ:

	Retail shop	*Hat manufacturer*	*Training college*
	£	£	£
Profit/(loss)	25,000	25,000	25,000
Increase in stocks	(5,000)	(50,000)	-
Increase in debtors	-	(40,000)	-
Increase in creditors:			
Purchases	65,000	20,000	500
Wage costs	2,000	1,000	2,000
Overhead costs	1,000	1,000	500
Increase in advance sales receipts	-	-	70,000
Cashflow	88,000	(43,000)	98,000

7.3 Activity

Exe plc has prepared a summary profit and loss statement and receipts and payments summary for its year ended 31 December 1997. These statements are reproduced below:

Profit and loss statement

	£	£
Sales		100,000
Cost of sales:		
Opening stocks	20,000	
Purchases	75,000	
	95,000	
Closing stocks	(42,000)	53,000
Gross profit		47,000
Wages costs	22,000	
Overhead costs	13,000	35,000
Net profit		12,000

Receipts and payments summary

	£		£
Receipts		Payments	
Customer payments	76,000	Creditors for purchases	62,000
		Wage payments	21,000
		Creditors for overhead	10,000
	76,000		93,000

Prepare a statement which reconciles the profit to the cashflow for the year.

7.4 Activity solution

		£
Net profit for the year		12,000
Increase in debtors		(24,000)
Increase in stocks		(22,000)
		(34,000)
Increase in creditors:		
Purchases	13,000	
Wages	1,000	
Overhead costs	3,000	17,000
Decrease in cash (£76,000 – £93,000)		(17,000)

8 CASH HANDLING PROCEDURES

8.1 Introduction

Much is said about the move towards 'a cashless society'. However, for the time being and many years to come businesses will have to handle case in the form of coins, notes and cheques.

8.2 Decisions which have to be made relating to the handling of cash involve:

(a) **Authority**, in terms of:

(i) who has the keys for the safe?
(ii) who has the duplicate keys for the safe?
(iii) who pays-in at the bank?
(iv) who signs cheques for payments?
(v) who countersigns cheques?
(vi) who decides when to pay a debt?
(vii) who distributes/makes-up wage packets?
(viii) who sorts out cash floats and petty-cash floats?

(b) **Systems**. Cash handling procedures will involve setting up sound and effective recording systems eg, cash books, receipt summaries, payment schedules etc, to track and record what is happening to the cash and bank balances.

(c) **Documentation**. This could involve using receipts which are issued for cash received, and receipts on which cash floats handed out to various personnel are signed for. Authorisations should be signed by a responsible official eg, to make certain payments above a specified amount. The aim is to ensure that all cash coming in or going out is accounted for and supported by documentary evidence.

(d) **Reconciliation**. This will form part of the internal control system ie, where work carried out by one person is independently checked by another person. The aim is to prevent and detect errors and fraud. In addition to the checks which are carried out in passing an invoice for payment which were mentioned in Chapter 8, it may also be possible to prove the cash balances via a reconciliation. This would take into account the opening balance, plus cash received less the cash paid out.

There are also bank reconciliations.

Another reconciliation to prove the cash sales figure could be prepared which takes account of stocks, purchases, and the average mark up.

(e) **Control accounts**. These provide an arithmetic check on the cash balances.

(f) **Audit**. It may also be possible to get the cash handling systems vetted, tested and reviewed by both internal and external auditors. They could also carry out random cash counts which act as a moral deterrent and help prevent fraud.

(g) **The imprest system**. This system is used for petty cash. The **imprest** is simply the balance which is available for use at the start of the period. If a company spends say, £120 petty cash in a period, the book plus vouchers would be checked and then £120 paid out of the main cash balance to the petty cashier. This £120 would make the amount in the petty cash equal to the imprest ie, the starting balance figure, which is the same for each period until management decide otherwise.

9 CENTRALISED CASH CONTROL

9.1 Introduction

Cash has to be managed and controlled so as to avoid errors and fraud.

There are definite advantages of having cash control centralised.

9.2 The advantages claimed for centralised cash control

(a) **The employment of specialist staff**. Staff who are more experienced and more highly qualified can be employed. This would tend not to be the case with a decentralised system.

(b) **Security**. Security in terms of who has the authority to handle cash, record cash, access the safe, pay-in at the bank, write cheques etc can be more tightly controlled. It should also be easier to afford better safes and cash handling equipment.

(c) **Recording**. Having just one major cash handling department ought to make the recording aspects easier and more accurate.

(d) **Control**. The verification of balances should also be easier to carry out. This could save both time and money.

9.3 Petty cash

Even when there is centralised cash control most organisations would also have a number of petty cash floats.

9.4 The treasury department

Centralised cash control may be operated within the treasury department, introduced in the next section.

10 THE TREASURY FUNCTION

10.1 Treasurership

Definition The function concerned with the provision and use of finance. It includes provision of capital, short-term borrowing, foreign currency management, banking, collections and money market investment.

10.2 The importance of cash within a business

The term 'treasurer', and therefore 'treasurership department', is an old one that has been resurrected in a modern context. This modern term is an import from the USA and essentially covers the following activities:

(a) Banking and exchange;
(b) Cash and currency management;
(c) Investment in short term assets;
(d) Risk and insurance; and
(e) Raising finance.

These roles have always existed, but the modern concept is to bring them all together and combine them under a corporate treasurer. All the areas above are concerned with managing the liquidity of a business. As previously discussed, a business must maintain an inflow of cash in order to survive and a further inflow of funds if it is to expand. Cash can be regarded as equally as important as profits. Certainly the business must be profitable in its existing and prospective activities, but the profitability objectives can only be achieved within the constraints imposed by funding requirements.

The functions and procedures of the treasury department are examined in greater detail in a later chapter.

11 SOURCES AND APPLICATION OF FINANCE

11.1 Sources of finance

One of the functions of the treasury department is the raising of finance, both short and long term.

There are many different sources of finances which are available to organisations. These may be grouped according to their timescale or whether they confer rights of ownership on the finance provider.

The following chart shows the types of finance available:

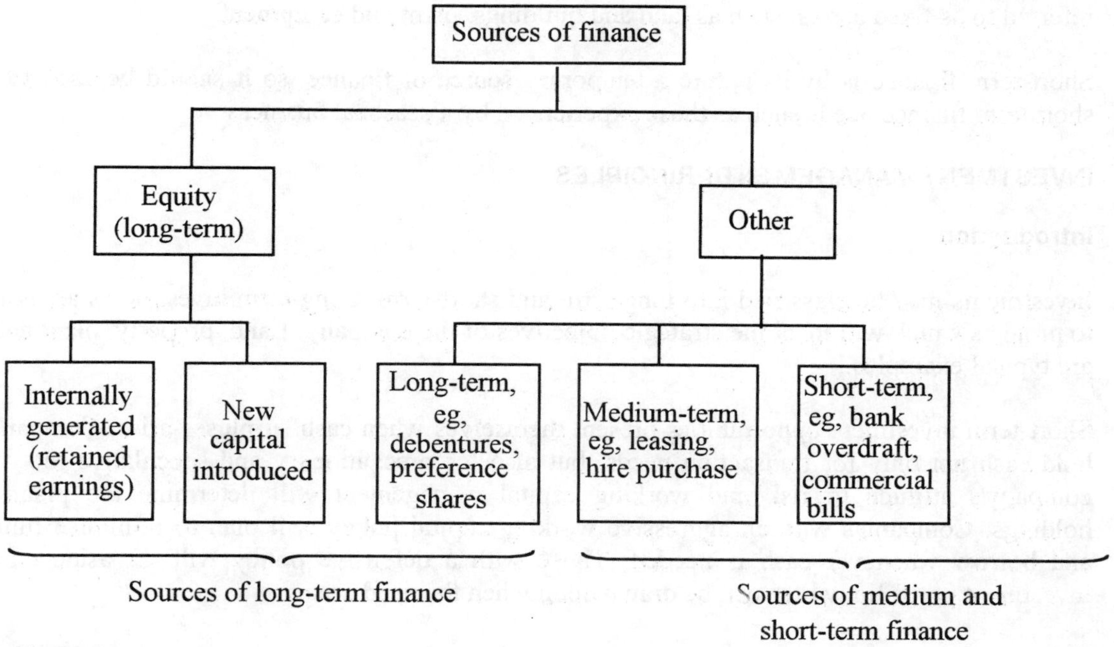

11.2 Equity finance

Equity is the term used to describe shareholders' funds (ie, the funds provided by the owners of the business).

As can be seen from the chart these are a long-term (ie, permanent) source of funds for the organisation.

Equity finance can be generated internally in the form of profits which are retained in the business rather than withdrawn by the owners, or they may be new amounts of finance introduced by the existing owners or by others who become owners as a result of their introduction of finance.

In limited companies these new amounts of finance are in the form of new issues of ordinary shares.

11.3 Other finance

These are sources of finance which are provided other than by the owners of the business. As can be seen by the chart these may be grouped according to their respective time spans.

For smaller businesses, most of the other finance provided will be obtained from high street lenders such as banks in the form of loans and overdrafts.

Conclusion

- There are many sources of finance available to businesses
- Sources of finance may be categorised as to whether they confer rights of ownership (equity finance) or not (other finance)
- Sources of finance may be categorised according to time span.

We are principally concerned with short term finance in this Unit; sources of such finance will be looked at in more detail later in this text.

11.4 Application of finances

The term 'Application of finances' is used to describe how the finances obtained are used within the business.

Typically long-term sources of finance are used to acquire long-term assets, more commonly referred to as fixed assets, such as land and buildings, plant and equipment.

Short-term finance is by its nature a temporary source of finance, so it should be used to finance short term finance needs such as those experienced by a seasonal business.

12 INVESTMENT MANAGEMENT PRINCIPLES

12.1 Introduction

Investments may be classified into long-term and short-term. Long-term investments are committed to projects which will meet the strategic objectives of the company. Land, property, plant and shares are typical examples.

Short-term investment opportunities present themselves when cash surpluses arise. Companies may hold cash not only for transaction needs, but also for precautionary and speculative motives. The company's attitude to risk and working capital management will determine the planned cash holdings. Companies with an aggressive working capital policy will plan to minimise funds held, and borrow whenever cash is needed. Those with a defensive policy will set aside cash in an investment portfolio, which can be drawn upon when the need arises.

This section introduces the basic principles of cash surplus short term investment; which is explored further in a later chapter.

12.2 Investing surplus cash

In this section surplus cash is defined as liquid balances held by a business which are neither needed to finance current business operations nor held permanently for short-term investment. Their availability is temporary, awaiting employment either in existing operations or in new investment opportunities (whether already identified or not).

The 'temporary' period can be of any duration from one day to the indefinite future date at which the new investment opportunity may be identified and seized.

The significance of this concept of balances held temporarily for conversion to other, more important business uses is the absolute priority which must be given to the avoidance of risk over maximising returns. The usual principle of finding the optimal mix between risk and return does not apply here because the investment is secondary and incidental to the ultimate business use of the asset, not an end in itself.

12.3 How does surplus cash arise?

Broadly, surplus cash can become available in the following ways:

(a) Overfunding;
(b) A reduction in operating or other assets;
(c) A surplus of retained earnings over the increase in net assets employed;
(d) Improved credit control;
(e) The sale of surplus fixed assets or surplus obsolete stocks;
(f) The nature of the business eg, journal subscriptions received by the publisher of the journal.

Overfunding can be deliberate or unintended. For example if a company finds its market growing, its fixed assets and working capital should also be growing over the years, and it may from time to time fund this growth of assets from share or long-term debt issues. If the company deliberately funds more than its current short-term debt so as to make the issue a worthwhile sum, then it will have surplus cash until the growth of its net operating assets catches up with its long-term funding.

A reduction in net operating assets occurs annually in all seasonal trades, or more irregularly where a trade runs into a more serious decline or indeed where the company deliberately reduces its working capital by improved efficiency or by a financial device such as factoring its receivables.

These are just a few illustrations of how surplus cash can become available.

A common problem is the build-up of surplus funds in an overseas subsidiary where local tax or exchange control regulations make the remittance of these funds to other parts of the group either illegal or uneconomic. Very often these problems are aggravated by economic or regulatory barriers to expansion projects which would absorb the funds. If no cure is visible, the cash may be outside the above definition of surplus cash.

12.4 Objectives in the investment of surplus cash

The objectives can be categorised as follows:

(a) Liquidity: the cash must be available for use when needed.

(b) Safety: no risk of loss must be taken.

(c) Profitability: subject to the liquidity and safety objectives mentioned above, the aim is to earn the highest possible after tax returns.

Each of these objectives raises problems which will be explored in a later chapter.

13 CHAPTER SUMMARY

In this chapter we have considered the importance of cashflow to a business and explained the principal reasons for differences between cashflow and profit.

We have also looked briefly at various aspects of cash management, including the role and functions of the the treasury department.

14 SELF TEST QUESTIONS

14.1 Define cash (1.1)

14.2 Define cashflow (1.2)

14.3 Define funds (1.3)

14.4 State the main purpose of cashflow management (2.1)

14.5 Define working capital (2.2)

14.6 Define current liabilities (2.2)

14.7 Define current assets (2.2)

14.8 Explain 'the operating cycle' (5.1)

14.9 Explain 'cash accounting' (6.1)

14.10 Explain 'accruals accounting' (6.2)

14.11 Explain why cashflow does not usually equal profits (7.2)

14.12 Explain 'equity finance' (11.2)

14.13 Explain 'application of finances' (11.4)

2 CASH BUDGETS

PATHFINDER INTRODUCTION

This chapter covers the following performance criteria and knowledge and understanding.

- A clear understanding of the main types of cash receipts and payments; regular revenue receipts and payments; capital receipts and payments; drawings/dividends and disbursements; exceptional receipts and payments (Element 14.1)
- Form and structure of cash budgets (Element 14.1)
- Lagged receipts and payments (Element 14.1)
- Computer models to assess the sensitivity of elements in the cash budget to change (eg, price, wage rate changes (Element 14.1)
- Cash flow accounting and its relationship to accounting for income and expenditure (Element 14.1)
- Liquidity management (Elements 14.2, 14.3, 14.4)
- Cash receipts and payments are monitored and controlled against budgeted cash flow (Element 14.1)
- Appropriate staff are consulted to determine the likely pattern of cash flows over the accounting period and to anticipate any exceptional receipts or payments (Element 14.1)
- Forecasts of future cash payments and receipts are in accord with known income and expenditure trends (Element 14.1)
- Cash budgets are prepared in the approved format and clearly indicate net cash requirements (Element 14.1)
- Significant deviations from the cash budget are identified and corrective action is taken within defined organisational policies. (Element 14.1)

Putting the chapter in context – learning objectives.

The previous chapter discussed the importance of cash management to the survival and growth of a business. One of the most important tools used in this area is the cash budget, or forecast. This can be used both to **plan** (for efficient and appropriate use of surpluses identified, and cost effective borrowing where required) and **control** (by the regular comparison of actual and budget cash flows).

This chapter considers the preparation and uses of the different types of cash budgets that may be required, and their reconciliation to budgeted profit and loss figures. The control aspect of cash budgets is also examined, and the use of computer software in both budget preparation and sensitivity analysis.

The planning functions of the cash forecast (investment of cash surpluses and raising of finance) will be considered in detail in later chapters.

At the end of this chapter you should have learned the following topics.

- The objectives of cash budget
- Preparation of a receipts and payments forecast
- How a projected change in cash balance can be reconciled to budgeted profits
- The purpose of a cleared funds forecast
- How the the working capital cycle can be used in balance sheet forecasts
- How cash flows are monitored using the cash budget
- The use of computer models to assess the sensitivity of elements in the cash budget for change

1 INTRODUCTION

1.1 Objectives of a cash budget

Definition A cash budget is a detailed forecast of cash inflows and outflows for a future time period, incorporating both revenue and capital items.

The objectives of a cash budget are to:

- anticipate cash shortages/surpluses and allow time to make plans for dealing with them
- provide a basis against which actual cashflow can be monitored.

1.2 Shortages

If a shortage of cash is forecast it will need to be funded. This can be achieved in a number of ways:

(a) by selling any short-term investments to release cash;

(b) by delaying payments to suppliers and/or increasing efforts to collect money due from customers;

(c) by borrowing in the forms of a loan or overdraft. The type of borrowing will be dependent upon the nature of the shortage; if it is a short-term problem an overdraft facility is usually preferable because interest is only charged to the extent that the facility is used. In comparison interest is charged on the full amount of any loan provided, whether it is used or not.

1.3 Surpluses

If a surplus is forecast it is important that it is used to earn income. This is done by investing it. Such investments are usually short-term, awaiting the accumulation of sufficient funds to make capital purchases to increase the size of the firm. Nevertheless, the interest earned on such short-term investments can be significant.

1.4 Contingencies

Receipts and payments forecasts are based on certain assumptions concerning the future, therefore they cannot be expected to be perfectly accurate. This is why organisations need to have a contingency which can be drawn upon if required, particularly when an unexpected cash shortage occurs. The size and form of such a contingency varies between organisations; it may be an overdraft facility or the permanent existence of short-term investments.

2 TYPES OF CASH BUDGET

2.1 Introduction

The AAT refer to two different types of cash budget (or forecast) in their guidance notes:

(a) receipts and payments forecasts;
(b) balance sheet forecasts.

2.2 Receipts and payments forecast

This is a forecast of cash inflows and outflows based on predicted sales and costs, and the timings of cashflows arising from these items. These forecasts are usually analysed into individual time periods which may be weeks, months or quarters.

The preparation of these forecasts is dealt with in detail below.

2.3 Balance sheet forecasts

This is a forecast derived from predictions of future balance sheets. Predictions are made of all items excepting cash, which is then derived as a balancing figure.

The preparation of these forecasts is also dealt with in detail below.

3 RECEIPTS AND PAYMENTS FORECASTS

3.1 Preparing receipts and payments forecasts

(a) Forecast sales.
(b) Forecast time-lag on converting debtors to cash, and hence cash receipts.
(c) Determine stock levels, and hence purchase requirements.
(d) Forecast time-lag on paying suppliers, and thus cash payments.
(e) Incorporate other cash payments and receipts, including such items as capital expenditure and tax payments.
(f) Collate this information so as to find the net cash flows.

3.2 Layout of a receipts and payments forecast

A tabular layout should be used with columns for the time periods (weeks, months, quarters) and rows for the receipts and payments.

3.3 Example

(a) **Revenue budget (ie, trading and profit and loss account)**

Six months to 31 December (all revenue/costs accrue evenly over the six months):

	£'000	£'000
Sales (cash received one month in arrears)		1,200
Cost of sales:		
Paid one month in arrear	900	
Paid in month of purchase	144	
Depreciation	72	
		1,116
Budgeted profit		84

(b) **Capital budget**

	£'000	£'000
Payments for new plant:		
July	12	
August	25	
September	13	
November	50	
		100
Increase in stocks, payable August		20
		120
Receipts: New issue of share capital (October)		30

(c) **Balance sheet**

	Actual 1 July £'000
Assets side:	
Fixed assets	720
Stocks	100
Debtors	210
Cash	40
	1,070
Liabilities side:	
Capital and reserves	856
Taxation (payable December)	30
Creditors - trade	160
Dividends (payable August)	24
	1,070

Prepare a cash budget for the six months to 31 December.

3.4 Solution

Cash budget for six months to 31 December

	Jul £'000	*Aug* £'000	*Sep* £'000	*Oct* £'000	*Nov* £'000	*Dec* £'000	*Total* £'000
Receipts:							
Sales	210	200	200	200	200	200	1,210
New issue of share capital	-	-	-	30	-	-	30
Payments:							
Exps & purchases	160	150	150	150	150	150	910
Exps & purchases	24	24	24	24	24	24	144
Plant	12	25	13	-	50	-	100
Stock	-	20	-	-	-	-	20
Tax	-	-	-	-	-	30	30
Dividends	-	24	-	-	-	-	24
	196	243	187	174	224	204	1,228
Surplus/(deficiency)	14	(43)	13	56	(24)	(4)	12
Opening balance	40	54	11	24	80	56	40
Closing balance	54	11	24	80	56	52	52

3.5 Reconciliation of profit and cashflow

The cash budget prepared above shows that the balance at bank has increased from £40,000 at the beginning of July to £52,000 at the end of December, an increase of £12,000. During the same period the revenue budget shows a profit of £84,000. Why is there a difference of £72,000?

There are two broad categories of causes of difference between profits and cashflow:

- items which are **not** included in both budgets; and
- differences in timing which affect profit/cashflow comparisons over a specific period.

Examples of items which do not appear in both budgets include:

- payments for new plant;
- receipts from the issue of share capital;
- payments of dividends; and
- payments of taxation.

These are not included in the statement of budgeted profit.

In addition, depreciation does not appear in the cash budget, it is a cost which reflects a cashflow which occurred in the past when the asset was acquired.

Examples of timing differences include changes in the levels of:

- stocks;
- debtors; and
- creditors

during the period.

We will now explain the difference of £72,000 referred to earlier, but first we need to calculate the changes in the levels of stocks, debtors, and creditors.

(a) **Stock**

There is a stock increase of £20,000 in August shown in the capital budget.

(b) **Debtors**

	£'000
The opening debtors (per balance sheet - 1 July)	210
Sales are paid one month in arrear so closing debtors at 31 December equal December sales	200
A reduction of	10

(c) **Creditors**

	£'000
The opening creditors (per balance sheet 1 July)	160
Closing creditors represent December cost of sales paid one month in arrears	150
A reduction of	10

(d) **The reconciliation**

	£'000	£'000	£'000
Profit as per revenue budget			84
Add: Non-cashflow item: Depreciation			72
			156
Adjust for timing differences:			
Increase in level of stock		(20)	
Decrease in level of debtors		10	
Decrease in level of creditors		(10)	
			(20)
			136
Adjust for cashflow not affecting profit:			
Receipts: New share capital		30	
Payments: Plant	(100)		
Taxation	(30)		
Dividends	(24)		
		(154)	
			(124)
Increase in cash balance			12

3.6 More involved cash flow workings

The above example had relatively simple workings for cash flows, being used principally to illustrate the layout of a cash budget and how it relates to profit. Other examples will need more thought in arriving at cash receipts from debtors, payments to suppliers etc, particularly when sales and purchases do not arise evenly over the period.

The following activities give you a chance to practise these skills before we work through a comprehensive example.

3.7 Activity

The budgeted sales for an organisation are as follows:

	Jan	*Feb*	*March*	*April*
	£	£	£	£
Sales	600	800	400	500

These are all sales on credit and debtors tend to pay in the following pattern.

	%
In month of sale	10
In month after sale	40
Two months after sale	45

The organisation expects a bad debt rate of 5%

What are the budgeted cash receipts from debtors in April?

3.8 Activity solution

	£
April sales 10% × 500	50
March sales 40% × 400	160
February sales 45% × 800	360
	570

3.9 Activity

You are given the following budgeted information about an organisation.

	Jan	*Feb*	*March*
Opening stock in units	100	150	120
Closing stock in units	150	120	180
Sales in units	400	450	420

The cost of materials is £2 per unit and 40% of purchases are for cash whilst 60% are on credit and are paid two months after the purchase. What are the payments in March for purchases?

3.10 Activity solution

Purchases in units	*Jan*	*Feb*	*March*
Sales	400	450	420
Less: Opening stock	(100)	(150)	(120)
Add: Closing stock	150	120	180
Production in units	450	420	480
	£	£	£
Purchases	900	840	960

Payment in March

	£
March purchases (960 × 40%)	384
January purchases (900 × 60%)	540
	924

3.11 A comprehensive example

The following budgeted profit and loss account has been prepared for Q plc for the four months January to April 1999:

	January £'000	*February* £'000	*March* £'000	*April* £'000
Sales	60	50	70	60
Production cost	50	55	32.5	50
Stock adjustment	(5)	(17.5)	20	(5)
Cost of sales	45	37.5	52.5	45
Gross profit	15	12.5	17.5	15
Admin/selling overhead	8	7.5	8.5	8
Net profit before interest	7	5	9	7

The working papers provide the following additional information:

(i) 40% of the production cost relates to direct materials. Materials are bought in the month prior to the month in which they are used, and 50% of them are paid for in the month of purchase. The remainder are paid for one month later.

(ii) 30% of the production cost relates to direct labour which is paid for when it is used.

(iii) The remainder of the production cost is production overhead. £5,000 per month is a fixed cost which includes £3,000 depreciation. Fixed production overhead costs are paid monthly in arrears. The variable production overhead is paid 40% in the month of usage and the balance one month later.

(iv) The administration and selling costs are paid quarterly in advance on 1 January, 1 April, 1 July and 1 October. The amount payable is £15,000 per quarter.

(v) Creditors on 1 January 1999 are expected to be:

Direct materials	£10,000
Production overheads	£11,000

(vi) The amounts expected to be received from customers during January to March are:

	£
January	69,600
February	56,944
March	56,470

(vii) The company intends to purchase capital equipment costing £30,000 in February which will be payable in March.

(viii) The bank balance on 1 January 1999 is expected to be £5,000 overdrawn. The bank balance on 1 December 1998 is expected to be £5,000 (positive).

(ix) Interest is payable/receivable on average monthly bank balances $\left(\frac{\text{opening + closing}}{2}\right)$ at the following rates:

Positive balances	interest receivable	1% per month
Overdrawn balances	interest payable	2% per month

Interest is payable/receivable in the following month.

Requirements:

(a) Prepare a cash budget for each of the months January to March 1999 for Q plc, showing clearly the bank balance at the beginning and end of each month.

(b) Explain how cash budgets are used in both feed-forward and feedback control mechanisms. Use your answer to (a) above to assist in your explanation.

3.11 Solution

(a)

	Jan	*Feb*	*Mar*
Receipts			
Sales	69,600	56,944	56,470
Interest (W2)			37
	69,600	56,944	56,507
Payments			
Capital			30,000
Admin and selling	15,000		
Labour (W1)	15,000	16,500	8,750
Overhead (W1)	15,000	12,600	10,800
Materials (W1)	21,000	17,500	16,500
		64	
	66,000c	46,664c	67,050c
Surplus / (Deficit)	3,600c	10,280c	(10,543)c
Balance b/fwd	(5,000)	(1,400)	8,880
Balance c/fwd	(1,400)	8,880	(1,663)

(b) Feed forward is the comparison of a budget with an objective to see if the proposed course of action achieves the objective set. If it does not then consideration can be given to changing the proposed course of action.

Feedback control is the comparison of a budget with the actual results to see if the target has been achieved.

Thus a cash budget can be used initially as part of a feed forward control system, and then once it has been agreed and thus become the target to be achieved, it is used as part of a feedback control system when it is compared with actual results.

W1 Production Cost

		January £	*February* £	*March* £	*April* £
Total		50,000	55,000	32,500	50,000
Materials 40% of total		20,000	22,000	13,000	20,000
50%		50% 50%	50% 50%	50% 50%	50%
	Paid Dec	Paid Jan	Paid Feb	Paid March	Paid April
	10,000	10,000	11,000	6,500	
		11,000	6,500	10,000	
		21,000	17,500	16,500	
Labour 30% of total		15,000	16,500	9,750	
		Paid Jan	Paid Feb	Paid Mar	
Production overhead (remainder = 30%)		15,000	16,500	9,750	
Fixed		(5,000)	(5,000)	(5,000)	
		10,000	11,500	4,750	
Creditor	40%	60%	40% 60%	40%	
		Paid Jan	Paid Feb	Paid March	
		4,000	6,000	6,900	
b/fwd (per question)		11,000	4,600	1,900	
Fixed payable (5,000 – 3,000 depreciation)		2,000	2,000	2,000	
		17,000	12,600	10,800	

W2 Interest:

February: $\left(\dfrac{(5{,}000) + (1{,}400)}{2}\right) \times 2\% = 64$ payable in February

March: $\left(\dfrac{(1{,}400) + 8{,}880}{2}\right) \times 1\% = 37$ receivable in March

3.12 Cash budgets and payment decisions

This unit is concerned with cash **management**; you must therefore be prepared to tackle an element of decision making in the process of preparing a forecast.

This may involve a requirement to hold a minimum cash balance or to remain within an overdraft limit, and the opportunity to take discounts from suppliers. The following example illustrates this possible scenario.

3.13 Example

At the end of December the management accountant has in front of him the company's budgeted profit and loss account figures for each of the months from the following January to June. The July and August budgets follow the same pattern as that for June. The budgets can be summarised as follows:

	January	*February*	*March*	*April*	*May*	*June*
Sales quantity	2,500	2,500	3,500	5,000	7,500	4,000
Production quantity	3,000	3,500	4,500	5,000	5,000	4,000
	£	£	£	£	£	£
Sales revenue	30,000	30,000	42,000	60,000	90,000	48,000
Factory cost of production	28,500	33,250	42,750	47,500	47,500	38,000
Stock adjustment	(4,750)	(9,500)	(9,500)		23,750	
Cost of goods sold	23,750	23,750	33,250	47,500	71,250	38,000
Selling and distribution costs	2,250	2,250	2,350	2,500	2,750	2,400
Administration costs	3,000	3,000	3,000	3,000	3,000	3,000
Profit	1,000	1,000	3,400	7,000	13,000	4,600
	30,000	30,000	42,000	60,000	90,000	48,000

The budgeted factory fixed overhead for the year is £140,000 and this is absorbed into the factory cost of production at the rate of £3.50 per unit. £32,000 of this overhead is depreciation of machinery and buildings, the remainder arises evenly throughout the year and is paid as it arises. Month end balances representing budgeted under or over absorbed overhead are carried forward and for the year as a whole the budgeted overhead is fully absorbed by the budgeted production. One quarter of the variable factory cost of production is direct material cost and the balance is predominantly manufacturing labour and similar services that are paid for as they arise. The planned direct material purchases of one month are determined by the planned production of the subsequent month. Suppliers are normally paid 30 days after the receipt of goods but it is possible to delay payment in some cases for another month. This course of action is only resorted to sparingly as the company does not wish to spoil its credit standing. 20% of the purchases attract a 5% discount for prompt (ie, immediate) settlement. 75% of customers settle their accounts in the month following the sale, 20% take another month's credit and the remaining 5% pay in the third month following the sale.

The company normally pays an interim dividend at the end of June and it is anticipated that the net payment to be made in the forthcoming June will be £30,000.

You are required to prepare the company's cash budget for the months of April, May and June assuming that the cash balance at the start of April is estimated at £5,000 and the company's policy is to maintain a month end cash balance no lower than £4,000 and no higher than £10,000. Surplus cash can be invested on a short term basis at 10% pa interest. No recognition has been given in the budgeted profit and loss accounts to any discount receivable or short term loan interest.

3.14 Solution

Cash budget

	April	*May*	*June*
Receipts			
Sales (W1)	39,000	54,900	81,600
	39,000	54,900	81,600
Payments			
Labour (W2)	22,500	22,500	18,000
Fixed overhead (W6)	9,000	9,000	9,000
Selling	2,500	2,750	2,400
Admin	3,000	3,000	3,000
Dividend			30,000
Suppliers (W7)	3,000	11,565	5,940
Investment (W8)		85	13,260
	40,000	48,900	81,600
Surplus/deficit	(1,000)	6,000	-
Bal b/f	5,000	4,000	10,000
Bal c/f	4,000	10,000	10,000

(W1)

Receipts

Month of sale

Received	*Jan*	*Feb*	*Mar*	*Apr*	*May*	*Total*
April	1,500	6,000	31,500	-	-	39,000
May		1,500	8,400	45,000	-	54,900
June			2,100	12,000	67,500	81,600

By way of illustration the entries relating to March sales are calculated as follows:

Total sales value = £42,000:

75%	is paid one month after the sale (ie, April)	=	£31,500
20%	is paid two months after the sale (ie, May)	=	£8,400
5%	is paid three months after the sale (ie, June)	=	£2,100

(W2)

	Jan	*Feb*	*Mar*	*Apr*	*May*	*June*
Production cost	28,500	33,250	42,750	47,500	47,500	38,000
Fixed (W3)	(10,500)	(12,250)	(15,750)	(17,500)	(17,500)	(14,000)
Variable	18,000	21,000	27,000	30,000	30,000	24,000
Materials (W4)	4,500	5,250	6,750	7,500	7,500	6,000
Other ie, labour	13,500	15,750	20,250	22,500	22,500	18,000

	Feb	*Mar*	*Apr*	*May*	*Jun*
Materials					
- discount available (W5)	1,050	1,350	1,500	1,500	1,200
- no discount	4,200	5,400	6,000	6,000	4,800

(W3)

Production quantity × Fixed Overhead Absorption rate of £3.50/unit.

(W4)

Materials are 25% of the variable cost.

(W5)

20% of the material costs relate to goods purchased from suppliers who offer a 5% discount for immediate settlement.

(W6)

Fixed overhead excluding depreciation (because it is not a cashflow item) is £140,000 - £32,000 = £108,000. This arises evenly and is therefore £108,000/12 = £9,000 per month.

(W7)

Supplier payments

April payment = May usage, received in April paid after discount = £1,425. April usage, received in March paid under normal terms = £1,575 (balance of cash available). Creditor c/fwd of £6,000 - £1,575 = £4,425 must be paid in May.

May payment	=	b/f	4,425
		May usage	6,000
		June usage at discount	1,140
			11,565
June payment	=	July usage at discount	1,140
		June usage	4,800
			5,940

(W8)

These are balancing entries.

Conclusion Receipts and payments forecasts are derived from a detailed analysis of income and costs and the expected timing of cashflows arising from those transactions.

4 SHORT-TERM FORECASTS

4.1 Introduction

The receipts and payments forecast illustrated above is suitable for medium-term planning and control purposes, but where management wish to control cashflow on a daily basis it is necessary to control cleared funds.

4.2 Cleared funds

Definition Cleared funds are those which are available for the organisation to spend immediately.

The amount of cleared funds is always likely to be different from the balance shown in the accounting records, as the banking system usually requires three working days for funds to become cleared. Monies received from overseas may take much longer.

4.3 Forecasting cleared funds

Large companies often plan and monitor their cashflow on a daily basis in order to maximise any interest receivable / minimise any interest payable. This is often part of the treasury function of a business and requires the use of cleared funds.

To forecast cleared funds judgement is needed as to the extent of any time delays which will occur between receipt and presentation of cheques received and issued together with an understanding of the bank clearing system. This is discussed further in a later chapter.

5 BALANCE SHEET FORECAST

5.1 Preparing a balance sheet forecast

This technique requires each element of the balance sheet except cash to be forecast; typically this may require forecasts of:

- changes to fixed assets (acquisitions and disposals)
- stock levels
- debtor levels
- creditor levels
- changes to share capital and other long-term funding (ie, debentures)
- changes to retained profits.

5.2 Example

Zed plc has the following balance sheet at 30th June 1998:

	£	£	£
Fixed assets			
Plant and machinery			192,000
Current assets			
Stock		16,000	
Debtors		80,000	
Bank		2,000	
		98,000	
Current liabilities			
Creditors	10,000		
Dividend	30,000	(40,000)	
			58,000
			250,000
Issued share capital			216,000
Retained profits			34,000
			250,000

(a) The company expects to acquire further plant and machinery costing £8,000 during the year to 30 June 1999.

(b) The levels of stocks and debtors are expected to increase by 5% and 10% respectively by 30 June 1999 due to business growth.

(c) Creditors and dividend liabilities are expected to be the same at 30 June 1999.

(d) No share issue is planned, and retained profits for the year to 30 June 1999 are expected to be £42,000.

(e) Plant and machinery is depreciated on a reducing balance basis at the rate of 20% per annum for all assets held at the balance sheet date.

5.3 Solution

	£	£	£
Fixed assets			
Plant and machinery [(192,000 + 8,000) × 80%]			160,000
Current assets			
Stock [16,000 × 105%]		16,800	
Debtors [80,000 × 110%]		88,000	
Bank (balancing figure)		67,200	
		172,000	
Current liabilities			
Creditors	10,000		
Dividend	30,000	(40,000)	
			132,000
			292,000
Issued share capital			216,000
Retained profits			76,000
			292,000

It can be seen that the forecast is that the bank balance will increase by £65,200 (ie, £67,200 - £2,000). This can be reconciled as follows:

		£
Retained profit		42,000
Add: Depreciation (20% of (£192,000 + £8,000))		40,000
		82,000
Less: Fixed asset acquired		(8,000)
		74,000
Increase in stock	800	
Increase in debtors	8,000	
		(8,800)
Increase in bank		65,200

5.4 Activity

Discuss the acceptability of the forecast bank balance in the above example, identifying any actions which management should consider.

5.5 Activity solution

The forecast is that the bank balance will increase by £65,200. This is significant and management should recognise the need to initiate a short-term investment plan to earn some interest on this money.

It is noticeable that the cost of new fixed assets is much less than the depreciation charge for the year, so there may be a requirement for capital investment in the following year.

5.6 The working capital cycle

Earlier in this text we referred to the management of working capital using the operating cycle. You should remember that this measures the number of days between payment to suppliers for raw materials and receipt from customer for the finished goods. This approach can be applied to balance sheet forecasts.

In the Zed plc example, now assume the following number of days applied during the year ended 30 June 1998:

Stock	49 days (based on materials)
Debtors	61 days (based on sales)
Creditors	30 days (based on materials)

If the following predictions of sales and materials apply to the year ended 30 June 1999:

Sales	£60,000
Materials	£150,000

then, assuming the number of stock, debtor and creditor days are to be unchanged, we can forecast the balance sheet at 30 June 1999 as follows:

			£
Fixed assets (as before)			
Plant and machinery			160,000
Current assets			
Stock ($^{49}/_{365}$ × £150,000)		20,137	
Debtors ($^{61}/_{365}$ × £600,000)		100,274	
Bank (balancing figure)		53,918	
		174,329	
Current liabilities			
Creditors ($^{30}/_{365}$ × £150,000)	12,329		
Dividend (as before)	30,000	(42,329)	132,000
			292,000
Issued share capital			216,000
Retained profits			76,000
			292,000

5.7 Activity

Reconcile the above forecast bank balance of £53,918 to the retained profit for the year of £42,000.

5.8 Activity solution

		£
Retained profit		42,000
Add: Depreciation (as before)		40,000
		82,000
Less: Fixed asset acquired		(8,000)
		74,000
Increase in stock	4,137	
Increase in debtors	20,274	
	24,411	
Increase in creditors	(2,329)	(22,082)
Increase in bank (£53,918 - £2,000)		51,918

6 MONITORING CASHFLOW

6.1 Introduction

Earlier in this chapter we stated that one of the objectives of a cash budget was to provide a basis against which actual cashflow can be monitored.

6.2 Cashflow reports

Regular reporting of actual versus budgeted cashflow should be carried out on a daily, weekly or monthly basis depending upon the size of the organisation and the frequency and value of their cash receipts and payments.

This is particularly appropriate if the organisation utilises a treasury function to maximise its reward from cashflow (ie, by earning interest on surpluses and minimising interest costs on deficits).

In common with all management reports the purpose of the report is to provide a basis for management decision-making to improve future performance. For this reason the report needs to be addressed to the manager who can control the cashflows.

6.3 Receipts

There are two main types of receipt which need to be considered: receipts from customers and investment income (eg, interest).

Cashflow receipts from customers are dependent upon

- the activity level of the organisation; and
- the time taken by customers to pay for the sales.

It is important to identify the cause of the difference in cashflow between budget and actual because the control action required will differ.

If the cause is a difference in the activity level then this is likely to also affect the cashflows in respect of purchases and expenses to the extent that they are variable with activity levels. The action required in respect of this cause should thus consider the net effect of the activity difference on cashflow.

If the cause is customers paying for items at a different time from that expected, then action needs to be taken to either amend the budget or take steps to change customers' payment practices.

6.4 Payments

Payments may be divided into three categories:

- those of a routine, recurring nature which are unrelated to activity (eg, rent, business rates);
- those of a routine nature which are related to activity (eg, payments to suppliers for purchases/expenses; wage payments);
- those of a non-recurring nature (eg, taxation, dividends, capital acquisitions).

As with income it is important to identify the type of payment and recognise that the control action required is different. In some cases the item may be uncontrollable.

One of the most controllable payment aspects is the time taken to pay suppliers. These need to be considered carefully, early payment may attract settlement discounts, whereas delaying payment may incur charges and eventually lead to the loss of future supplies.

6.5 Revising forecasts

It is important that comparisons of actual cashflows are against meaningful targets, so from time to time it may be necessary to revise the cashflow forecasts to take account of earlier period differences and the management action used to resolve them.

In these instances it is advisable to identify in any reports both the original cash budget and the latest forecast, because it is the original cash budget which is part of the organisation's budgeting strategy.

7 COMPUTERISED CASH FLOW MODELS

7.1 Introduction

Computer models provide an easy way of monitoring cash flows. The most suitable format is that of various **spreadsheet** packages now available on most micros - Supercalc, Multiplan, Lotus 1-2-3, Jazz and Excel are among the better known.

The following simplified example is on Jazz, but similar results would be achieved with any of the above packages. In this example the cash flow data has been reduced to balance brought forward, receipts and payments:

	A	**B**	**C**	**D**	**E**
1		Jan	Feb	Mar	April
2					
3	Opening balance	1,000	1,100	1,000	550
4	Add: Receipts	700	800	500	850
5	Less: Payments	600	900	950	400
6					
7	Closing balance	1,100	1,000	550	1,000
8					

This table could equally well have been prepared manually, but in fact the columns containing balances consist of relationships, rather than numeric values:

	A	B	C	D	E
1		Jan	Feb	Mar	April
2					
3	Opening balance	1,000	=B7	=C7	=D7
4	Add: Receipts	700	800	500	850
5	Less: Payments	600	900	950	400
6					
7	Closing balance	=B3+B4–B5	=C3+C4–C5	=D3+D4–D5	=E3+E4–E5
8					

In order to understand the second table, it must be appreciated that the columns are labelled from left to right alphabetically, A, B, C, etc, and the rows numerically from the top down, 1, 2, 3, etc. Each cell is defined by the letter of the column and the number of the row, and calculations are by reference to cells rather than numbers.

Thus the opening balance for every month except January equals the previous month's closing balance. Similarly the closing balance is the Opening balance + Receipts – Payments.

The great advantage of this approach becomes apparent when applied to a large and complex flow projection:

(a) this program can handle up to 8,192 rows and 234 columns, enough to accommodate a very complex model (though most micros would run out of memory if all the cells were used);

(b) if any figure is amended, all the figures will be immediately recalculated;

(c) the results can be printed out without going through an intermediate typing phase; and

(d) most programs can also represent the results graphically eg, the above balances can be shown in a bar diagram:

Closing cash balances

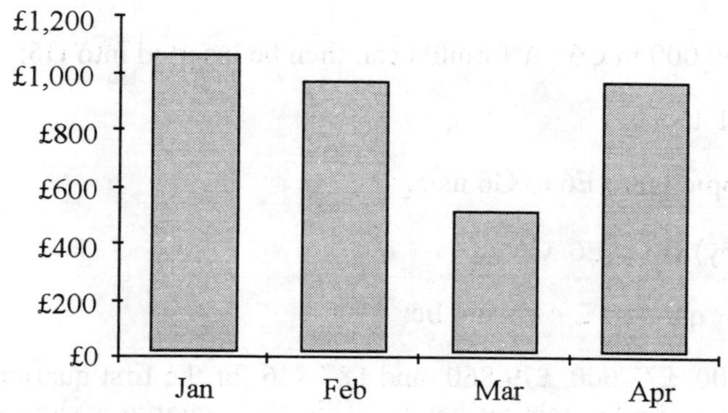

In total spreadsheet cash flow models represent a very powerful tool for use by the accountant.

7.2 Example of a cash budget

The following worksheet illustrates a screen showing part of a budgeting spreadsheet that has been set up for a cash budget.

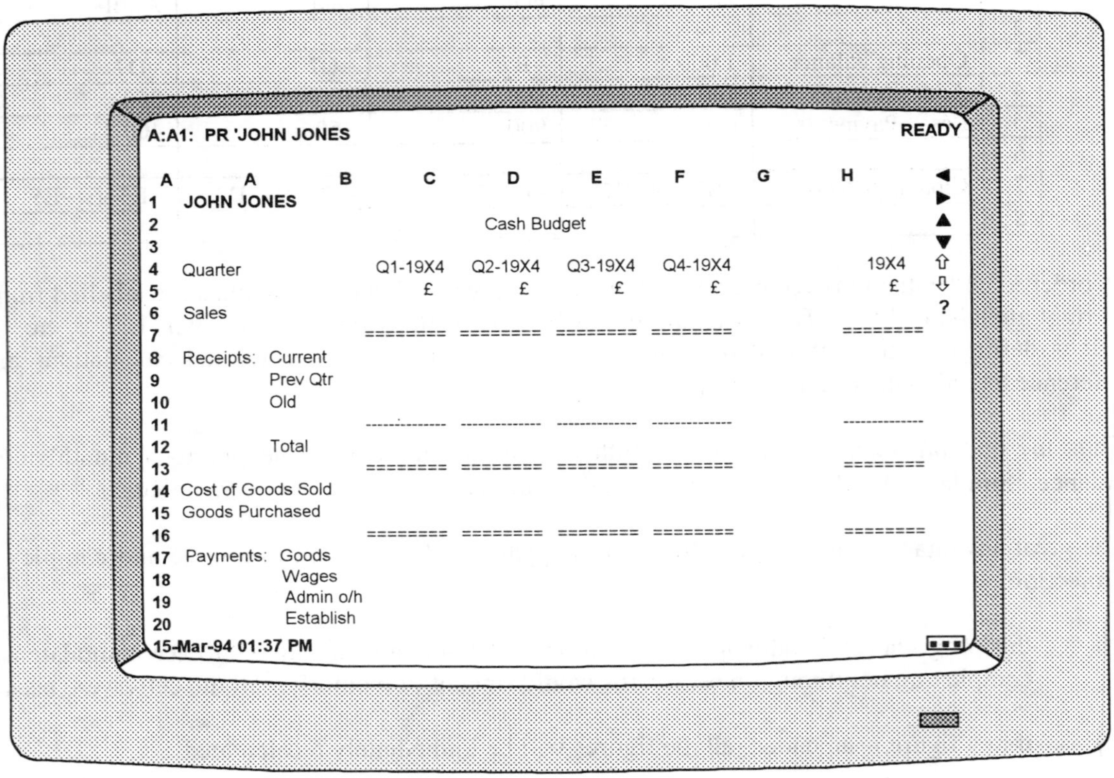

It is not the purpose of this unit or text to teach you how to use a spreadsheet. The following therefore simply attempts to give a good overview of how a spreadsheet can be used to produce part of a cash budget.

(a) **Quarterly sales**

Sales are expected to be £60,000 in quarter 1, increasing in volume by 10% per quarter.

Thus insert £60,000 in C6. A formula can then be inserted into D6:

+C6*1.1

This can be copied into E6 to G6 using:

/ C(opy) D6 ↲ E6..G6 ↲

The figures for quarters 2-4 should be:

£66,000, £72,600, £79,860 (and £87,846 for the first quarter of 19X5 which will be needed to find purchases below. This 19X5 quarter is shown in column G.)

Total sales revenue (@SUM(C6..F6)) is £278,460.

(b) **Receipts**

50% of sales are expected to be received in the quarter that the sale is made, 40% is received one quarter later and 10% received two quarters later.)

The formulae: for cell F8 will be F6*0.5

for cell F9 will be E6*0.4

for cell F10 will be D6*0.1

These can be copied into rows C, D and E.

In cells H8..H10 an @SUM function is required to add the total of columns C to F. In row 12 the three elements of receipts can be totalled. The result is shown below.

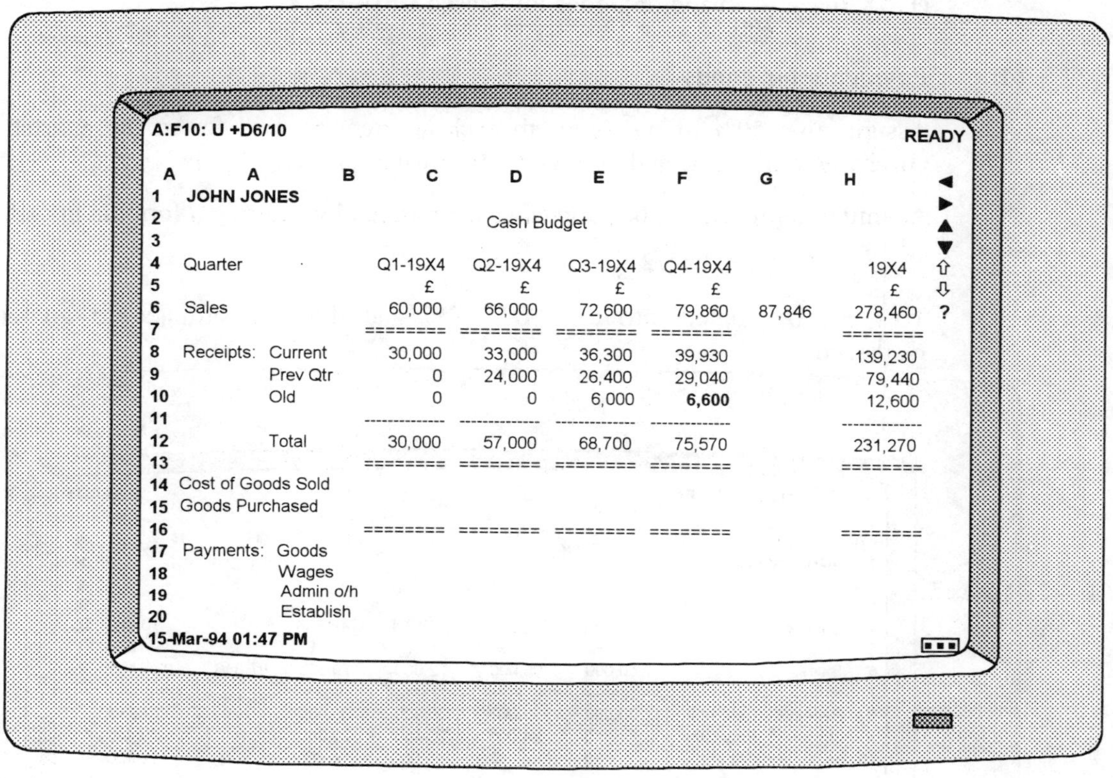

A:F10: U +D6/10 READY

A	A	B	C	D	E	F	G	H
1	JOHN JONES							
2				Cash Budget				
3								
4	Quarter		Q1-19X4	Q2-19X4	Q3-19X4	Q4-19X4		19X4
5			£	£	£	£		£
6	Sales		60,000	66,000	72,600	79,860	87,846	278,460
7			========	========	========	========		========
8	Receipts:	Current	30,000	33,000	36,300	39,930		139,230
9		Prev Qtr	0	24,000	26,400	29,040		79,440
10		Old	0	0	6,000	**6,600**		12,600
11			-------------	-------------	-------------	-------------		-------------
12		Total	30,000	57,000	68,700	75,570		231,270
13			========	========	========	========		========
14	Cost of Goods Sold							
15	Goods Purchased							
16			========	========	========	========		========
17	Payments:	Goods						
18		Wages						
19		Admin o/h						
20		Establish						

15-Mar-94 01:47 PM

(c) **Cost of sales and purchases**

The company will use a mark up on cost of 60%. 1½ months stock is to be held, therefore purchases in a quarter will correspond to 50% of the current quarter's cost of sales plus 50% of the next quarter's, the exception being quarter 1 of 19X4 when sufficient goods will be purchased to satisfy the next 4½ months.

The formula for cell C14 can be worked out by looking at the cost structure:

Cost of goods sold	+	profit	=	sales revenue
100	+	60	=	160

Cost of goods sold are $\frac{100}{160}$ times sales revenue.

The formula for cell C14 is:

+C6*100/160

When this is copied into rows D to G, the figures that appear are:

£37,500, £41,250, £45,375, £49,912.5 (and £54,903.75)

The cost of goods purchased shown in cell C15 must be:

+C14+D14/2

However in D15 (and copied into E and F) will be:

+D14/2 + E14/2

The totals can be shown in row H. The total of the Cost of Goods Sold is £174,037.50 (£278,460 × $\frac{100}{160}$) and of Goods Purchased £201,489.4.

(d) **Payments for goods**

Assume that 50% of purchases in each quarter are paid for in the quarter in which the purchases were made and 50% in the following quarter.

A similar approach can be adopted as for receipts by entering a formula in cell C17:

+C15/2 + B15/2

This can be copied into cells D17..F17 and the row summed to give the following worksheet.

A:H17: U @SUM(C17..F17) READY

A	A	B	C	D	E	F	G	H
1	JOHN JONES							
2				Cash Budget				
3								
4	Quarter		Q1-19X4	Q2-19X4	Q3-19X4	Q4-19X4		19X4
5			£	£	£	£		£
6	Sales		60,000	66,000	72,600	79,860	87,846	278,460
7			========	========	========	========		========
8	Receipts:	Current	30,000	33,000	36,300	39,930		139,230
9		Prev Qtr	0	24,000	26,400	29,040		79,440
10		Old	0	0	6,000	6,600		12,600
11			--------------	--------------	--------------	--------------		--------------
12		Total	30,000	57,000	68,700	75,570		231,270
13			========	========	========	========		========
14	Cost of Goods Sold		37,500	41,250	45,375	49,912.5	54,903.75	174,037.5
15	Goods Purchased		58,125	43,312.5	47,643.75	52,408.13		201,489.4
16			========	========	========	========		========
17	Payments:	Goods	29,062.5	50,718.75	45,478.13	50,025.94		**175,285.3**
18		Wages						
19		Admin o/h						
20		Establish						

15-Mar-94 01:55 PM

7.3 Use of computer models in sensitivity analysis

As we saw above, a cash budget spreadsheet is generally set up with certain input values (sales price, volume, wage rates etc,) which are then processed via formulae to produce cash receipts and payments. If we wish to assess the impact on monthly cash flows of changes in the inout values - for example selling price variations - this can be done simply and quickly by changing the relevent input value and the spreadsheet will adjust accordingly. This is an example of the use of financial modelling in 'what if' or sensitivity analysis.

7.4 Split between data and logic

An example of financial modelling, concerning the revenue incorporated into a cash budget, may be expressed as follows:

Input	Sales quantity eg, 10 Sales price eg, £5
Calculation	Sales revenue = Sales quantity × Sales price
Output	£50

The model contains a calculation or logical relationship between some of the variables. The model receives input data regarding the value to be given to certain variables. The output is then determined by the model applying a calculation to this input data. This calculation is the logical relationship between the input and output data.

This demonstrates a very important aspect of financial modelling: the model is built up in such a way that the data to be input is separate from the calculation that will be performed on that data. This means that different sets of data may be input to the model, but the calculation of the output will remain unchanged. Thus, in the above example, the effect on revenue of raising sales price by £1 can immediately be seen. By entering £6 into the model and not £5, the output of £60 will immediately be shown. Thus, the data has been changed although the calculation using the data remains unchanged. Financial models split the data input from the calculation to be performed on the data, which means that the actual calculation can be used again and again for any input.

This changing of the input data is called '*what if*' analysis. The financial modeller is able to determine what the change in the output is if certain changes are made to inputs. This sort of analysis would not be possible with a purely manual system, because of the time that would be spent in recalculating the model at every point for one simple change in the input data.

A financial model, then, allows a split to be made between data and the logic that will be applied to that data. It then follows that 'what if' analysis can be used to find the changes that take place in the output when certain changes are made to the input data.

7.5 General note on sensitivity analysis

In the example above it was assumed that a spreadsheet would be used to construct the cash budget model. In a modern business environment this may well be the case, although this does not always follow. If a set of quick jottings on the back of an envelope will solve the problem, then this is all that is necessary. Due to the powerful 'what if' analysis on spreadsheets it is unlikely now that envelopes will suffice except for the most simple of problems.

7.6 Activity

Drake Ltd wishes to create a spreadsheet model to forecast its cash requirements for the production of a new product. The company has determined the following:

Initial sales in month 1	200 units increasing at a rate of 10% a month for the first 6 months.
Selling price:	Initially £200 per item, but it wishes to review this price. All sales revenue cash flows occur in the month after the sales have occurred.
Machine	A new machine needs to be purchased costing £40,000 payable in month 1.
Material costs	£45 per unit. Sufficient raw material is purchased in a month to meet the requirements for the next month. No buffer stock is held. Materials are paid for when purchased.
Other variable costs	40% of sales, occurring in month of sale.

Fixed cost	£10,000 per month, payable in the same month.
Opening cash balance	£10,000 available in month prior to month 1 (month 0).

Design a spreadsheet to assist the company to examine its cashflow (show just the first two months and the month prior to month 1, with the appropriate initial sums and formulae).

Comment how you might use the spreadsheet to determine overdraft/loan requirements.

7.7 Activity solution

	A	B	C	D
1	**CASH**	**BUDGET**	**MODEL**	
2	MONTH	1	2	3
3	SALES (units)	200	B3*1.10	C3*1.1
4	PRICE	200	B4	C4
5	REVENUE	B3*B4	C3*C4	D3*D4
6	=========	=======	========	========
7	**CASH**	**FLOWS**		
8	MONTH	0	1	2
9	**INFLOWS**			
10	REVENUE		B5	C5
11	--------------	--------------	--------------	--------------
12	**OUTFLOWS**			
13	MACHINE		40,000	
14	MATERIAL	45*B3	45*C3	45*D3
15	VAR COST		0.4*B5	0.4*C5
16	FIX COST	10,000	B16	B16
17	TOTAL	@SUM (B13.B16)	@SUM (C13.C16)	@SUM (D13.D16)
18	=========	=========	=========	=========
19	OPENING BALANCE	10,000	+B22	+C22
20	CASH IN	B10	C10	D10
21	CASH OUT	B17	C17	D17
22	CLOSING BALANCE	B19+B20–B21	C19+C20–C21	D19+D20–D21
23	=========	=========	=========	=========

The above spreadsheet is one of several layouts that might be used. The first part determines the amount of revenue each month, but not the timing of the revenue cash flows.

The second part deals with the cash flows particularly the problem of ordering and paying for material in the previous month to its use.

The third section brings the totals of the cashflows together and determines the closing balance for each month, which is the opening balance for the next month.

Management can examine the spreadsheet closing balances to see the months in which there is a negative balance and hence a need for a loan, overdraft or some injection of cash. They can also identify where there is a surplus of cash which could be invested.

The spreadsheet needs some amendments if the pricing decision needs to be addressed. A monthly profit and loss account with annual totals needs to be included. Then sensitivity analysis on the price could be carried out to determine the effect on profits and cashflows.

8 SELF TEST QUESTIONS

8.1 What are the objectives of a cash budget? (1.1)

8.2 How may a forecast cash shortage be funded? (1.2)

8.3 Why are contingencies necessary? (1.4)

8.4 Identify the two types of cash budget. (2.1)

8.5 Why is there a difference between profit and cashflow? (3.5)

8.6 What are cleared funds? (4.2)

8.7 What is the working capital cycle? (5.6)

8.8 When monitoring cashflow receipts what are the two main causes of differences between actual and expected values? (6.3)

8.9 When monitoring cashflow payments, what are the three categories of payment to be considered? (6.4)

8.10 Why is it important to revise cashflow forecasts? (6.5)

8.11 Explain the use of spreadsheets in cash budget sensitivity analysis. (7.2)

3 FORECASTING TECHNIQUES

PATHFINDER INTRODUCTION

This chapter covers the following performance criteria and knowledge and understanding.

- Basic statistical techniques for estimating future trends: moving averages, allowance for inflation (Element 14.1)
- Forecasts of future cash payments and receipts are in accord with known income and expenditure trends

Putting the chapter in context – learning objectives.

Having studied the methods of preparing a cash budget, it is time to look at how some of the figures can be estimated in practice. In particular, sales figures for example often need to be estimated by considering the past history of sales and projecting estimates into the future. Similarly, inflation needs to be taken into account, as revenues or costs may increase because of inflation as well as because of real changes in activity.

Time series analysis is a method of analysing data produced over a period of time.

At the end of this chapter you should have learned the following topics.

- Explain the different factors that cause the shape of a time series graph
- Understand the additive model for the actual value of a period
- Understand what the trend of a series is
- Be able to determine the trend of a series by the method of moving averages
- Understand what is meant by seasonal variation
- Calculate the seasonal variation
- Understand how to use time series analysis for forecasting purposes
- How indices, in particular the RPI, can be used to incorporate inflation into forecasts.

1 TIME SERIES ANALYSIS

1.1 Introduction

Definition A time series is a set of observations taken at equal time intervals.

The observations might be taken hourly, daily, weekly, monthly, quarterly or annually.

The observations may be monetary such as sales figures or costs totals, or non-monetary such as temperature measurements or numbers of people.

1.2 Examples of time series

Examples of time series might include the following:

- quarterly sales totals;
- annual profit figures;
- weekly payroll totals;

1.3 Basic aims of time series analysis

A time series shows how a value of a particular variable (sales, unemployment etc) has changed over time in the past. The aim of time series analysis is to use this historical data to form a model from which *future* values may be predicted. This will be useful to businesses and the government in planning future strategy and budgets.

Initial analysis breaks the time series down into components, each of which is generally easier to project into the future than the original time series. These projections can then be combined into an overall forecast.

For example, suppose you were asked to predict the next three values of the following series:

2, 2, 1, 4, 6, 6, 5, 8, ?, ?, ?

Not particularly easy! However, you will find the following two series somewhat easier:

1, 2, 3, 4, 5, 6, 7, 8, ?, ?, ? (Answer: 9, 10, 11)

+1, 0, -2, 0, +1, 0, -2, 0, ?, ?, ? (Answer: +1, 0, -2)

Now note that the sum of corresponding values of these two series gives the original series (1 + 1 = **2**, 2 + 0 = **2**, 3 + (-2) = **1**, 4 + 0 = **4** etc), and thus the predictions for the next three values of the original series can be obtained by adding together the separate predictions for the 'sub-series';

9 + 1 = 10; 10 + 0 = 10, 11 + (-2) = 9.

This simple example illustrates the basic principles of time series analysis. In this case, the original time series was broken down into two components - a **trend**, the underlying movement (steadily upwards), and a **seasonal** or **cyclical variation**, a regular rise and fall over a specific period of time (repeating every four periods). The summing of these to get the original series illustrates the **additive model.**

In practice, and all future examples, the numbers will not be so nice, and it will not be so easy to identify/project the underlying components. However, in working through the methods for their estimation, do not lose sight of what you are trying to achieve, as illustrated by this simple example.

2 SHAPE OF A TIME SERIES GRAPH

2.1 Introduction

The observations of a time series are often shown on a graph. The observations are plotted against time to give an overall picture of what is happening. Time is always plotted on the horizontal axis and the observations on the vertical axis.

There are a variety of different factors that cause a time series to have the results that it does and therefore the graph to have its particular shape. Some of these factors are long term and some short term. Some factors are due to the economy as a whole whereas others are specific to that particular business.

The four main factors that are of interest when analysing a time series are:

(a) long-term trends;
(b) cyclical variations;
(c) seasonal variations;
(d) residual or random variations.

2.2 Long-term trends

This is the way in which the graph of a time series appears to be moving over a long interval of time when the short-term fluctuations have been smoothed out. The rise or fall is due to factors which only change slowly eg,

(i) increase or decrease in population;
(ii) technological improvements;
(iii) competition from abroad;
(iv) inflation.

2.3 Cyclical variations

This is the wave-like appearance of a time series graph when taken over a number of years. Generally, it is due to the influence of booms and slumps in industry. The distance in time from one peak to the next is often approximately 5 to 7 years. The cyclical variations represent long-term economic changes and are only noticeable if a time series spans a considerable number of years.

2.4 Seasonal variations

This is a regular rise and fall over specified intervals of time. The interval of time can be any length - hours, days, weeks etc, and the variations are of a periodic type with a fairly definite period eg,

(i) rises in the number of goods sold before Christmas and at sale times;
(ii) rises in the demand for gas and electricity at certain times during the day;
(iii) rises in the number of customers using a restaurant at lunch-time and dinner time.

These are referred to under the general heading of 'seasonal' variations as a common example is the steady rise and fall of, for example, sales over the four seasons of the year.

However, as can be seen from the examples, the term is also used to cover regular variations over other short periods of time.

They should not be confused with cyclical variations (see above) which are long-term fluctuations with an interval between successive peaks greater than one year.

2.5 Residual or random variations

This covers any other variation which cannot be ascribed to the three factors discussed above. This is taken as happening entirely at random due to unpredictable causes eg:

(i) strikes;
(ii) fires;
(iii) sudden changes in taxes;
(iv) loss of goodwill

Not all time series will contain all four elements. For example, not all sales figures show seasonal variations.

2.6 Example

The following data are the quarterly sales figures for Barb Ltd, a retailer of barbecue equipment and accessories, for three years.

	Quarter 1	*Quarter 2*	*Quarter 3*	*Quarter 4*
	£'000	£'000	£'000	£'000
19X1	121	188	290	88
19X2	125	201	301	102
19X3	146	227	318	103

The time series graph is plotted as follows:

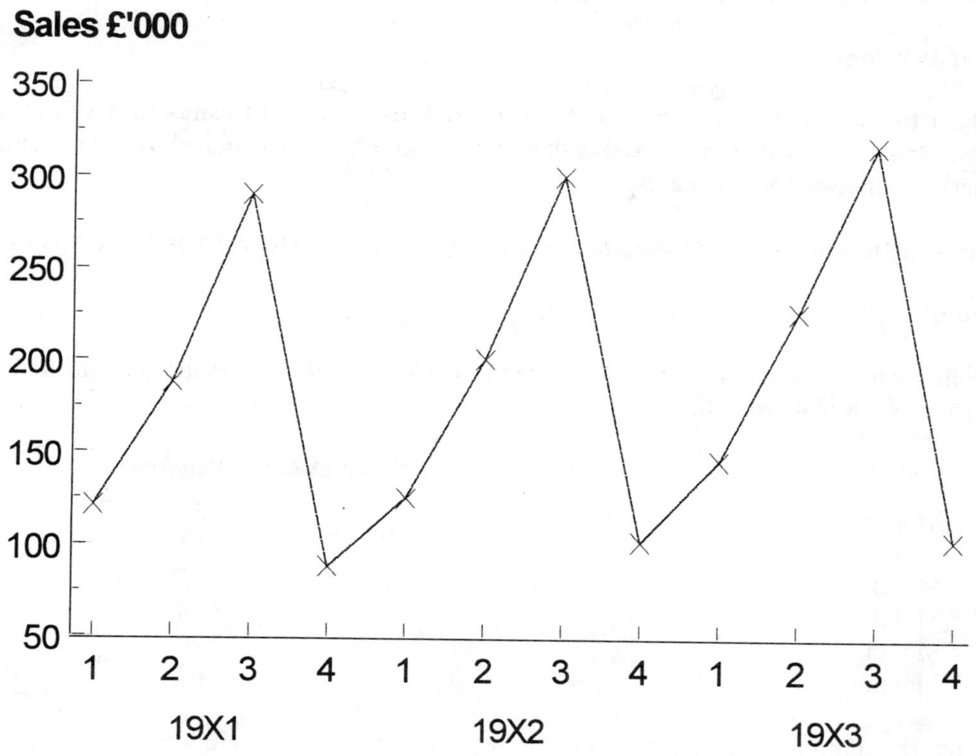

Distinguish the factors that would appear to be causing the graph to be this shape.

2.7 Solution

Trend - it would appear that the trend is one of a general increase in sales as on the whole each quarter's figure is above that of the same quarter in the previous year.

Cyclical variations - as the period covered by the time series is only 4 years there are no evident cyclical variations.

Seasonal variations - as might be expected for a retailer of barbecue equipment there would appear to be very definite seasonal variations. Sales are at their highest in the third quarter, the summer months, and drop dramatically in quarter 4 as winter approaches.

Random variations - it is not particularly easy to identify random variations from the graph but an example might be the 19X3 quarter 2 sales figure which appears to show a rise from previous quarter 2 sales figures out of proportion to the general rise (trend).

3 TREND OF A TIME SERIES

4.1 Introduction

Each figure in a time series will be made up of possibly as many as four different components. These four components are:

- the trend component;
- the cyclical component;
- the seasonal component;
- the random or residual component.

When these four components are combined this will give the actual figure for each period.

The trend of a time series is the way that the time series tends to move overall. The trend is a rough estimate of how the time series increases or decreases over time.

3.2 Moving averages

If a linear trend cannot be assumed, another method must be used to smooth out the fluctuations in the time series. The simplest method is that of moving averages, which shows, on average, how the time series increases and decreases.

The best way to illustrate the calculation of a moving average is to use a simple example.

3.3 Example

The following information is available concerning the number of employees in a manufacturing concern for each of six months:

	Number of employees
Month 1	50
Month 2	54
Month 3	65
Month 4	58
Month 5	70
Month 6	68

Calculate the trend of these figures using a three figure moving average and then plot the trend on the time series graph.

3.7 Solution

The steps in the calculation are as follows:

Step 1 Calculate a three month total for each successive three month period (the choice of averaging period - here three months - is discussed after illustration of the technique).

The first moving total will therefore be months 1 to 3 employees:

$$50 + 54 + 65 = 169$$

Then months 2 to 4:

$$54 + 65 + 58 = 177$$

Then months 3 to 5 etc.

Step 2 Produce an average for each three month period by dividing by 3.

Thus months 1 to 3:

$$\frac{169}{3} = 56$$

months 2 to 4:

$$\frac{177}{3} = 59$$

This can be laid out best in the form of a table.

Tutorial note: the three month moving total and the three month moving average are shown in the middle of the time period, ie, on the line of, or against, the middle figure for the three years. Therefore the month 1 to month 3 moving figures are shown in the month 2 line and the month 2 to month 4 figures in the month 3 line. There will therefore be no moving totals or moving averages for month 1or month 6.

Month	*Number of employees*	*3 month moving total Step 1*	*3 month moving average Step 2*
Month 1	50	-	-
Month 2	54	169	56
Month 3	65	177	59
Month 4	58	193	64
Month 5	70	196	65
Month 6	68	-	-

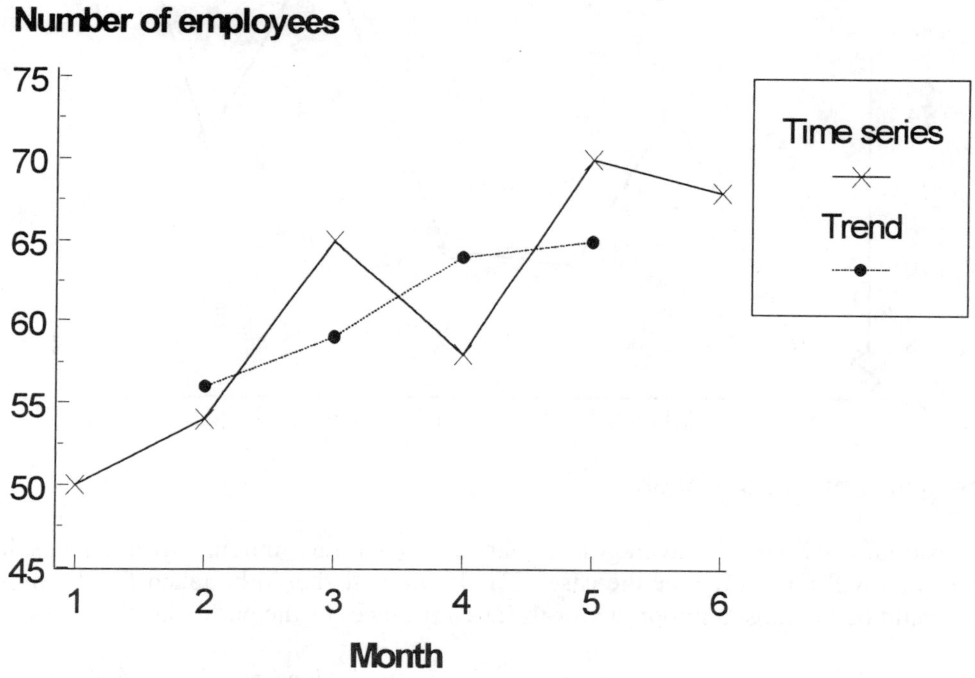

3.8 Activity

The data given is the daily temperature reading for one week in July.

	Temperature (F)
Monday	68
Tuesday	74
Wednesday	70
Thursday	71
Friday	78
Saturday	73
Sunday	80

Calculate the trend of these temperatures using a three figure moving average and plot the trend on the time series graph.

3.9 Activity solution

Day	*Temperature*	*3 day moving total Step 1*	*3 day moving average Step 2*
Monday	68	-	-
Tuesday	74	212	71
Wednesday	70	215	72
Thursday	71	219	73
Friday	78	222	74
Saturday	73	231	77
Sunday	80	-	-

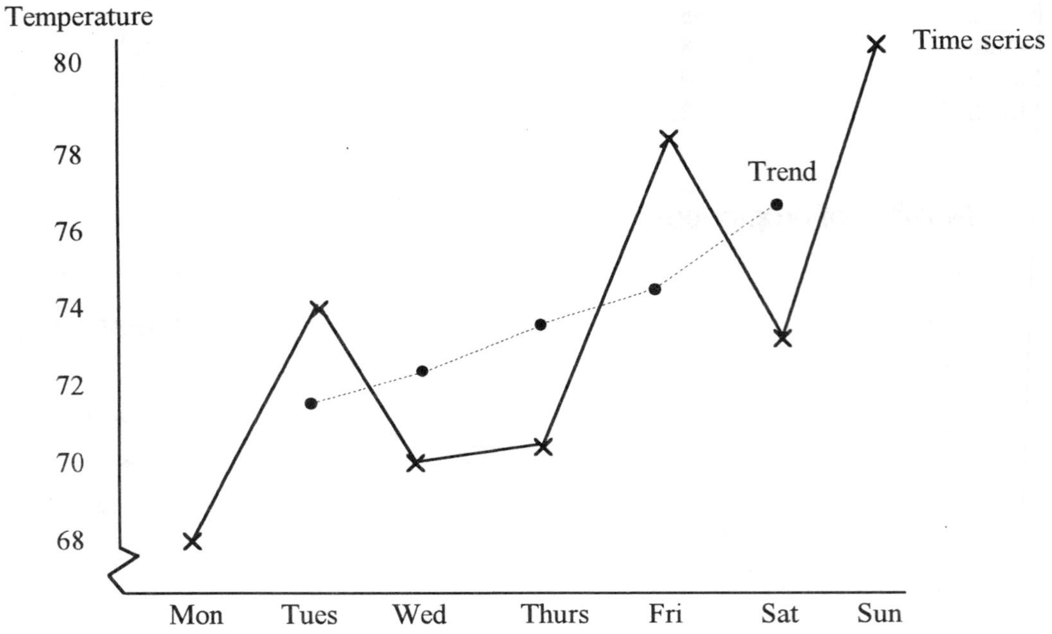

3.10 Choice of moving average figure

In the examples of moving averages, so far, a three figure moving average has been chosen. However this will not always be the case. The figure that should be taken for the moving average period should be the most appropriate for the circumstances of the particular time series.

If it is known that there is a cycle for a time series over which seasonal variations tend to occur then the moving average period that should be chosen is one that covers the entire cycle.

3.11 Examples of moving average periods

- A time series covers a number of years and it is apparent from the time series that there is in general a six year cycle. A six year moving average would be the most appropriate in this case as this would cover the entire six year cycle.

- Figures are given for monthly sales for four years and those sales vary throughout the year. A twelve month moving average might be chosen as this would cover the entire annual cycle of sales variations.

- Figures are given for daily numbers of customers in a restaurant for a two month period and the number of customers varies significantly for each day of the week. A seven day moving average might be most appropriate in order to cover the whole week.

- Figures are given for quarterly sales and there appears to be four distinct quarterly seasons to the sales. A four period moving average to cover the entire year might be chosen as the most appropriate.

3.12 Moving averages and even number periods

Earlier in the paragraph it was noted that the moving total and moving average relate to the mid-point of the time period chosen. If the moving average period is an odd number then the mid-point will be a specific time period. However if an even number is chosen for a moving average then the mid-point of that period will be between specific time periods.

3.13 Example of the problem

For example the following four years of sales figures are given:

	£'000
19X1	100
19X2	120
19X3	160
19X4	180

The total for these four periods is 560 and therefore the average is 140 (560/4).

This average of 140 relates to the middle of the four year period therefore somewhere between 19X2 and 19X3. This would be shown in the averaging table between the lines for 19X2 and 19X3 as follows:

Year	*Sales*	*Moving total*	*Moving average*
19X1	100		
19X2	120		
		560	140
19X3	160		
19X4	180		

The problem with this is that the trend line must relate to specific time periods in order both to be plotted on the graph and to be used in further calculations with seasonal variations.

This problem is solved by taking a moving average of the moving average. This is known as centring the moving average.

3.14 Example

Look back at the graph for our earlier example Barb Ltd (2.6). The seasonal variations appear to be repeated every four quarters. Thus a four quarter moving average will be appropriate. The sales figures for Barb Ltd were as follows:

	Quarter 1 £'000	*Quarter 2* £'000	*Quarter 3* £'000	*Quarter 4* £'000
19X1	121	188	290	88
19X2	125	201	301	102
19X3	146	227	318	103

Using a four period moving average calculate the trend of these figures, and plot the trend on the graph for this time series. Work to the nearest £1,000.

3.15 Solution

Step 1 calculate each four period moving total and position this figure in the middle of the four quarter time period.

Step 2 calculate each four period moving average by dividing the total by four and also position this figure in the middle of the four quarter time period.

Step 3 calculate a two period moving average of each of the four period moving averages. This will give the trend at specific time periods.

This example would therefore be tackled as follows:

Step 1 calculate the four period moving totals:

19X1: Quarter 1 to quarter 4

$$121 + 188 + 290 + 88 = 687$$

X1 Quarter 2 to X2 quarter 1

$$188 + 290 + 88 + 125 = 691$$

X1 Quarter 3 to X2 quarter 2

$$290 + 88 + 125 + 201 = 704$$

etc.

Step 2 calculate the four period moving averages:

19X1: Quarter 1 to quarter 4

$$\frac{687}{4} = 172$$

X1 Quarter 2 to X2 quarter 1

$$\frac{691}{4} = 173$$

X1 Quarter 3 to X2 quarter 2

$$\frac{704}{4} = 176$$

etc.

Step 3 calculate two period moving averages of the four period moving averages in order to give the trend. These figures will now relate to a specific time period.

Trend for quarter 3

$$\frac{172 + 173}{2} = 173$$

Trend for quarter 4

$$\frac{173+176}{2} \quad = \quad 175$$

etc.

The completed table is now shown:

Quarter	*Sales*	*Four period moving total Step 1*	*Four period moving average Step 2*	*Trend Step 3*
19X1 - 1	121			
2	188			
		687	172	
3	290			173
		691	173	
4	88			175
		704	176	
19X2 - 1	125			178
		715	179	
2	201			181
		729	182	
3	301			185
		750	188	
4	102			191
		776	194	
19X3 - 1	146			196
		793	198	
2	227			199
		794	199	
3	318			
4	103			

Tutorial note: when calculating the trend all of the numbers have been rounded to the nearest £'000.

The trend can now be plotted on the time series graph (showing an **approximate** linear trend).

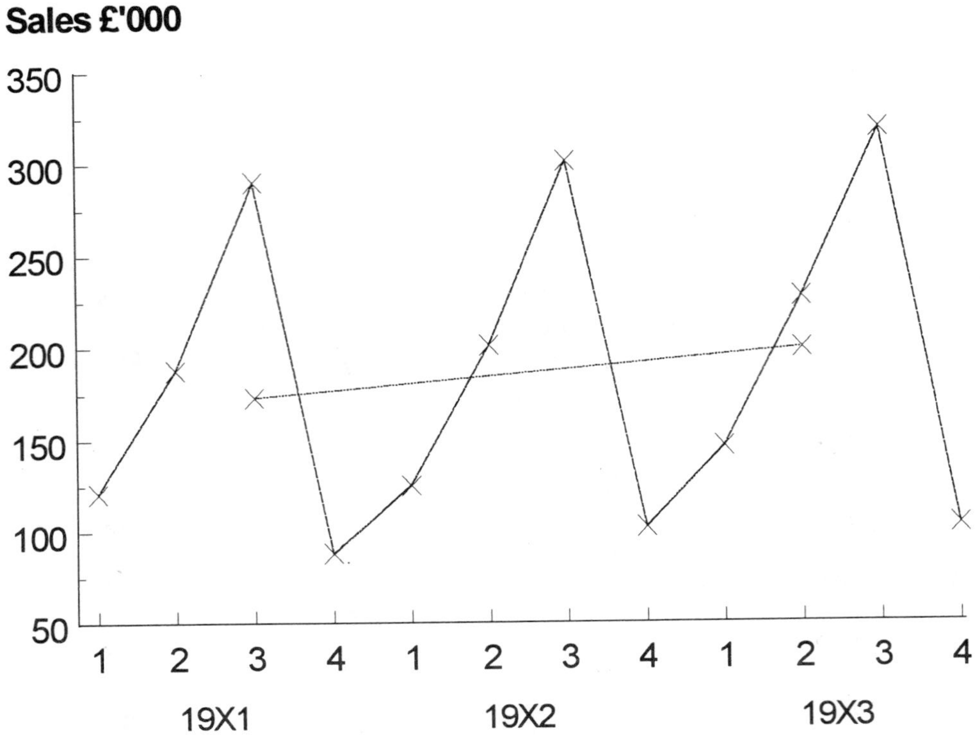

3.16 Activity

Ski Fun Ltd owns a number of chalets in Switzerland that it lets out for holidays. Given below is data showing the number of people who stayed in the chalets each quarter for a period of 5 years.

	Quarter 1	*Quarter 2*	*Quarter 3*	*Quarter 4*
19X5			92	195
19X6	433	324	95	202
19X7	486	347	98	218
19X8	499	360	104	236

Calculate the trend of the number of visitors using a four period moving average rounded to the nearest whole number where necessary.

3.17 Activity solution

Quarter	*Numbers*	*Four period moving total Step 1*	*Four period moving average Step 2*	*Trend Step 3*
19X5 - 3	92			
4	195			
		1,044	261	
19X6 - 1	433			262
		1,047	262	
2	324			263
		1,054	264	
3	95			271
		1,107	277	
4	202			280
		1,130	283	

19X7 -	1	486			283
			1,133	283	
	2	347			285
			1,149	287	
	3	98			289
			1,162	291	
	4	218			293
			1,175	294	
19X8 -	1	499			295
			1,181	295	
	2	360			298
			1,199	300	
	3	104			
	4	236			

4 SEASONAL VARIATIONS

4.1 Introduction

In the examples considered in detail up to now, as in most instances, the data provided by the time series was monthly or quarterly figures for a few years, say three or four. This precludes the analysis of cyclical variations, and thus this type of time series will be analysed into the trend and seasonal variations. Seasonal variations are common movements in the figures of the time series at different times of the year.

4.2 Examples of seasonal variations

Many product sales will vary with the season:

- ice cream sales will tend to be highest in the summer months;
- greetings cards sales will reach peaks at Christmas, Easter, Mothers and Fathers days;
- many retail outlets will have winter and summer sales where increases in volume of sales will be noted.

Other types of time series may also have seasonal variations:

- the number of restaurant customers is likely to be higher at weekends than in the week;
- production in a manufacturing organisation may be lower on Friday than it is earlier in the week.

4.3 Additive model

The additive model for a time series is as follows:

$$A = T + C + S + R$$

In a short term time series that only covers a few years there will be no cyclical variations but there are likely to be seasonal variations. The model will therefore simplify to:

$$A = T + S + R$$

4.4 Method of calculating seasonal variations

The method of calculating seasonal variations has four steps:

Step 1 calculate the trend of the time series using appropriate moving averages. In most cases the four quarters of the year will be the seasons and therefore a four period moving average will be most suitable. As this is an even number period the figures will need to be centred in order to calculate the trend at specific time periods.

Step 2 use the additive model for a time series:

A = T + S + R

- the actual figure for each period will be made up of the trend, the seasonal variation and the residual variation. This can therefore be rearranged to give:

A - T = S + R

- if the trend component for each period is removed from the actual figure for the period then the remaining figure will be the seasonal variation plus any residual element.

Step 3 in order to remove the residual element from the totals calculated in step 2, the next step is to average the seasonal variations for each season.

Step 4 finally check that the seasonal variations total to zero and adjust if necessary.

4.5 Example

Returning to the example of Barb Ltd used throughout this chapter the trend was calculated in a previous paragraph. These calculations will now be continued to determine the seasonal variations.

4.6 Solution

Step 1 calculating the trend has already been performed.

Step 2 for each sales value deduct the trend to leave only the seasonal and residual elements.

Quarter	*Sales* (A)	*Four period moving total*	*Four period moving average*	*Trend* (T)	*Seasonal + residual variations* (A - T)
19X1 - 1	121				
2	188				
		687	172		
3	290			173	117
		691	173		
4	88			175	-87
		704	176		
19X2 - 1	125			178	-53
		715	179		
2	201			181	20
		729	182		
3	301			185	116
		750	188		
4	102			191	-89
		776	194		
19X3 - 1	146			196	-50
		793	198		
2	227			199	28
		794	199		
3	318				
4	103				

Step 3 average the seasonal figures in order to remove the residual element.

	Quarter 1	*Quarter 2*	*Quarter 3*	*Quarter 4*
19X1	-	-	117	-87
19X2	-53	20	116	-89
19X3	-50	28	-	-
	-103	48	233	-176
Average	$\frac{-103}{2}$	$\frac{48}{2}$	$\frac{233}{2}$	$\frac{-176}{2}$
=	-52	24	117	-88

Tutorial note: as might be expected for a barbecue equipment retailer there are distinct seasonal variations in sales. Sales for quarter 2 and for quarter 3, spring and summer, are above the trend values whilst the quarter 1 and quarter 4 figures are generally well below the trend values.

Step 4 finally check that the seasonal variations total to zero and adjust if necessary.

Seasonal variations from step 3

Quarter 1	-52
Quarter 2	24
Quarter 3	117
Quarter 4	-88
	1

This difference should be spread across all four seasonal variations. However as the resulting adjustment would be just 0.25 for each season it makes more sense to simply adjust one of the figures by 1. The most appropriate figure to adjust is the largest as this will have the smallest relative effect.

In this case therefore the quarter 3 seasonal variation should be adjusted by subtracting the difference of +1.

117 - 1 = 116

The four seasonal variations are therefore:

Quarter 1	-52
Quarter 2	24
Quarter 3	116
Quarter 4	-88

All four seasonal variations now total to zero (-52 + 24 + 116 - 88 = 0)

4.7 Activity

The trend calculations for the earlier activity, Ski Fun Ltd, are given below. Continue the calculations in order to determine any seasonal variations that there might be in the figures.

Quarter		*Numbers*	*Four period moving total*	*Four period moving average*	*Trend*
19X5	3	92			
	4	195			
			1,044	261	
19X6	1	433			262
			1,047	262	
	2	324			263
			1,054	264	
	3	95			271
			1,107	277	
	4	202			280
			1,130	283	
19X7	1	486			283
			1,133	283	
	2	347			285
			1,149	287	
	3	98			289
			1,162	291	
	4	218			293
			1,175	294	
19X8	1	499			295
			1,181	295	
	2	360			298
			1,199	300	
	3	104			
	4	236			

4.8 Activity solution

Step 1 calculating the trend has already been performed.

Step 2 for each actual value deduct the trend to leave only the seasonal and residual elements.

Quarter		*Numbers*	*Trend*	*Seasonal + residual variations*
		(A)	*(T)*	*(A - T)*
19X5	3	92		
	4	195		
19X6	1	433	262	171
	2	324	263	61

	3	95	271	-176
	4	202	280	-78
19X7	1	486	283	203
	2	347	285	62
	3	98	289	-191
	4	218	293	-75
19X8	1	499	295	204
	2	360	298	62
	3	104		
	4	236		

Step 3 average the seasonal figures in order to remove the residual element.

	Quarter 1	*Quarter 2*	*Quarter 3*	*Quarter 4*
19X6	171	61	-176	-78
19X7	203	62	-191	-75
19X8	204	62	-	-
	578	185	-367	-153
Average	$\frac{578}{3}$	$\frac{185}{3}$	$\frac{-367}{2}$	$\frac{-153}{2}$
=	193	62	184	-77

(Tutorial note: as might be expected the seasonal variations are quite great. The quarter 1 seasonal variation is the highest above the trend as the first three months of the year are the height of the skiing season. Quarter 2 is still above the trend reflecting later seasonal skiers. Quarter 3, the summer months, is understandably well below the trend whilst quarter 4 is moving back towards the trend.*)*

Step 4 finally check that the seasonal variations total to zero and adjust if necessary.

Seasonal variations from step 3

Quarter 1	193
Quarter 2	62
Quarter 3	-184
Quarter 4	-77
	-6

This difference of six could be spread amongst all four seasons' figures by deducting -1.5 from each variation. An alternative however is to deduct -3 from each of the two large variations for quarters 1 and 3.

Quarter 1	193 - (-3)	=	196
Quarter 3	-184 - (-3)	=	-181

The four seasonal variations are therefore:

Quarter 1	196
Quarter 2	62
Quarter 3	-181
Quarter 4	-77

These four now total zero.

4.9 Cyclical variations

Introduction

In an earlier paragraph cyclical variations were explained. Cyclical variations are essentially economic booms and slumps that appear every few years. This will cause there to be some sort of pattern to the peaks and troughs of the time series. Cyclical variations are therefore relevant to a time series that is made up of a number of years of information. The method for calculating cyclical variations is very similar to that for calculating seasonal variations; however it is unlikely that you will have to deal with these.

4.10 Residual or random variations

Residual or random variations are those that are not caused by the trend of the figures or the seasonal/cyclical variations that affect the figures. Therefore these are effectively whatever is left if the trend and seasonal/cyclical factors are removed from the actual data.

The residual variations indicate to some extent how much the time series is affected by other factors. If a time series has large residual variations then it will be highly affected by factors other than the trend of the numbers and the seasonal/cyclical variations.

5 FORECASTING USING TIME SERIES ANALYSIS

5.1 Introduction

The principal use of the time series analysis that has been studied in this chapter is as an aid to forecasting results for future periods.

5.2 Technique

The technique for forecasting future results involves the following steps:

Step 1 estimate the trend for the future period.

For the purposes of this unit this will be done by extending the trend line on the time series graph and reading off the figure at the future point in time that is being used in the forecast.

Step 2 apply the appropriate seasonal adjustment (or cyclical adjustment) in order to determine the forecast figure.

It is not possible to forecast residual or random variations as they are unforeseeable by their very nature.

5.3 Example

Given below is the time series graph for Barb Ltd showing the original time series and the trend.

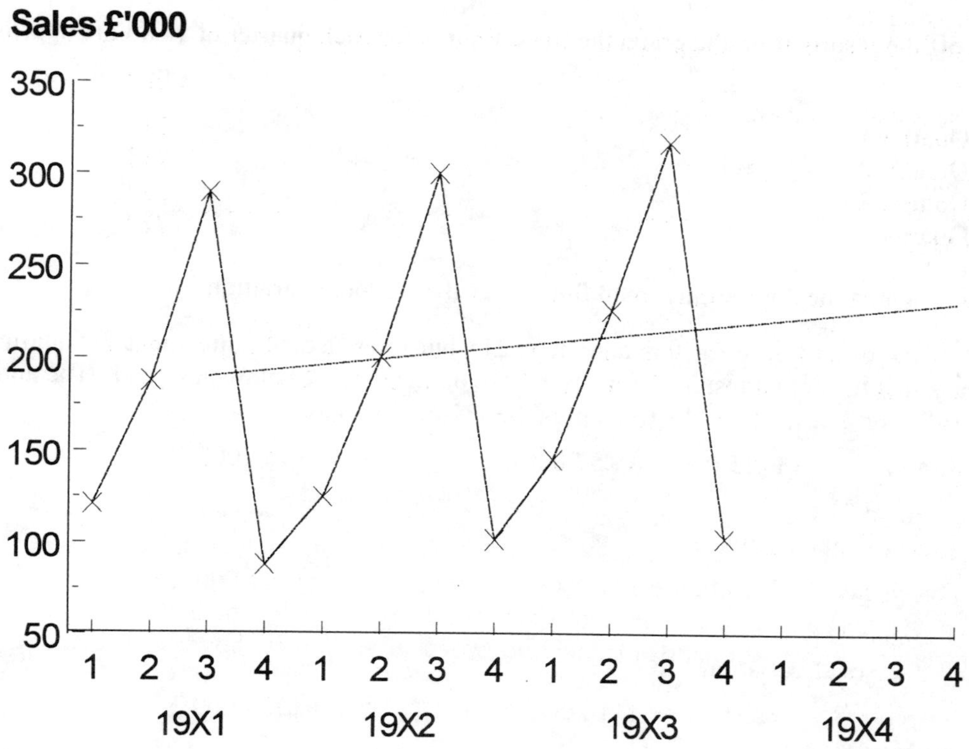

The seasonal variations for Barb Ltd are:

Quarter 1	-52
Quarter 2	24
Quarter 3	116
Quarter 4	-88

From this information estimate the values of sales for each quarter of 19X4.

5.4 Solution

Step 1 estimate the trend figure for each of the quarters of 19X4.

This can be done by extending the trend line on the graph and reading off the relevant figures. This is also known as extrapolation.

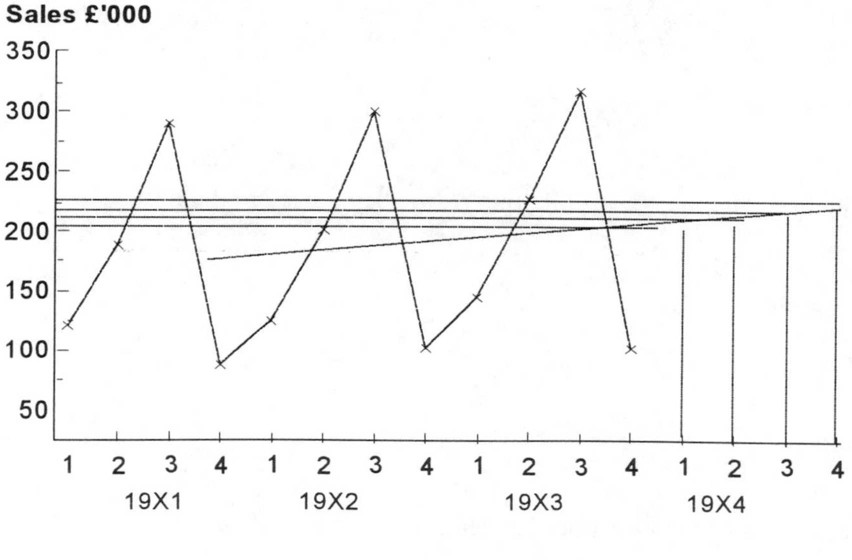

Reading off the results from the graph the trend figures for each quarter of 19X5 are approximately:

	£'000
Quarter 1	215
Quarter 2	218
Quarter 3	222
Quarter 4	227

Step 2 adjust the appropriate trend figures for the seasonal variation.

Quarter 1 - the trend figure for this quarter is 215 but the seasonal adjustment for quarter 1 is -52. This means that the actual results for quarter 1 are on average 52 below the trend. The anticipated or forecast sales for quarter 1 are the trend plus the seasonal variation.

Forecast £215,000 + (- £52,000) = £163,000

Quarter 2 - trend 218
seasonal variation 24

Forecast £218,000 + £24,000 = £242,000

Quarter 3 - trend 222
seasonal variation 116

Forecast £222,000 + £116,000 = £338,000

Quarter 4 - trend 227
seasonal variation -88

Forecast £227,000 + (-£88,000) = £139,000

5.5 Activity

Given below is the time series graph for Ski Fun Ltd showing the time series and the trend. The seasonal variations for Ski Fun Ltd are also given.

From this information estimate the approximate number of chalet visitors for each of the four quarters of 19X9.

The seasonal variations are as follows:

Quarter 1	196
Quarter 2	62
Quarter 3	-181
Quarter 4	-77

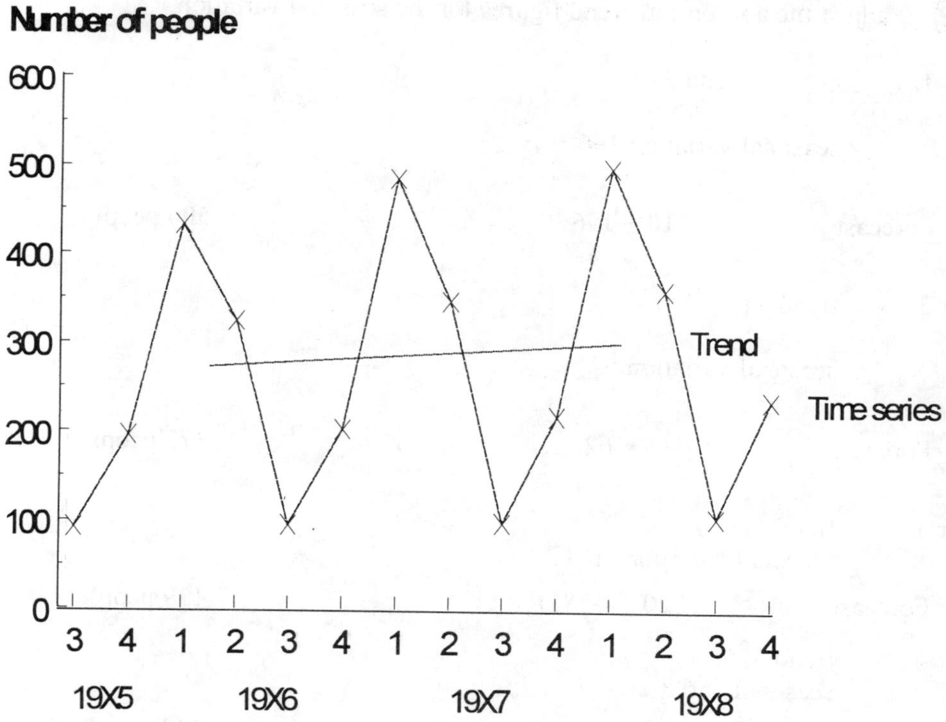

5.6 Activity solution

Step 1 extend the trend line on the graph in order to estimate the future trend numbers.

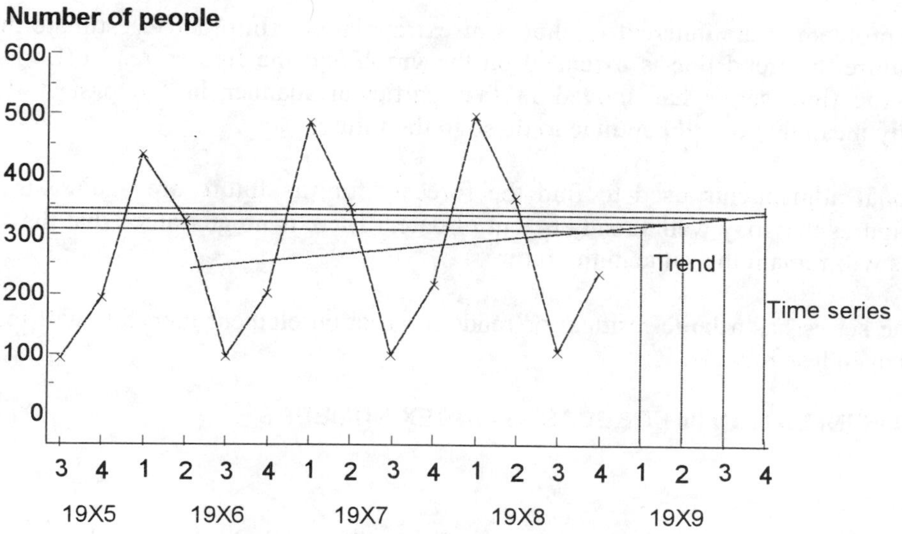

Reading off from the graph the appropriate figures for the trend for 19X9 are as follows:

	Number of people
Quarter 1	310
Quarter 2	315
Quarter 3	320
Quarter 4	325

Step 2 adjust the appropriate trend figures for the seasonal variation.

Quarter 1	-	trend 310		
		seasonal variation 196		
	Forecast	310 + 196	=	506 people
Quarter 2	-	trend 315		
		seasonal variation 62		
	Forecast	315 + 62	=	377 people
Quarter 3	-	trend 320		
		seasonal variation -181		
	Forecast	320 + (-181)	=	139 people
Quarter 4	-	trend 325		
		seasonal variation -77		
	Forecast	325 + (-77)	=	248 people

5.7 Problems with forecasting

There are a number of problems with using time series analysis in order to estimate or forecast future results.

- the main problem is the inherent weakness of extrapolation. In order to estimate the trend for the future the trend line is extended on the graph and the figures read off. However although the time series has moved in that particular manner in the past it does not necessarily mean that it will continue to do so in the future.

- the seasonal adjustments used to find the forecast for the future are again based upon historic figures that may well already be out of date. There is no guarantee that the seasonal variations will remain the same in the future.

- if the time series has a large residual or random variation element then this will make any forecasts even less reliable.

6 ALLOWANCE FOR INFLATION IN FORECASTS - INDEX NUMBERS

6.1 Introduction

The time series analysis in the previous section used past (historic) data to develop a model to predict future values. This may be used in the context of cash budgeting to predict future sales revenue, costs etc.

However, in times of significant inflation, this may lead to inappropriate forecasts, for two reasons:

- the past data will have been affected by different rates of inflation, distorting the picture given by the trend estimate; and

- future cash flows will be affected by future rates of inflation.

Thus it is important that the impact of inflation is recognised within the budgeting process, which involves the measurement of past inflation and the prediction of future rates. This will often be done by the use of index numbers, commonly the Retail Price Index (RPI). Before considering the RPI in particular, we shall first briefly look at the principles of index numbers in general.

6.2 Simple index numbers

Definition An index is a technique for comparing, over time, changes in some property of a group of items (eg, price, quantity consumed etc,) by expressing the property each year as a percentage of some earlier year.

The year that is used as the initial year for comparison is known as the base year.

Index numbers are used in a variety of situations and to measure changes in all sorts of items. As the uses of index numbers are so diverse, there are also many different ways of calculating or measuring index numbers. We shall illustrate the principles with a simple index.

Definition a simple index is one that measures the changes in either price or quantity of a single item.

There are two types of simple index:

- a price index;
- a quantity index.

These simple indices are also known as relatives giving either a price relative or a quantity relative.

6.3 Simple index measurement

A simple index measures the percentage change for a single item in comparison to the base year. The index can measure either the price of the item or the quantity of the item that was sold.

If the index is a price index then this will show the percentage increase in price of the item since the base year. If the index is a quantity index then this will show the increase in quantity or volume sold since the base year.

6.4 Calculation of a simple index

The formulae for calculating simple indices are:

$$\text{Simple price index} = \frac{p_1}{p_0} \times 100$$

$$\text{Simple quantity index} = \frac{q_1}{q_0} \times 100$$

Where p_0 is the price at time 0
p_1 is the price at time 1
q_0 is the quantity at time 0
q_1 is the quantity at time 1

(***Tutorial note:*** the concept of time 0, time 1 and so on is simply a scale counting from any given point in time. Thus, for example, if the scale started on 1 January 19X0 it would be as follows:

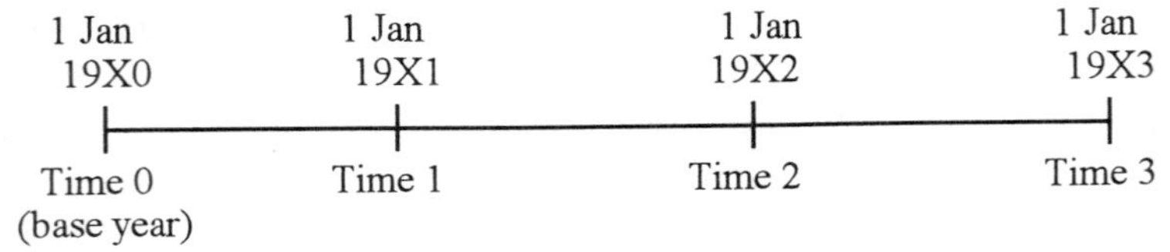

The starting point is chosen to be most convenient for the problem under consideration.*)*

6.5 Example - price index

If a commodity costs £2.60 in 19X4 and £3.68 in 19X5, calculate the simple price index for 19X5, using 19X4 as base year (ie, time 0).

6.6 Solution

$$\text{Simple price index} = \frac{p_1}{p_0} \times 100$$

$$= \frac{3.68}{2.60} \times 100$$

$$= 141.5$$

This means that the price has increased by 41.5% of its base year value ie, its 19X4 value.

6.7 Example - quantity index

6,500 items were sold in 19X8 compared with 6,000 in 19X7. Calculate the simple quantity index for 19X8 using 19X7 as base year.

6.8 Solution

$$\text{Simple quantity index} = \frac{q_1}{q_0} \times 100$$

$$= \frac{6{,}500}{6{,}000} \times 100$$

$$= 108.3$$

This means that the quantity sold has increased by 8.3% of its 19X7 figure.

6.9 Activity

A product which cost £12.50 in 19X0, cost £13.65 in 19X1. Calculate the simple price index for 19X1 based on 19X0.

6.10 Activity solution

$$\text{Simple price index} = \frac{p_1}{p_0} \times 100$$

$$= \frac{13.65}{12.50} \times 100$$

$$= 1.092 \times 100$$

$$= 109.2$$

This means that the price has increased by 9.2% on its base year price of £12.50.

7 WEIGHTED INDICES

7.1 Introduction

In the previous paragraph simple indices were discussed. A simple index measures changes either in price or quantity of a single item. What is perhaps more practical and useful is the calculation of an index that measures overall changes in either price or quantity of a number of different items.

7.2 Weighted index measurement

A weighted index measures the change in overall price or overall quantity of a number of different items compared to the base year. In order to be able to do this for a price index there are two steps to the calculations to be performed:

Step 1 calculate the price relative (simple price index) for each of the items.

Step 2 these price relatives must then be weighted in some suitable manner in order to produce an overall price index.

Similarly if a quantity index is to be calculated:

Step 1 calculate the quantity relative (simple quantity index) for each of the items.

Step 2 these quantity relatives must then be weighted in some suitable manner in order to produce an overall quantity index.

7.3 Example

Suppose that an organisation produces three products. Information about the selling prices of these three products for the last two years are as follows:

	Selling price 19X1 £	*Selling price 19X2* £
Product A	2	3
Product B	9	10
Product C	25	30

In order to produce a weighted index of the overall price increase over the period, weightings are to be assigned to each of the three products as follows:

	Weighting
Product A	4
Product B	5
Product C	1

Calculate a weighted price index for 19X2 for these three products with 19X1 as the base year.

7.4 Solution

Step 1 Calculate the price relative or simple price index for each of the products.

Product A $\quad \frac{3}{2} \quad \times \quad 100 \quad = \quad 150$

Product B	$\frac{10}{9}$	×	100	=	111
Product C	$\frac{30}{25}$	×	100	=	120

Step 2 Weight the price relatives on the weighting basis given.

	Price relative	Weighting	Total
	$\frac{P1}{P0} \times 100$	W	$W \times \left(\frac{P1}{P0} \times 100\right)$
A	150	4	600
B	111	5	555
C	120	1	120
		10	1,275

$$\text{Weighted price index} = \frac{1,275}{10}$$

$$= 127.5$$

The selling price of the three products together has therefore increased by 27.5% from 19X1 to 19X2.

7.5 Selection of weightings

In the example in the previous paragraph weightings for each of the items to be included in the index were given. These are likely to reflect the relative significance of the individual products, measured by, for example, the physical sales quantity of each product or their total sales value.

8 INDEXES AND INFLATION

8.1 Introduction

In the previous paragraphs the basic construction and interpretation of simple and weighted indices have been considered. In this paragraph a common practical use (and commonly examined use) for indices will be discussed.

The indices that have been constructed in the earlier paragraphs, whether simple or multi-item, are capable of providing additional information to management regarding the price or volume of its sales or inputs. However one question that has not yet been addressed is how to use such indices to take account of inflation in cash budgeting.

8.2 The Retail Price Index (RPI)

In the UK the generally accepted measurement of general price inflation is the Retail Price Index, which is an example of an aggregative index.

Definition an aggregative price index is a price index that compares the total expenditure in one year on a particular collection of goods with the total expenditure in the base year on those same goods.

The Retail Price Index (RPI) is constructed using the prices of a list of goods and services used by most households in the UK. The total cost of those goods and services each month is compared to the cost in the base month, currently January 1987, in order to produce what is effectively a cost of living index.

The prices of the list (or basket) of goods and services are collected monthly by a survey amongst representative retail outlets. The weights assigned to these prices in order to construct a price weighted index are value weights according to the proportion of £1,000 spent by the average household on each item. These weights are updated annually from surveys of household expenditure.

The index is divided into fourteen main groups eg, food, catering, alcohol etc, and these in turn are divided into subgroups eg, food is subdivided into bread, cereals etc. Separate index numbers are given for each subgroup, each group and for the index as a whole.

8.3 Specific price indices

Organisations however not only face general inflation but also specific price changes in their inputs (raw materials and wages) and their outputs (sales). There are a number of published statistics from the Central Statistical Office showing specific price indices for different sectors of industry.

8.4 Use of indices to account for inflation

An organisation can choose to compare its results and costs to a general inflation index such as the RPI or a specific price index for its inputs or outputs. This is done by stripping out the effects of inflation leaving only the 'real terms' increase or decrease in sales or costs.

Whichever type of index is used by an organisation will be a management decision and will help to provide a more realistic comparison between the results of different periods. If the general or specific increases in prices are taken out of an organisation's results then this will leave only the real or genuine increase (or decrease) due to selling price, sales volume and costs.

8.5 Method

A series of costs or revenues over a period of time can be adjusted for inflation in one of two ways:

- all figures can be reduced to base year figures by stripping out the effects of inflation.
- all figures can be inflated to current year prices.

8.6 Example

Suppose that an organisation has the following sales over a number of years. The specific index that relates to those sales is also given:

	Sales £'000	*Specific price index*
19X1	140	112
19X2	150	118
19X3	154	128
19X4	160	135
19X5	170	140

Remove from these sales figures the effect of the specific price changes for this product in order to give the real increase or decrease in sales for the period.

8.7 Solution

In order to remove the effects of inflation two different methods can be used:

(a) all figures can be reduced to base year figures by stripping out the effects of inflation.
(b) all figures can be inflated to current year prices.

(a) **Reduction or deflation of sales figures**

The sales figures for each year are deflated or reduced by dividing by the price index for the year being considered and multiplying by the index for the earliest year.

19X1 $£140,000 \times \frac{112}{112} = £140,000$

19X2 $£150,000 \times \frac{112}{118} = £142,373$

19X3 $£154,000 \times \frac{112}{128} = £134,750$

19X4 $£160,000 \times \frac{112}{135} = £132,741$

19X5 $£170,000 \times \frac{112}{140} = £136,000$

(b) **Inflation to current year prices**

This is done by dividing each year's figures by the index for that year and then multiplying by the current year, 19X5, index.

19X1 $£140,000 \times \frac{140}{112} = £175,000$

19X2 $£150,000 \times \frac{140}{118} = £177,966$

19X3 $£154,000 \times \frac{140}{128} = £168,438$

19X4 $£160,000 \times \frac{140}{135} = £165,926$

19X5 $£170,000 \times \frac{140}{140} = £170,000$

Each set of calculations tells the same story. The actual sales figures appear to be increasing each year. However when the specific price changes of those products are taken into account using the price index the picture is different.

Whether the prices are deflated by stripping out the effects of inflation or inflated to current prices the resulting information is the same:

- 19X2 sales have increased in real terms. Even after taking price inflation into account the real sales figure is greater.

- sales in 19X3 and 19X4 have both reduced in real terms. Despite the appearance of increases from £150,000 to £154,000 for 19X3, and then from £154,000 to £160,000 for 19X4, when inflation is taken into account the real sales figures have in fact decreased.

- finally the sales for 19X5 have increased not only on paper from £160,000 to £170,000 but also in real terms as the amount of increase in sales has been greater than the specific price increases over the same period.

8.8 Activity

Given below are the sales figures of an organisation and the Retail Price Index for a number of years.

	Sales £'000	*Retail price index*
19X4	500	131
19X5	510	139
19X6	540	149
19X7	580	154
19X8	650	164

Restate the sales figures for each year on the following bases:

(a) deflating each year's sales in order to take out the effect of inflation;
(b) restating each year's figures in terms of 19X8 prices.

Briefly comment on the figures that are revealed.

8.9 Activity solution

(a) Deflation of figures

19X4 $£500{,}000 \times \frac{131}{131} = £500{,}000$

19X5 $£510{,}000 \times \frac{131}{139} = £480{,}647$

19X6 $£540{,}000 \times \frac{131}{149} = £474{,}765$

19X7 $£580{,}000 \times \frac{131}{154} = £493{,}377$

19X8 $£650{,}000 \times \frac{131}{164} = £519{,}207$

(b) Inflation to current year prices

19X4 $£500{,}000 \times \frac{164}{131} = £625{,}954$

19X5 $£510{,}000 \times \frac{164}{139} = £601{,}727$

19X6 $£540{,}000 \times \frac{164}{149} = £594{,}362$

19X7 $£580{,}000 \times \frac{164}{154} = £617{,}662$

19X8 $£650{,}000 \times \frac{164}{164} = £650{,}000$

Comment

The sales figures alone show increases year after year. However once inflation is taken into account the result is different.

Both sets of figures, once deflated by one method or the other, show that in real terms sales values decreased in 19X5 and 19X6 and increased again in 19X7 and 19X8. By 19X8, even in real terms, sales were higher than in 19X4.

8.10 Inflation and cash budgeting

Of course, cash budgets have to incorporate the actual cash flows expected in the future. This means that they must include expected levels of inflation. Where cash budgets for, say, sales revenue, are based upon a projected trend obtained from analysis of past data affected by inflation, the procedure would be as follows:

- put the historic data to be used onto a comparable inflation base, eg, by inflating to the current year, as above
- use this adjusted data to determine a trend, as in the earlier section on time series analysis
- project the trend to the required future point(s) in time
- adjust the projections for the expected rates of inflation (using estimates of future values of the RPI or specific price indices) from the current year to the year of the projected value.

9 SELF TEST QUESTIONS

9.1 What is a time series? (1.1)

9.2 What four factors accumulate to comprise a time series? (2.1)

9.3 Write down the equation for the additive model for a time series (4.3)

9.4 What are the problems with forecasting from time series analysis? (5.7)

9.5 Explain how the RPI is determined each month. (8.2)

9.6 Explain how inflation may be accounted for in a forecast based upon a time series (8.10)

4 THE ECONOMIC BACKGROUND

PATHFINDER INTRODUCTION

This chapter covers the following performance criteria and knowledge and understanding.

- The basic structure of the banking system and the money market in the UK. (Element 14.2)
- A basic understanding of Government monetary policies (Element 14.2)
- Account is taken of trends in the economic and financial enviornment in managing cash balances (Element 14.2).

Putting the chapter in context – learning objectives.

The first chapter of this book was concerned with the importance of cash and cashflow, both to accountants specifically and the corporate sector in general. This chapter concentrates on the banking system, the operation of which is crucial to the amount of cash or money available for use by firms. Moreover, banks are involved intimately in the money transmission process, without which no company could operate effectively; and additionally, they provide considerable amounts of funding for the corporate, as well as the personal and public sectors. This chapter provides a basis for understanding the material contained in the next three chapters; making use of the concepts developed here to examine the effect of money supply changes on the price of money – ie, the rate of interest.

At the end of this chapter you should have learned the following topics.

- The meanings and relevance of money, creation of money and the monetary base within a banking system
- The functions of the commercial banks, the Bank of England and the discount houses
- The control of the money supply; monetary policy
- The link between money and inflation
- The workings of the Monetary Policy Committee.

1 MONEY AND THE BANKING SYSTEM

1.1 What is money?

Definition Money is anything which is generally accepted as a medium of exchange or in discharge of a debt.

Anything may serve as money if it is acceptable and if it continues to fulfil the necessary functions to the satisfaction of the community.

In past societies, all sorts of exotic and primitive forms of money (eg, shells and animal hides) have existed but in a modern community, with a reasonably stable economic and financial system, the following survive as the most commonly accepted forms of money.

(a) **Token coins**

Used chiefly for small cash transactions and acceptable up to limited amounts. These have little inherent value, unlike the gold and silver coinage used in earlier times.

(b) **Paper**

Modern paper money is now either cash in its own right, eg Bank of England notes which in Britain is unlimited legal tender (which means that it must be accepted in payment of a debt), or an instruction to transfer credit from one bank to another, eg a cheque. Some forms of 'quasi-money' come close to fulfilling these requirements. For example, a Bill of Exchange is a more sophisticated and very old form of money. This is essentially the acceptance of an obligation to pay a definite amount at a stated time and place. It can be passed from hand to hand and becomes a means of payment. It is also used in foreign trade to arrange transfers of bank credit, although the Domestic Bill of Exchange has received increasing favour in recent years.

However, because a bill of exchange is not generally accepted, it really cannot be classified as money. Although it may be acceptable in the business fraternity, you could not buy groceries with one!

(c) **Bank credit**

The most important form of modern money is bank credit, ie the amounts standing to the credit of bank customers in the books (or magnetic tape, etc) or computer memory banks of the banking institutions. As a result, paper is being replaced by other means of transferring bank credit, eg credit cards and computer instructions. Indeed bank credit in the UK is twenty times more important than cash in circulation.

2 THE CREATION OF MONEY

2.1 Introduction

A fascinating thing about money is the way banks can create it. This section considers how this is done in a modern banking system.

2.2 Money creation under a fractional reserve system

A **fractional reserve system** is one where banks only keep part of their assets in the form of cash to repay investors. The rest of the assets are in the form of investments which cannot easily be converted into cash, eg

The banking system - Balance sheet end of Day 1

	£		£
Share capital	100	Fixed assets	100
Customer deposits	1,000	Cash	1,000
	1,100		1,100

In this simple example, share capital finances fixed assets. The customer deposits represent current accounts of customers. A bank therefore has a liability to repay all of these on demand.

However, since few customers want to withdraw their cash at once, a bank only has to hold say 10% (£100) in the form of 'cash' (in practice, mainly deposits at the central bank). The rest can be loaned to other customers. If a bank loans £900 to customers, the balance sheet will look as follows:

The banking system - Balance sheet end of Day 2

	£		£
Share capital	100	Fixed assets	100
Customer deposits	1,000	Loans	900
		Cash	100
	1,100		1,100

Note that there is now only £100 cash in the bank, the remaining £900 is in circulation and will eventually be spent and deposited back with either the same or, more likely, other banks within the banking system. The balance sheet will now look as follows:

The banking system - Balance sheet end of Day 3

	£		£
Share capital	100	Fixed assets	100
Customer deposits (1,000 + 900)	1,900	Loans	900
		Cash (100 + 900)	1,000
	2,000		2,000

2.3 How much money is there in the above system?

The vital point to grasp is that the economy started with £1,000 cash.

Day 3 -When this £900 is deposited back in the banking system the money in the economy is still £1,900 - the amount of customer deposits at the banks. Notice that the cash backing for deposits is $\left(\frac{1,000}{1,900}\right)$ = 53%, well above the 10% safety margin. There is clearly plenty of scope to create more money.

Conclusion The amount of money in the economy (ie, the amount people can spend) has increased from £1,000 to £1,900.

2.4 Activity

What factors are likely to limit the ability of a bank to create credit in this way?

2.5 Activity answer

Ultimate, it is the size of the cash reserve (called the 'reserve ratio') which limits this process. This depends on:

- notions of prudence on the part of the bank itself. This will be governed by past experience.
- government regulations stipulating a minimum reserve ratio.
- how much cash the public want to keep to hand. This limits the return flow of cash to the bank.
- the extent to which cheques and credit cards are used. If all transactions are done without cash, then none need leave the bank.

Other factors are:

- Presence of other banks in the system. Some recipients of expenditures financed by bank loans may deposit their receipts in a different bank. The ability of the first bank to create credit is thus limited but the credit-creation capacity of the banking system as a whole is unimpaired.

- The demand for loans by the population.

3 THE MONETARY BASE

3.1 Introduction

The money supply is looked at in more detail later in the text but for the moment just note that one key measure of this is the **monetary base**.

Definition This is defined as the amount of cash in the economy.

The monetary base is referred to as 'high powered money' precisely because it is the basis of all lending. You will remember that banks create deposits based on the cash they start with – the more cash they hold, the more deposits they can create.

3.2 The money multiplier

Definition The **money multiplier** gives the change in the money supply for a £1 change in the quantity of the monetary base.

Thus we can write

Money supply = money multiplier × monetary base

3.3 Activity

What is the maximum amount of credit that the monetary base in the previous example can support?

3.4 Activity answer

With a 10% reserve ratio, £1,000 of cash can support customer deposits of £10,000. If there is sufficient demand for loans, the final balance sheet will look like this;

The Banking System—Balance at end of the lending process

	£		£
Share capital	100	Fixed assets	100
		Loans	9,000
Customer Deposits (1,000 + 9,000)	10,000	Cash	1,000
	10,100		10,100

In this case, £1,000 cash has been used to create money of £9,000. The change in bank deposits is given by $\left[\text{initial deposits} \times \frac{1}{\text{reserve ratio}}\right] = £1,000 \times \frac{1}{10\%} = £10,000$. The bank multiplier is thus 10, and the credit multiplier is 9 ie, $\left[\frac{\text{new loans}}{\text{initial deposit}}\right] = \frac{£9,000}{£1,000}$

4 THE COMMERCIAL BANKS

4.1 The primary banks

The primary banks are also known as retail banks, and consist of all banks who participate in the Bank of England's clearing system. The main commercial banks are the big high street ones, Barclays, Lloyds-TSB, Midland, Natwest, Abbey National and a number of Northern Ireland and Scottish banks, such as the Bank of Scotland. In addition, there has been an increase in the number of such banks with the demutualisation of some of the larger building societies, eg, Halifax and Northern Rock.

4.2 Secondary banks

These are principally the merchant banks, foreign banks and consortium banks, and almost all are London-based. They are sometimes referred to as the wholesale banks because they have few, if any, branches and deal only in very large amounts of money obtained either directly from personal, business and public sector customers or via brokers in the City money markets.

The distinction between primary/retail and secondary/wholesale banks has become increasingly blurred over time as a result of the diversification of services and the acquisition or setting up of subsidiary institutions. In particular, the primary banks have moved into those forms of business (eg, term lending) that were previously the preserve of the secondary banks.

4.3 The clearing banks

The members of the London Bankers' Clearing House are closely linked with the Scottish Clearing Banks. The Clearing Houses are systems for simplifying daily payments so that all the thousands of individual customer payments are reduced to a few transfers of credit between the members. The bulk of the business is transacted by the big four - Barclays, Lloyds, Midland and National Westminster. Most payments made by transfers of bank credit within the UK pass through the various clearing systems of these banks.

5 THE BANK OF ENGLAND

5.1 Introduction

The Bank of England is the UK's central bank.

Definition A country's central bank is the bank which is used by the government to manage its monetary policy and to supervise its financial system. It acts as banker to other banks in the system.

The Bank of England was set up in 1694 as a private company and was nationalised in 1946. It has a number of roles in the economy, most of which are common to central banks of all countries. They are described below.

5.2 Functions of the Bank of England ('The Bank')

(a) The Bank is responsible for issuing notes and coins; it is the only institution which has the power to do this in England and Wales.

(b) The government uses the Bank as its banker for departments which are temporarily in financial deficit, by providing 'Ways and Means Advances'. It keeps the accounts of government departments, which operate in exactly the same way as standard bank accounts.

(c) A more important aspect of its role as government's banker is that it manages the issue and redemption of government securities such as Treasury Bills and gilts. If there is need for short-term funds to cover a temporary excess of expenditure over receipts, the Bank will raise money in the markets either by the sale of gilt edged securities ('gilts'), loans with 5 to

15 years to maturity, or by the sale of Treasury Bills, which are loans with 90 days to maturity. The issue of Treasury Bills is crucial to the working of the traditional market and is considered more fully below.

It also gives advice to the government on general financial matters, including making recommendations on possible strategies for controlling the rate of growth of the money supply and influencing the exchange rate. In 1997, the Bank was given the responsibility for setting short term interest rates via its monthly Monetary Policy Committee meeting, after which an announcement is made relating to the level of the base rate for the following month.

(d) It is the bankers' bank. The UK clearing banks hold accounts at the Bank, which are subject to certain controls. The accounts are primarily used to clear cheques at the end of every day. For example, if Nat West customers have drawn £3 million in cheques payable to Lloyds customers, while Lloyds customers have written £2 million of cheques payable to Nat West customers, the net £1 million will be taken out of the Nat West account and paid into the Lloyds account at the end of the day.

(e) The Bank manages the **Exchange Equalisation Account** and the country's reserves of foreign currencies and other assets suitable for overseas transactions. It also deals with all aspects of foreign monetary affairs, representing the UK in trade negotiations.

(f) Probably its most important function is to supervise the monetary and banking system. The collapse of the Bank of Credit and Commerce International (BCCI) brought into question the monitoring abilities of the Bank of England. Luckily, however, this type of incident is rare.

(g) The banking system is based on confidence and is potentially vulnerable to collapse. The Bank oversees the system, acting as lender of last resort.

Definition If the banking system needs funds, then, as a last resort, it will be able to obtain them from the Bank of England. The Bank therefore acts as lender of last resort.

Conclusion The Bank of England, as the UK's central bank, has maintained a pivotal role within the financial and monetary system. Its influence has increased recently, as a consequence of the government granting it additional interest rate fixing powers in 1997.

6 DISCOUNT HOUSES

6.1 Underwriting the Treasury Bill issue

The discount houses have a special relationship with the Bank of England. They underwrite the whole of the weekly Treasury bill issue, which is the means whereby the government raises short-term finance.

Definition Treasury Bills are short-dated (91 days) government securities issued by the Bank of England each Friday, originally designed to finance shortfalls in government revenue over expenditure.

6.2 Taking clearing banks' surplus funds

The clearing banks lend money at short notice to the discount houses. This is an invaluable benefit to the banks - it enables them to lend surplus funds on the agreement that they will be returned when 'called for'. There are two types of lending:

- overnight money - the banks lend the money at the end of the working day and call it back as required at the start of business the following day;

- money at call - the banks lend money to the discount houses on the understanding that they can call it back whenever it is needed.

6.3 Borrowing from the Bank of England

The discount houses are committed to take up the weekly Treasury Bill tender. The *quid pro quo* is that the Bank of England will act as lender of last resort to the discount houses and lend them money if they run short of cash.

6.4 Acting as intermediary for the Bank's monetary policy - open market operations

The discount houses thus have a pivotal role in the implementation of the Bank of England's monetary policy. We shall take an overview of this now and then put it all in context a little later.

The Bank can squeeze the clearing banks' cash by selling Treasury Bills or other government stocks in the market at attractive rates. The financial institutions, including some banks, will be the main purchaser and cash will therefore flow from the clearing banks to the Bank of England. This will put pressure on the clearing banks' ratio of cash held to deposits; we used 10% in our earlier example. The clearing banks will then call back their money at call from the discount houses who may not have the available cash - they might have had to take up a large Treasury Bill issue which will again result in cash flowing to the Bank of England.

We thus have the position where the Bank of England has squeezed cash out of the system.

The Bank will now lend cash to the beleaguered discount houses who can then repay the clearing banks and restore equilibrium to the system. The possible consequence of this process will be a general increase in short term interest rates. A shortfall in the supply of cash will increase its price, other things being equal.

7 CONTROL OF MONEY SUPPLY

7.1 Introduction

In this section, consideration is given to how money supply is controlled. Control is administered by the Bank of England but policy is, of course, the responsibility of the Government of the day.

The main weapons available to control the supply of bank credit created by the private sector banking system are the following.

7.2 Open market operations

These are now used chiefly for day-to-day control, bearing in mind that the Bank must ensure that there is a sufficient supply of money at any particular time to finance normal business transactions.

At this stage, you may wish to revise the explanation of the creation of bank credit outlined above. Remember that the total amount of additional money created depends on:

(a) the amount of cash in the banking system which may be used to create further deposits; and

(b) the proportion maintained between this cash and the amount re-lent as fresh loans to customers.

There is normally a stable ratio between the cash retained by the banks and the amount of loans to customers.

It is now easy to understand the principle underlying the open market operations. Suppose the Government makes a new issue of bonds and sells these on the open market. Private and non-bank institutional customers will buy the bonds and pay for them by cheques drawn on their accounts with a commercial, probably a clearing, bank. When the cheque is cleared, credit passes from the normal commercial banking system to the accounts of the central bank. Thus the effective amount of 'cash' in the private commercial banks is reduced. As they want to maintain the prudent ratio between 'cash' and loans, they will have to cut back on their lending or, alternatively call in some of their already existing loans. Either way, the total amount of bank deposits, and therefore money supply, is likely to decrease.

Should the Bank desire to increase the capacity of the clearing banks to lend to customers, it can purchase bonds on the open market. Credit then passes from the central bank to ordinary banking customers. The Government can, of course, adjust the prices of bonds in accordance with its desire to buy or sell, and it is this price of bonds that determines the rate of interest in the market.

7.3 Interest rates

Interest rate control represents an important mechanism available to the government. A situation where money supply growth appears excessive is likely to be met with a response of high interest rates. Such a strategy makes it more expensive for customers to borrow from the banking system, thereby reducing the demand for borrowed funds and simultaneously diminishing the credit-creating ability of these institutions.

Conclusion In theory the government has in its armoury a number of weapons to control money supply, but in practice reliance is placed on two - open market operations and interest rates.

8 MONETARY POLICY:- BOND PRICES AND INTEREST RATES

8.1 Introduction

The relationship between bond prices and interest rates provides the key to understanding monetary policy. We give some detailed attention to this as the corporate treasurer needs to understand how government policy will affect the cost of finance and also the yield on short-term investments.

Governments finance their activities mainly by tax revenue. When there is a shortfall between tax revenue and planned expenditure, the government needs to borrow – this is called the net cash deficit in the UK. Most borrowing is achieved by issuing government stock which is a form of bond. Variations in the demand and supply of bonds will affect interest rates as explained below.

Conclusion A shortfall between tax revenue and government expenditure triggers a need to borrow—the net cash deficit (NCD). Most borrowing is achieved by selling bonds.

8.3 Bonds

Definition A bond is issued by the government as a means of borrowing. It is like an IOU: the purchaser lends the government money, in exchange for which the government agrees to pay interest.

Bonds come in many different forms, but here we will be interested primarily in irredeemable bonds.

Bonds may be redeemable, in which case the government will repay the initial loan at some specified future date; or irredeemable, in which case the loan remains in place forever. The following discussion applies to both types of bond, but we concentrate on irredeemable bonds, for the sake of simplicity.

A bond has a nominal value and a market value.

Definition The **nominal value** of a bond is its face value. The **market value** is the amount for which the bond may be bought and sold. There is no connection between the nominal and the market values, though the majority of bond issues are at a price fairly close to the nominal value - ie, £100.

For example, a £100 nominal value bond might be sold for £120, its market value. The £100 is simply a unit of measurement used to specify the quantity of bonds which are being traded, in much the same way as kilos are used to specify quantities of vegetables, say.

The interest payable on a bond is the 'coupon' rate, or simply 'coupon'.

Definition The coupon on a bond multiplied by the bond's nominal value gives the annual interest payable on the bond.

Example: a bond has a coupon of 4%. How much interest will the holder of £100 nominal value of the bond receive each year?

Solution: bonds are generally issued in units of £100 nominal value. A £100 nominal value, 4% bond would pay £100 × 4% = £4 interest each year.

Note that the amount of interest is fixed at £4 per annum, regardless of the **market** value of the bond. The holder of the bond could have paid £2 or £200 for the bond; he will get £4 interest, whatever the price was.

8.4 Activity

Suppose a holder of a 4% coupon, £100 nominal value bond had paid £20 for the bond. What annual rate of return is the investor getting on his investment?

8.5 Activity solution

As before, the interest paid on the bond is £4 per annum. The investor has invested £20 in the bond, so he is getting an annual return of £4 on £20, a percentage return of £4/£20 = 20% per annum.

The percentage rate of return achieved on a bond depends on the original price paid for it. The example in the activity would give the same answer if it had asked for a percentage return on a building society account balance of £20, which paid the account holder £4 interest each year.

8.6 The relationship between bond prices and the general rate of interest

Bond prices are inversely related to the general rate of interest in the economy. If interest rates rise, bond prices will fall, and vice versa. (In fact this relationship also applies to other assets, such as shares.)

You can see why in the following activity.

8.7 Activity

(a) The bond in the question above had a market price of £20. What can be inferred about the going rate of interest in the economy?

(b) Suppose the going rate of interest were 10%. How much would the bond cost?

8.8 Activity solution

(a) From the previous activity, we know that when the bond has a price of £20 it yields an annual return of 20%. Therefore the going rate of interest in the economy must be approximately 20% also. If the going rate of interest were higher than 20%, no one would buy the bond. If the going rate of interest were lower than 20%, the bond would be an extremely attractive investment, and everyone would want to buy it. This would drive up its price, changing the rate of return it yields (since the **absolute** amount of interest is fixed at £4 per annum).

(b) For example, if the going rate of interest were 10%, everyone would rush to buy the 20%-yielding bond. The price of the bond would rise until it, too, gave a percentage return of 10%. In fact, the price would rise to £40, since this gives a 10% return: £4/£40 = 10%.

In the above activity, when the rate of interest **halved** from 20% to 10%, the price of the bond **doubled** from £20 to £40. This was because the coupon is fixed according to the nominal value of the bond, so the only way in which the **percentage** rate of return on the bond can change is if its market value changes. To **reduce** the rate of return on the bond, the market value must **rise**; and vice versa.

Conclusion The price of bonds is inversely related to changes in the general level of interest rates.

It should now be clear why government sales of bonds (which drive down bond prices) spark interest rate increases and vice versa.

It is important now to explain exactly why the government may want to control the money supply. Quite simply, excessive money in the system is thought to drive inflation. This relationship is explained by the Quantity Theory of Money.

9 THE QUANTITY THEORY OF MONEY : THE LINK BETWEEN MONEY AND INFLATION

9.1 The quantity theory of money

The quantity theory of money is expressed as follows:

$$MV = PT$$

where:

M = the money supply (money stock)
V = the velocity of circulation
P = the average value of transactions in a period
T = the number of transactions that takes place in a period

Definition The velocity of circulation is the frequency with which the money stock is spent.

An example will explain:

Suppose the money supply in an economy consists of £1 million. In any given week, every £1 coin buys £2 worth of goods. For example, I might spend £1 on groceries and the grocer might then spend half the money (50p) on a newspaper and the other 50p on a light bulb. My £1 has paid for a total of £2 worth of goods. It has changed hands twice: once when I bought the groceries, half again when the grocer bought the newspaper, and another half when the grocer bought the light bulb.

The stock of money in this economy (M) is £1 million, and the velocity of circulation (V), the frequency or speed with which the monetary unit, £1, is spent, is 2.

Returning to the example, the number of transactions which took place was three. If everyone in the economy were to carry out the same transactions in a week, the total number of transactions (T) would be 3 million.

Finally, the average value of the transactions (P) is $\frac{£(1+0.5+0.5)}{3} = \frac{£2}{3}$. In the economy in general one can think of the average value of transactions as being measured by a price index, such as the RPI.

Putting the figures together in the quantity theory of money equation, we have:

$$£1{,}000{,}000 \times 2 = \frac{£2}{3} \times 3{,}000{,}000$$

ie, £2,000,000 = £2,000,000

All the quantity theory is saying is that the money spent in a period equals the total amount of money received in that period.

9.2 Activity

The money supply in an economy equals £100 million. The average good costs £250 and the number of transactions carried out in a week is normally about 400,000. What is the velocity of circulation?

9.3 Activity solution

MV = PT and, rearranging, V = PT/M, where here:

M = £100,000,000
P = £250
T = 400,000

Therefore, V = (250 × 400,000)/100,000,000 = 1.

9.4 The relationships between the variables

As it stands, the quantity theory of money is simply a fact: total expenditure equals total receipts. It becomes a theory when the relationships between the variables are examined.

The velocity of circulation, V, is thought to be fairly stable at least in the medium-to-long-term, governed by payment patterns established in the economy. T, the number of transactions which takes place, essentially depends on the number of goods available to buy. This is fixed by the productive capacity of the economy and changes only relatively slowly over time (currently about 2% p.a.). If the money supply is determined by the government then the price level is dependent on the values of the other three variables.

Looking at the equation MV = PT, you can see that if V is stable and T grows in line with the growth rate of the underlying economy, then if the government allows the money supply to grow faster than this underlying growth rate, prices will rise and the economy will suffer inflation.

Conclusion Excessive growth in the money supply causes inflation. To avoid inflation, the money supply should only be allowed to grow at a rate corresponding to the growth rate in productive capacity. This is called the 'Monetary Golden Rule'.

9.5 Assessment

Controlling the money supply in practice is not easy; as stated above, some people doubt whether the government really can control it, largely because new forms of money usually emerge as substitutes for the forms under control. Various targets have been established in the past, aimed at various definitions of the money supply.

Current policy is to set a target for inflation and to set, in parallel, monitoring ranges for M_0 and M_4. M_0 is broadly the monetary base, consisting of notes and coins in circulation. M_4 includes M_0 as well as bank and building society deposits. The argument for M_0 is that it is this which gives the banks a base on which to create credit, so that if this is controlled, so will credit creation be controlled. Equally, M_4 must be controlled as this is the broad monetary measure. Other ways of controlling credit creation were covered earlier.

Since 1980, the government has abandoned direct monetary controls and has used interest rates to control monetary growth. Through the Bank of England's dealings in the money markets and its function as lender of last resort, it can in practice manipulate the general level of short-term interest rates.

Conclusion Current thinking is to contain inflation by controlling interest rates. Interest rate changes then impact on the demand for credit.

9.6 The impact of interest rate changes

Interest rates have a powerful impact on exchange rates. For a country like the United Kingdom, heavily engaged in international trade, variations in exchange rates are extremely significant. The years 1997 and 1998 witnessed significant strength of sterling, partly caused by high short term interest rates. In consequence, industries heavily dependent on export markets suffered considerably, resulting in factory closures and higher unemployment.

A policy of high interest rates is designed to discourage borrowing by both the industrial and personal sectors. Insofar as this is successful, aggregate demand in the economy will decrease, thereby possibly leading to a recession with an associated increase in the level of unemployment. At the extreme, not only may industrial unrest develop, but the seeds may be sown for perhaps more fundamental social discontent.

10 THE CURRENT POLICY STANCE : HOW IT WORKS

10.1 The Monetary Policy Committee

The UK government places major reliance on control of interest rates in order to pursue a target rate of inflation, currently 2½% p.a. Interest rates are set on a month-by-month basis by the nine-person Monetary Policy Committee (MPC) currently comprised of four academics, one business person and four bank insiders, including the Governor, Mr Edward George. The MPC takes a view on the likely cause of inflation in the light of recently published economic indicators, such as the level of High Street spending and industrial production, and sets the key base rate of interest accordingly, on which all other interest rates are based.

Conclusion The MPC focuses on controlling inflation by controlling interest rates.

10.2 The relationship with government borrowing

The interest rate determined will have to be consistent with the government funding programme eg, if the government wants to sell a large amount of bonds and the MPC lowers interest rates, there will be tension. To accommodate this, the Bank could buy-in existing bonds but to do so may have to print money, which itself could create inflationary pressure. Suffice to say that a specific interest rate policy designed to control expenditure in the economy and hence the rate of inflation needs to be buttressed by open market operations. The policy is thus designed to influence the demand for money. If the demand falls, for example, the amount of credit required to accommodate people's spending, and hence the money supply, will be lower.

These relationships are expressed in the following diagram.

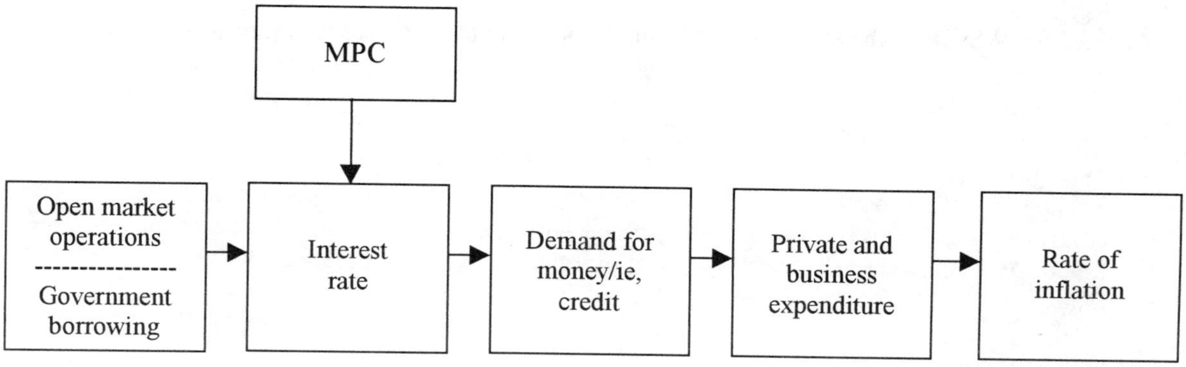

10.3 The future

The important reason for setting up the MPC was to attempt to remove interest rate decisions from the political arena, establishing a system similar to that existing in many EU countries, and thus to prepare the way for the UK's eventual membership of EMU and the introduction of the Euro.

Euro notes and coins are not scheduled to enter circualtion until 2002, although once the eleven founder states fix their exchange rates in Janaury 1999, they will relinquish control over setting of interest rates to the New European Central Bank (ECB), whose primary responsibility is to maintain price stability.

The ECB will be headed by a former Dutch central banker who will preside over the ECB's governing council, made up of the eleven heads of the relevant central banks who will meet every month to determine the cost of borrowing.

The ECB is expected to combine the methods of the present German Bundesbank and the Bank of England. The Bundesbank has a target for growth in money supply and restricts the money supply when its growth threatens to breach the limits. Because monetary growth may be hard to measure, and hence control, in the new system (eleven different economies), the ECB is expected to reinforce its monetary targets with a Bank of England style inflation target.

11 SUMMARY

This chapter has explained how the monetary and banking system operates. In particular, we looked at the process of credit creation by retail banks and how it can be controlled by the monetary authorities. The UK authorities endeavour to control interest rates (supported by open market operations) in order to influence the level of expenditure in the economy which might create inflationary pressure if unchecked. It is important for company cash managers to understand the determinants of interest rates for two broad reasons – firstly, interest rates constitute the cost of borrowing for firms temporarily short of funds, and secondly, they determine the returns available on investing short-term cash surpluses.

12 SELF TEST QUESTIONS

12.1 What is money? (1.1)

12.2 What are the restrictions on the creation of money? (2.5)

12.3 How are the money supply, multiplier and base linked? (3.3)

12.4 Give examples of a primary and a secondary bank. (4.1/2)

12.5 Give five functions of the Bank of England (5.2)

12.6 What role do the discount houses play in the workings of the Bank of England? (6)

12.7 Why does the sale of government bonds lead to increases in interest rates? (8)

5 BANKS AND THEIR CUSTOMERS

PATHFINDER INTRODUCTION

This chapter covers the following performance criteria and knowledge and understanding.

- An understanding of bank overdrafts and loans; terms and conditions; legal relationship between bank and customer (Element 14.2)

Putting the chapter in context

The relationship between the cash manager of a business and its banker is a very important one, and this chapter starts by examining the obligations of both parties. It then goes on to consider the legal aspects and administrative procedures relating to cheques and the banking system in general, information which is essential for the effective management of cash.

At the end of this chapter you should have learned the following topics.

- The relationship between banker and customer
- The law relating to cheques
- The law relating to cheque crossing and endorsements
- Distinguishing valid and invalid forms of payment
- The operation of the clearing bank system
- General services offered by banks
- Duties of the bank/banker
- Lending decisions for personal customers and corporate customers

1 BANKER AND CUSTOMER

1.1 Introduction

When a business has any spare cash it is unlikely to keep much of it on the premises in the form of notes and coins. The vast bulk of the cash will be paid into a business bank account from which the business can then either withdraw the money in cash or make payments by cheque at a later date. It is therefore important to understand the principles of the relationship that exists between the bank and the business.

1.2 Nature of the relationship

As indicated earlier the basic relationship is that of debtor and creditor; as such it is a form of contract. If the customer has a credit balance, the bank is the debtor. The bank is under a contractual duty to honour the customer's cheques so long as there is a sufficient credit balance or an agreed overdraft facility.

As cheques are not presented for acceptance before payment, a bank has no liability to the payee and no obligation to make payment to him out of available funds.

1.3 Duties of the customer

(a) It was held in **London Joint Stock Bank v MacMillan (1918)** that a customer owes to his bank a duty in drawing cheques to take reasonable care to exclude the possibility of alteration. In that case, a cheque was signed for the amount of £2 in figures and without any amount in words. A dishonest employee altered the figure to £120 and wrote in the same amount in words; the bank paid £120 and debited the customer's account. It was held that the customer must bear the loss made possible by his lack of care. However, in **Slingsby v District Bank (1932)**, a gap was left after the payee's name into which a rogue wrote words to enable him to obtain payment. It was held that leaving this gap was not negligent.

(b) A customer usually receives periodic bank statements but owes **no legal duty to the bank to examine them and draw attention to unauthorised debits, etc.**

(c) To inform the bank of any theft or forgery: **Greenwood v Martin's Bank (1993).**

1.4 Duties of the banker or bank

A banker owes the following duties to a customer in relation to cheques drawn by the customer. A bank must therefore:

- Take reasonable care when honouring such cheques

- Honour the customer's cheques to the extent that he is in credit or up to the limit of any agreed overdraft.

  If the banker wrongfully dishonours a cheque (ie, refuses to pay it and usually returns it marked 'refer to drawer') the customer can claim damages.

  Gibbons v Westminister Bank (1939)

  Mrs Gibbons, having paid money into her account, drew a cheque for payment of her rent. When the landlord presented it to the bank it was dishonoured. The bank had put the money paid in by Mrs. Gibbons into the wrong account and therefore thought Mrs. Gibbons had insufficient funds to meet the cheque and had refused to pay it. Mrs. Gibbon's landlord required her to pay cash after this. Mrs. Gibbons sued the bank, but because she could not prove any special damages she was awarded nominal damages only.

  A trader, however, may get substantial damages without proof of special damages, because if a cheque is wrongfully dishonoured, this may damage his credit rating.

  The customer **may** also be able to sue in the tort of defamation. In **Jayson v Midland Bank (1968)** it was held that the words 'refer to drawer' were capable of being defamatory by innuendo.

- Obey the customer's signature by ensuring that only cheques signed by him or his authorised agent are paid out of the customer's account.

  A bank is required to know whether the signature on a customer's cheque is genuine and cannot usually debit his account if it pays on a forged cheque or one which bears a material alteration or if payment has been effectively countermanded.

  However, a customer may lose this protection if he has facilitated the fraud by his negligence (**MacMillan** above) or if, on becoming aware of it, he has left the bank in ignorance.

Greenwood v Martin's Bank Ltd (1933)

Greenwood's wife forged his signature to certain cheques whereby she drew £410 out of his account at the defendants' bank. In 1929 the wife disclosed this fact to Greenwood and persuaded him not to inform the bank. In 1930 Mrs. Greenwood committed suicide and Greenwood then notified the bank of the forgeries and claimed that the bank was not entitled to debit his account with the £410. **Held:** Although ratification had no application to a forged signature, the plaintiff was estopped from alleging the forgeries. His silence until after his wife's death caused the bank to lose their right of action against the forger. The silence of the husband produced estoppel because the relationship of banker and customer is such that the customer is under an obligation to the banker if he is aware that a cheque bears his forged signature.

- not pay a 'post-dated' cheque before the due date, since he will render himself liable if the customer countermands the cheque before that date.

- not 'cash' a crossed cheque drawn by the customer by paying it over the counter unless the crossing has been 'opened' by the customers writing 'pay cash' and the bank is happy that the person presenting the cheque is its true owner.

- give reasonable notice to the customer before withdrawing overdraft facilities.

- not close the customer's current account where it is in credit, without first giving reasonable notice to the customer.

- he must not wrongfully pay a cheque since he owes the customer a contractual duty to take reasonable care when handling the customer's business: **Ligget (Liverpool) Ltd v Barclays Bank (1928)**, where the plaintiff company had told the bank that two directors' signatures were required on all cheques drawn on the company's account. The bank carelessly paid cheques signed by only one director. **Held**: The bank was not entitled to debit the account. However, it was entitled to subrogation (ie, to stand in the shoes of people who had been paid by the cheques which had been wrongly paid by the bank).

- Keep confidential all information which it may have about a customer's affairs but it is released from this duty when the customer gives his consent (eg, to a banker's reference) or the law or public interest requires disclosure or where the banker acts to protect his own interests.

- Not pay a cheque crossed 'a/c payee' to a person other than the payee.

As already stated, it is the duty of the bank to its customer to honour his cheques up to the limit of available funds. If the bank fails to do so the payee has no remedy but the customer can recover damages for the prejudice to his reputation, which will be presumed without specific evidence of loss if he carries on a business.

1.5 Countermand payment ('Stopping cheques')

The authority of a bank to pay on a customer's cheques is terminated:

(a) on countermand of payment;

The countermand must be in writing, unambiguous and contain the necessary details to enable the bank to identify which cheque has been countermanded (eg, the date, payee, amount, cheque number etc.) It must be sent to the branch on which it is drawn. It is not effective until the bank has actual notice of it.

Curtice v London City and Midland Bank (1908)

Curtice drew a cheque on his bank and on the same day, after business hours, countermanded payment by telegram. The telegram was put in the letterbox and, owing to the negligence of the bank's servants, did not reach the manager until two days' later. In the meantime, the cheque was cashed. **Held:** The cheque was not countermanded because:

- countermanding means actual notice to the banker, there being no such thing as a constructive countermand; and
- the bank was not, although they reasonably might accept, bound to accept an unauthenticated telegram as authority to stop payment. (On this basis a telephone call or fax would probably also not suffice.)

If the bank pays a cheque despite it having been countermanded it cannot debit the customer's account. It may however recover the money from the payee if it can be shown to have been paid under a mistake of fact and not just due to the bank's own negligence.

(b) on notice of a customer's death or mental disorder;

(c) on notice of bankruptcy or , in the case of a company, of commencement of winding up; or

(d) on service of a court order in favour of a judgement creditor charging a customer's credit balance with payment of the judgement debt.

1.6 Activity

1. If a bank wrongfully dishonours a customer's cheque, what rights does the customer have?

2. Can a bank pay a post-dated cheque before the due date?

3. When can a bank release confidential information about its customer?

4. Will a telephone call or fax be acceptable by a bank in order for them to countermand their customer's cheque?

1.7 Solution

The answers to the above are included in 1.4 and 1.5. From an illustrative point of view, it is useful when possible to back up the answer by reference to decided case law.

1.8 Conclusion

Both customer and bank/banker have duties to each other. In addition to the debtor/creditor relationship, they may also be joined together by a contract eg, a lending contract. Banks can and do make mistakes from time to time so it is most important that their customers do check their bank statements / loan statements to ensure that they are in fact correct. Bankers do have to behave in a professional and responsible manner; if they don't, and for example cause their customer a loss of goodwill, the bank could be liable for damages.

2 THE LAW RELATING TO CHEQUES

2.1 Introduction

In many businesses a large proportion of cash receipts will be in the form of cheques. It is also likely that most business payments will be made by cheque. Therefore it is necessary for students to understand the law as it relates to cheques.

2.2 Cheques

A cheque is a form of negotiable instrument and most of the legal aspects that surround it stem from its legal definition.

Definition In legal terms a cheque can be defined as " an unconditional order in writing, addressed by one person to another, signed by the person giving it, requiring the bank to pay on demand a sum certain in money to, or to the order of, a specified person or to bearer."

Each of the elements of this definition will now be considered in turn.

2.3 Unconditional order in writing

For a cheque to be valid then it must have no conditions attached to it. It must simply be an order to pay money. For example, 'pay S Hampton £100 if I have more than £250 in my account' would be unacceptable

The fact that it must be in writing includes print. In theory a cheque may be written on any material but in practice most cheques are completed on pre-printed bank-produced cheques. An example of a pre-printed cheque is shown below.

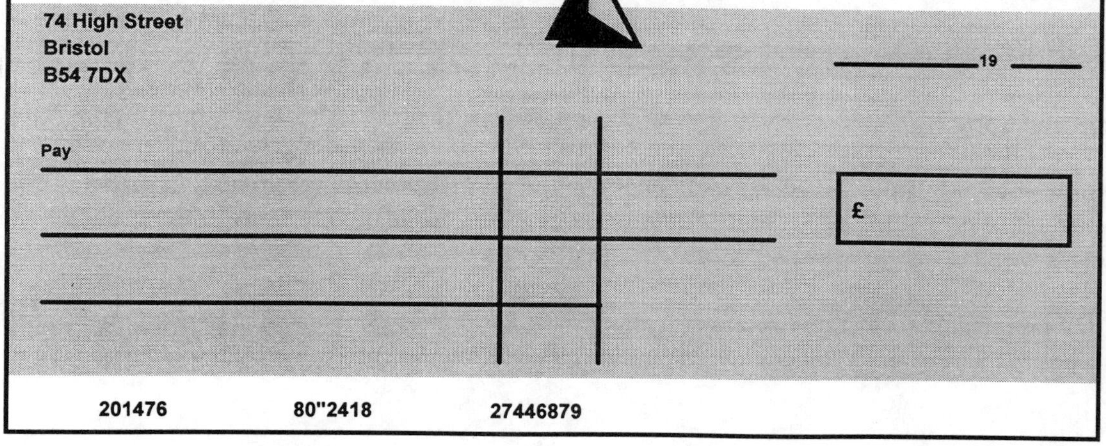

2.4 Parties to a cheque

The next part of the definition concerns the parties to the cheque, ".... addressed by one person to another, signed by the person giving it, requiring the bank ...".

There are three parties to a valid cheque:

- The drawer is the customer of the bank who writes out the cheque. The drawer must sign the cheque.
- The drawee is the bank on which the cheque is drawn, to whom it is addressed. Therefore the drawee is the customer's bank.
- The payee is the person in whose benefit the cheque has been drawn ie, the person who is to be paid.

2.5 On demand

A cheque is payable on demand. Therefore as soon as it is presented to the bank it should be paid. However, if a cheque is drawn up but is post dated (given a date later than the current date) then it cannot yet be paid by the bank and the bank should refuse to pay it. It could however be presented on or after the due date (but see below).

Cheques are paid by banks when they are presented to the bank for payment. This is when the receiver of the cheque pays it into a bank. Banks will generally pay cheques on demand but do tend to regard a cheque that is presented more than six months after it has been written as "stale". Such a cheque would usually be returned to the drawer with an appropriate description.

2.6 Sum certain

The amount to be paid must be stated clearly. On pre-printed cheques the amount is required to be stated in both words and numbers. If there is a difference between the amount stated in words and the amount specified in numbers then theoretically the amount stated in words is the amount payable. However, in practice the cheque will normally be returned to the drawer and marked "words and figures differ".

2.7 Holder of a cheque

A final element of the terminology surrounding cheques is that the holder of a cheque is the person who is in possession of a cheque which is either payable to him/her or is payable to bearer. However bearer cheques (cheques payable to whoever holds them) are not common in practice.

3 CHEQUE CROSSINGS AND ENDORSEMENTS

3.1 Introduction

If a person, or business, receives a cheque then the normal process would be to pay that cheque into a bank account. However, in some circumstances it may be desired to transfer the cheque to another party.

For example suppose that A receives a cheque for £100 from B. A also happens to owe C £100 and wishes to transfer the £100 cheque to C. This can be done by endorsement of the cheque.

3.2 Endorsement

Definition A cheque is endorsed simply by signing the back of it. However, there are a number of different types of endorsement including:

- An endorsement in blank is where the drawee simply the signs the back of the cheque. This cheque is then converted to a bearer cheque which is payable to the holder ie, whoever happens to be in possession of it. The problem with this is that if a third party (neither A, B nor C) became the holder then such a cheque would be payable to that party. The security of such a cheque is clearly minimal and this sort of endorsement is rarely used.

- A special endorsement deals with this specific problem by stating the person to whom the cheque is now to be payable. A special endorsement therefore consists of the name of the party to whom the cheque is now payable (C) together with the signature of the drawee (A) on the back of the cheque. Thus if Alan Smith receives the cheque from Barry John and wishes to pay the cheque to Charles Jones he would endorse the back as follows:

> *Pay Charles Jones*
>
> *Signed Alan Smith*

This cheque can now be paid to Charles Jones and Charles Jones can pay it into his bank.

3.3 Preventing an endorsement

The fact that cheques can be endorsed clearly presents security problems. In general, an endorsement means that the cheque is paid to someone other than the original person for whom it was intended. This may be desirable, but clearly opens the way for fraud.

One way of preventing any endorsement is to write the name of the payee with the added word 'only'. Thus if Alan Smith receives a cheque from Barry John that looks as follows,

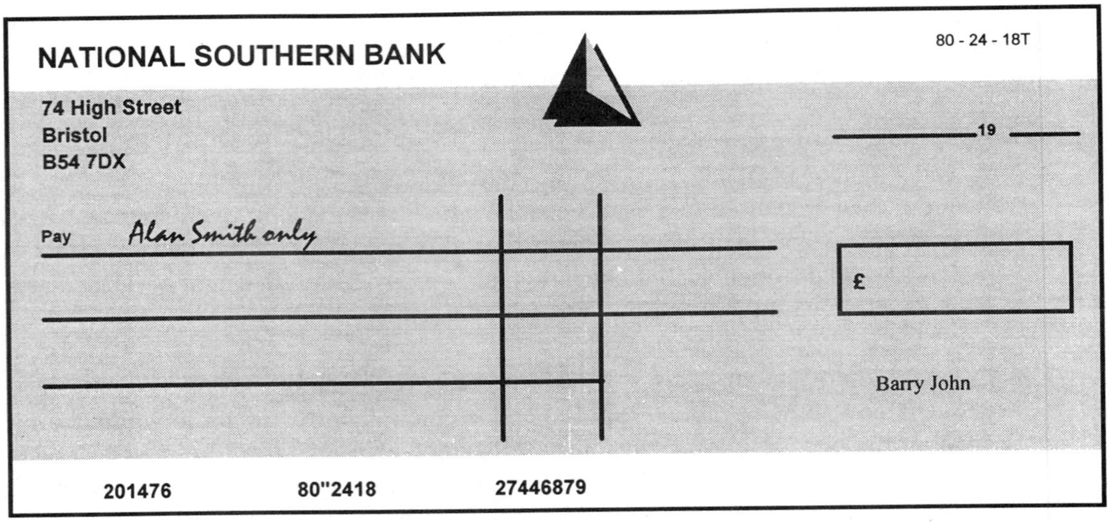

3.4 Crossed cheques

You will notice that the cheque illustrated earlier in this chapter had two vertical parallel lines running down it. This is known as a crossing and this type of cheque is a crossed cheque.

The purpose of a crossing is to ensure that payment on the cheque is made directly into a bank account rather than in cash. Therefore, in general, a crossed cheque cannot be paid in cash by a bank.

Thus if Alan Smith receives a cheque which has no crossing on it from Barry John, Alan Smith could endorse the back of the cheque as follows:

> *Please pay cash*
>
> *Signed Alan Smith*

He could now present this to a bank and the bank would pay him cash over the counter. He would not need to have a bank account.

However, if the cheque is crossed with two vertical lines as shown below, it has to be paid into a bank account and Alan Smith could not endorse it 'please pay cash' as above and could not receive cash for this cheque.

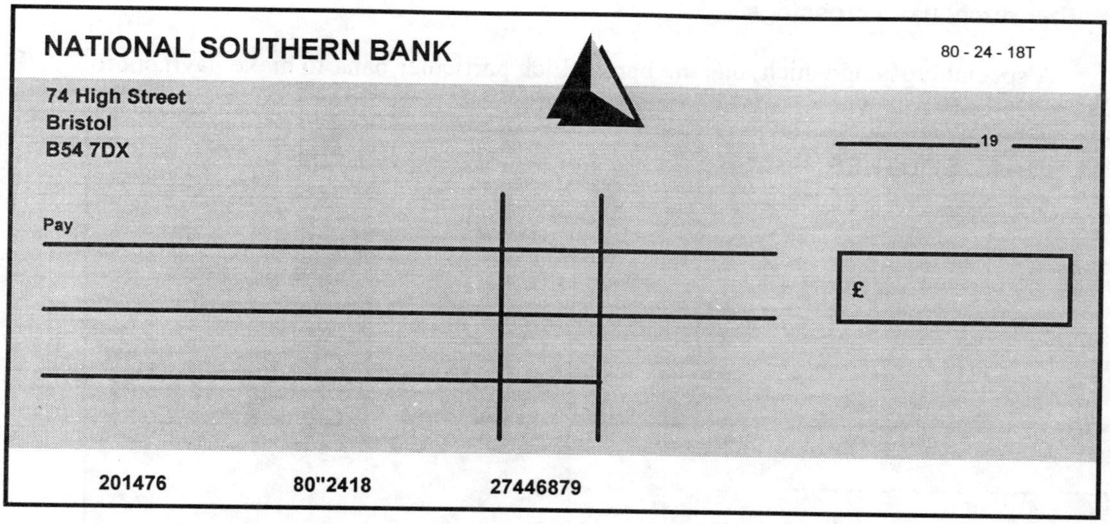

3.5 Cheques crossed 'A/c payee'

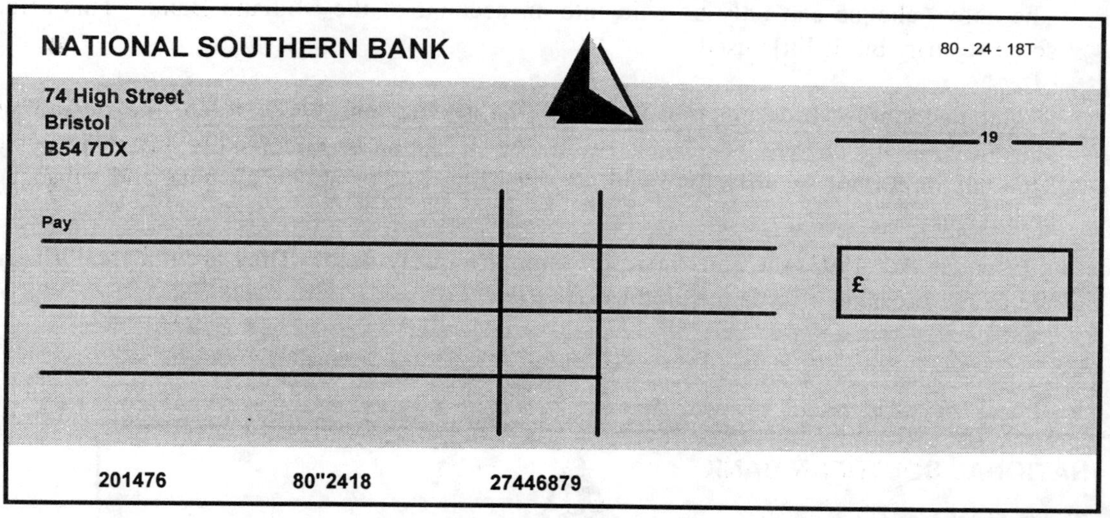

The above cheque is crossed with the words 'A/c payee' (or 'A/C payee only' and be used).

Since the Cheques Act 1993, this is now the most common form of crossing.

Such a crossing means that the cheque can only be paid into the bank account of the payee.

This has the same effect as writing the payee's name followed by 'only', but is a statutory protection and most banks now print cheques crossed 'a/c payee' so that the drawer and the payee are fully protected.

3.6 Two other rarely used crossings

(a) A special crossing which tells the bank which particular bank to make payment to.

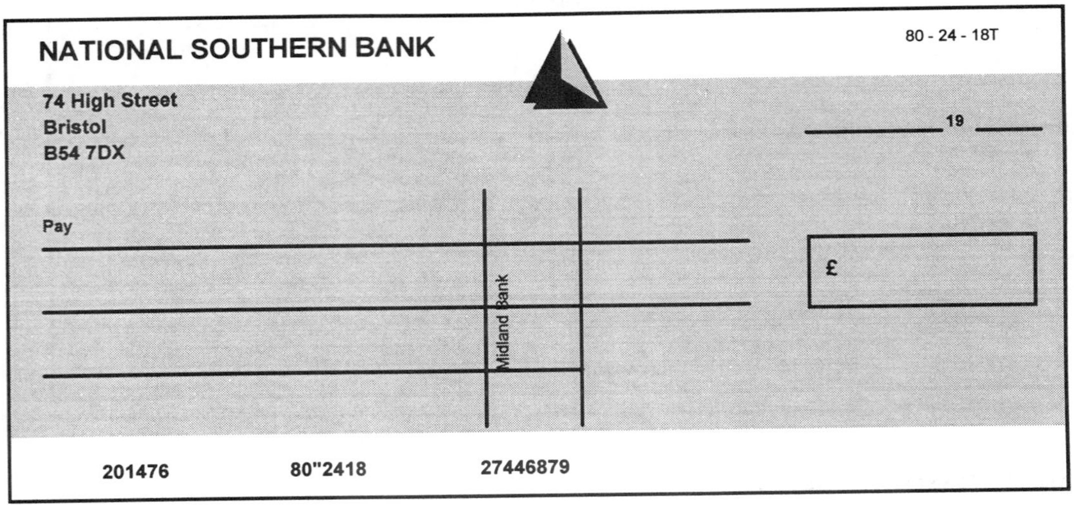

The above cheque can only be paid into an account of the Midland Bank. This affords some security but is little used.

(b) a "not negotiable" crossing means that if the cheque has been stolen, the person who currently has the cheque has no legal title to it. It cannot be endorsed to any other person. This has important security implications regarding lost or stolen cheques and subsequent endorsements.

Since the Cheques Act 1993, the above two crossing are rarely used. They are not totally secure and the 'a/c payee' crossing affords the greatest security.

3.7 Activity

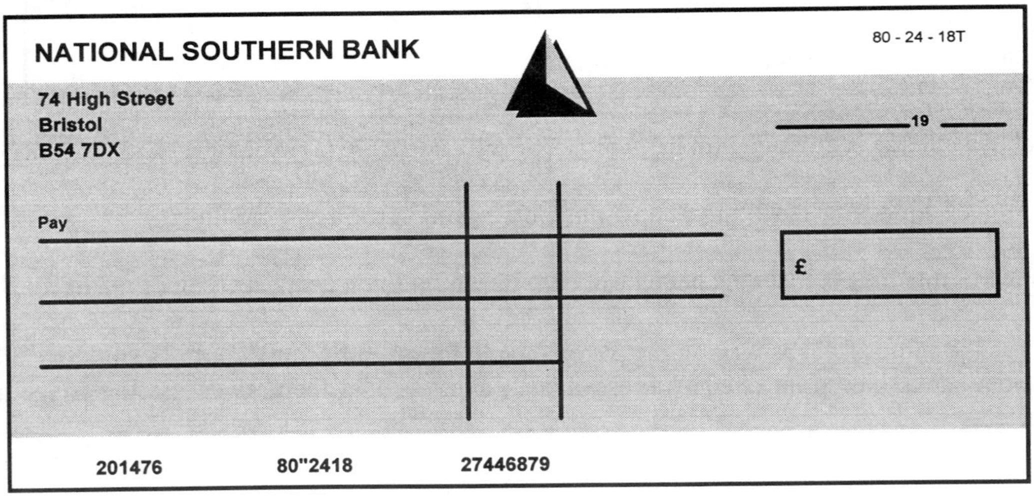

Complete the above cheque, making it payable to D. Bekum Plc for £6,250.39p, date it 1st January 20X3, also cross it so that it can only be paid into D. Bekum Plc's account and no one else.

3.8 Solution

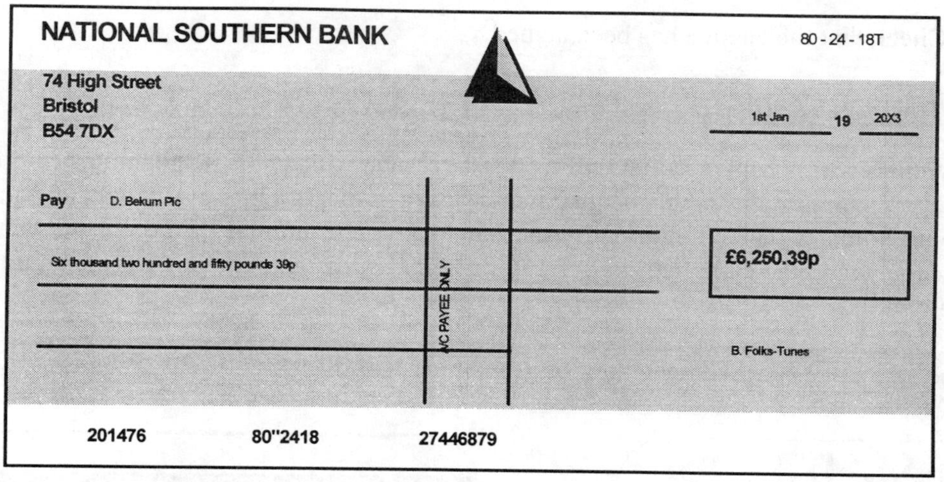

Points worthy of note:

- the cheque should be dated, and
- made out to D. Bekum plc
- figures should be expressed both in words and numbers (as illustrated), and should be in agreement with each other
- it should be signed by whosoever is authorised to sign it
- the crossing needed here is 'A/C Payee only'.

4 RECOGNISING VALID AND INVALID CHEQUES

4.1 Introduction

It has already been noted that many business receipts are likely to be in the form of cheques. Therefore it is important that you are able to distinguish between a valid and invalid cheque.

4.2 Validity of cheques

In strict legal terms, provided that a cheque meets the requirements of the legal definition considered in an earlier paragraph of this chapter, then the cheque will be valid.

4.3 Pre-printed cheques

Most cheques will be written out on pre-printed bank cheques and there are certain details that should always be checked before a cheque is accepted from a customer.

(a) The date of the cheque should be checked. A post dated cheque cannot theoretically be paid by a bank until that date and therefore usually post dated cheques will not be acceptable. When checking the date also check the year (particularly in the first few weeks of a new year).

(b) Check that the payee details have been filled in showing the business's correct name.

(c) Check that the amount is correct in both words and figures. If the words and figures differ request the customer to alter the incorrect element and to sign or initial the alteration.

(d) Check that the cheque has been signed.

4.4 Cheque guarantee cards

All individuals with a bank account will tend to be issued with a cheque guarantee card by the bank. If a cheque is supported by a cheque guarantee card then this is a guarantee that a cheque written by the account holder will be honoured by the bank up to the amount of the cheque guarantee card. Most cheque guarantee cards will be for £50 or £100; cards guaranteeing payments up to £250 are less common.

A cheque guarantee card will usually look something like this:

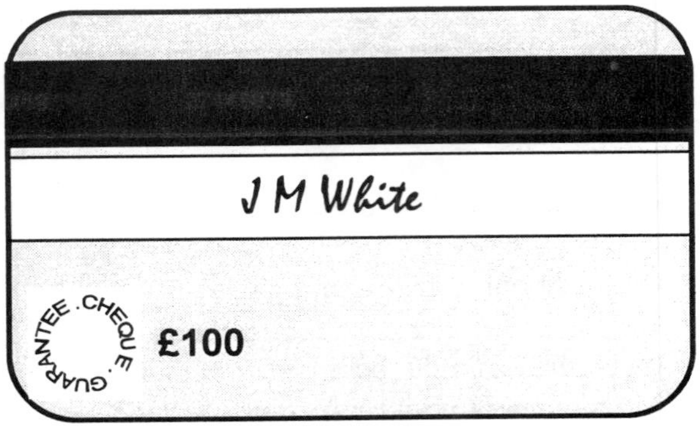

4.5 Acceptance of cheques

It is normal business practice that cheques from individuals are only accepted if accompanied by a valid cheque guarantee card.

Cheques should only be accepted up to the amount of the cheque guarantee card as, if the cheque is any larger, then the bank is not bound to honour it. Only one cheque supported by a cheque guarantee card can be used for each transaction so it is not possible to write out a number of cheques that are all guaranteed for the one transaction.

4.6 Example

Suppose that a purchase is to be made by cheque of an item costing £70 but the purchaser only has a £50 cheque guarantee card. It is not valid to write out one cheque for £50 and another for £20.

4.7 Procedure with cheque guarantee cards

When a cheque is taken together with a cheque guarantee card then the following procedures should be followed:

(a) Check whether the bank details (bank name, account name, account number, sort code) agree with that on the cheque.

(b) Check that the cheque does not exceed the amount of the guarantee card.

(c) Check that the card has not already expired by reference to the expiry date.

(d) Compare the signature on the cheque to the specimen signature on the cheque guarantee card.

(e) Write on the back of the cheque the guarantee card number, guarantee amount and expiry date of the card. The cheque is only supported by the cheque guarantee card if the number is written on the back by the receiver of the cheque, not the payer.

5 THE CLEARING BANK SYSTEM

5.1 Introduction

So far in this chapter the legal aspects and validity of cheques have been discussed. In this paragraph the process of actually banking a cheque will be considered.

5.2 Clearing banks

Definition A bank which accepts deposits of money from persons and businesses and provides them with a payments transmission service and various saving and loan facilities (Collins Dictionary of Business).

Banks such as Midland, National Westminster, Barclays and Lloyds are clearing banks and settle the amount of cheques drawn on them and payable into their accounts through what is known as the clearing system.

5.3 The clearing system

In outline, the clearing system operates in the following manner:

- All cheques paid into, say, Lloyds branches in a day are sent to Lloyds head office. They are sorted into piles according to the bank that the cheques are drawn on, for example all cheques drawn on Midland Bank are grouped together.

- This process will take place in each of the clearing bank head offices' clearing departments.

- The end result might be that for that particular day Lloyds require £18m from Midland to cover the cheques paid into Lloyds branches that are drawn on Midland bank accounts. Midland in turn requires £24m from Lloyds for cheques paid into Midland branches drawn on Lloyds accounts. This is settled by Lloyds paying the difference of £6m to Midland through the accounts that each of the clearing banks hold at the Bank of England.

- Each individual cheque is then sent to the branch on which it has been drawn. If the cheque is valid and the account has sufficient funds then the account will be debited with the amount of the cheque and the payee's account credited.

- Cheques drawn on other banks or building societies are dealt with in the same system with one of the clearing banks acting as their agent.

- Cheques do not leave the branch if both the drawer and the payee have an account at that branch. Cheques are dealt with at head offices if the drawer and payee have accounts at different branches of the same bank.

5.4 Example

Suppose that A writes a cheque to B for £120. A's bank is the Wadhurst branch of Barclays and B pays the cheque into his own bank, the Tenterden branch of National Westminster.

The process that follows can be summarised into the following steps:

Step 1 The Tenterden branch of National Westminster sends all of the cheques paid in that day to National Westminster head office for clearing.

Step 2 National Westminster head office sorts all of the cheques received from its branches into bundles of cheques drawn on each of the other clearing banks. These bundles are totalled to determine the amount owed by each of the other banks.

Step 3 The cheques drawn on other banks are sent to the Bankers Clearing House and exchanged with the other clearing banks in order to determine the net amount due from/to each of the clearing banks.

Step 4 All cheques drawn on Barclays branches and paid into other banks are then sent to Barclay's head office.

Step 5 The cheques are then sent by Barclays head office to each individual Barclay's branch. Therefore A's cheque would now be sent to the Wadhurst branch of Barclays.

Step 6 The Wadhurst branch of Barclays will check that the cheque written by A is valid and that he has enough funds in his account to cover the amount. If this is the case then A's account with Barclays will be debited and B's account with National Westminster will in turn be credited.

5.5 Timing of the clearing system

This whole process of clearing cheques takes three working days. The implications of this are as follows:

- when B pays the cheque into his bank account it will be three working days before the amount credited to his account is technically cleared; and
- when A gives his cheque to B it will be three working days until A's account is debited even if B pays the cheque into his bank straight away.

5.6 Dishonoured cheques

Not all cheques will necessarily be paid by the paying bank. For example if the cheque is incorrectly drawn up or the drawer does not have sufficient funds in his bank account then the drawer's bank will not pay on the cheque. The cheque will be dishonoured.

5.7 Example

Continuing with the previous example suppose that, when A's cheque is sent to the Wadhurst branch of Barclays, it is discovered that A does not have enough funds in his account (or overdraft facility). Then the Wadhurst branch will not debit A's account. Instead the cheque will be marked "refer to drawer" and returned to the Tenterden branch of National Westminster. The cheque will then, in turn, be sent back to B and B must contact A within a reasonable time in order to sort out the problem.

6 OTHER SERVICES OFFERED BY BANKS

6.1 Introduction

The main subject considered in this chapter so far has been the law relating to banks and cheques. However, banks now offer many more services other than the provision of a cheque account. Some of the services relevant to this Unit are discussed below.

6.2 Standing orders

The most common form of payment out of a current account is a payment by cheque. However it is also possible to instruct a bank to make regular payments to a third party by means of a standing order.

A standing order is an instruction to the bank by the payer to pay a certain amount on a regular basis (usually monthly) to a third party. This removes the need for anyone within the business to remember to make the payment and to write a cheque. The types of regular payments that are made by standing order are items such as insurance premiums or hire purchase payments.

Standing orders will be considered in more detail in a later chapter of the study text.

6.3 Direct debits

A bank will also pay a third party on behalf of a customer by a direct debit. This is very similar to a standing order, the main difference being that it is the receiving business that initiates the direct debit and specifies the amount. Also, the amount and frequency of payment can vary with a direct debit.

The types of payments that a business might make using a direct debit include payments of regular bills such as telephone and heating. Again this area will be discussed in more detail later in the study text.

6.4 Credit transfer

A credit transfer is a further method of instructing a bank to make a payment to a third party. This is usually done by the customer filling out a credit transfer form in favour of the third party. This form is typically attached to the bottom of a bill received by the customer and, when completed, is then handed into the bank and the funds are transferred from the payer's bank account to the payee's bank account.

This method of payment is suitable for one off payments or irregular payments to suppliers. Credit transfer forms (Bank Giro Credit) are often found attached to bills such as gas, electricity and telephone.

6.5 Credit cards

Banks do not just offer services within the cheque account system but also a wider range of services such as the provision of credit cards. In this country all of the major banks can offer customers a VISA and/or an Access card.

The customer can then use this card to purchase goods on credit and will receive a monthly statement detailing the purchases made and the amount due. If the full amount due is paid off within a specified time scale then there is no interest charge. However, if there is an outstanding amount left on the card, then interest will be charged by the bank on this. There is also sometimes a yearly fee charged by the banks for the use of the credit card. A typical credit card is illustrated below.

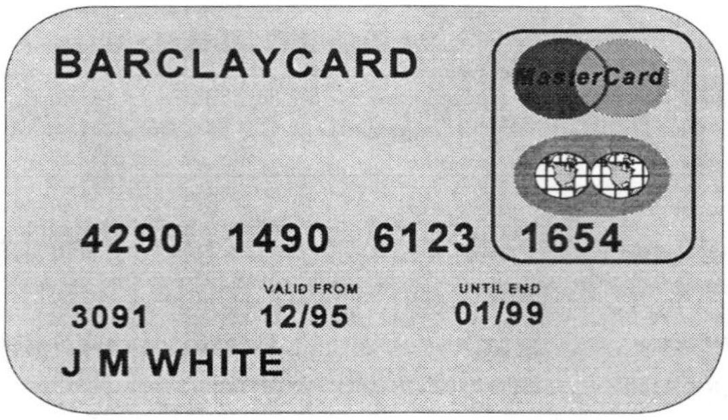

6.6 Debit cards

A debit card is a method of making a payment straight from an individuals bank account but without writing a cheque.

If goods are purchased using a debit card (which looks similar to a credit card) then the card is processed in the same way as a credit card with a voucher being signed by the purchaser. The difference is that the purchaser's bank account is debited immediately with the amount of the purchase.

Debit cards currently in issue include Barclays Connect card and Midland and National Westminster's Switch system.

Depending upon the type of debit card that is used the processing will take place either through the credit card system or through an EFTPOS system.

6.7 EFTPOS systems

EFTPOS stands for "electronic funds transfer at the point of sale". EFTPOS systems mean that it is possible to have an automatic transfer of funds from the customers bank account to the sellers bank account at the time that the sale is made.

6.8 Telegraphic Transfer and Mail Transfer

Telegraphic Transfers (TT) and Mail Transfers (MT) are methods of payment made by a bank on behalf of a customer by electronic transfer of funds from the customer's account to that of the bank account of the party to be paid. A Telegraphic Transfer is one where the customer's bank sends its instructions using the telecommunications system whereas with a Mail Transfer the instructions are sent through the postal system.

These methods of payment are quick but they will only be used in limited circumstances for large payments that are required quickly.

6.9 Deposit accounts

Banks do not only provide customers with current accounts from which they can make payments by cheque. Banks will also offer a variety of medium to long term deposit accounts. The precise details of the terms of different deposit accounts will depend upon the policy of the individual bank.

However in most cases deposit accounts will have the following characteristics:

- they will offer interest on any funds held in the deposit account. The rate of interest may become higher the larger the amount that is deposited.

- there will sometimes be a time restriction on withdrawals. For example a 60 day deposit account will usually mean that if funds are withdrawn without 60 days notice then some sort of penalty will be charged.

If a business has spare cash then it may make sense to hold this in a deposit account and therefore earn interest on it rather than it earning no money in a current account. However the business must first ensure that no penalties are likely to be incurred by early withdrawal of the funds if they are urgently needed.

Some banks now offer current accounts which pay interest on credit balances over a certain amount or in the account for a certain period of time. This combines in some measure the benefits of current accounts and deposit accounts although the interest rate will usually be lower than that on a deposit account.

6.10 Night safe

Many high street banks offer a night safe service. This is where it is possible to deposit cash into a secure night safe in the bank by actually posting it through a designated hole in the wall in the bank.

This is particularly useful for businesses that have large amounts of cash takings that they cannot deposit during normal bank opening hours. Instead they can be put into the bank's night safe and automatically be dealt with the following day.

6.11 Activity

Explain briefly how a direct debit differs from a standing order and the types of payment which it may be used for.

6.12 Solution

(See 6.3) However, you should also note that direct debit is becoming more popular for credit control purposes. For example a debtor may not be granted the usual credit terms but be allowed to receive goods and/or services by agreeing to pay by direct debit.

6.13 Banking Services

Conclusion Banks do provide a multitude of services to individual customers and corporate customers. They have numerous product offerings aimed at both small and large business. They can provide overdrafts and loans, including multi-million pound loans. They can be of great assistance if the business concerned has established a good working relationship with them. The banks on their part may in certain cases put in more time and effort into serving and servicing their key customers, personal or corporate.

7 BANK ACCOUNTS

7.1 Types of account

There are nowadays many different types of accounts which can be used by individuals or businesses, the principal ones being as follows:

- Current Account

  Is an account with a cheque book which can be used to pay money out of the account. Money can be lent on this type of account. When a bank lends money to a customer, interest is paid to the Bank by the customer.

- Loan Account/Personal Loan Account

  Money is always lent on these types of account, with repayment by regular instalments. Interest is also paid to the bank by the customer.

- Deposit Account/Savings Account

  This is an account upon which money can be saved. The customer is here lending money to the Bank and so the Bank pays interest for the use of the money. However the customer has no cheque book but is able to withdraw the money whenever required.

7.2 Bank lending

One of the Bank Manager's main tasks is to lend money. As the money lent belongs to customers of the Bank, care has to be taken to make sure that the Bank will be repaid.

There are several ways in which money can be borrowed from a Bank.

7.3 Bank Overdrafts

The customer is allowed to take more out of the account than has been put into it. The overdraft is for any amount up to a certain figure and normally for a short length of time eg, the customer is allowed to borrow up to £1,000,000 secured on its assets, the limit to be reviewed on an annual basis.

Bank overdrafts from the clearing banks and merchant banks offer a very flexible source of finance which is ideal for assisting in providing working capital. It must be noted, however, that a certain proportion of the working capital should be regarded as a fixed investment and financed from long-term sources of funds. Amounts can be repaid or withdrawn as and when appropriate. If the concern requires more on overdraft an increase can be negotiated quite speedily with the bank. In some cases the banks may ask for security or a guarantee. It is, however, a fact of business life, that many organisations look upon and use their bank overdraft as a long-term source of funds.

For many companies their bank overdraft can be one of their highest forms of borrowing and also **secured** by a fixed or floating charge on their assets. More proof is provided by the banks themselves, in that they do try to get organisations to convert a certain proportion of their overdraft into a term loan. You should note that if an overdraft is treated as long term, then this will affect the liquidity ratios and gearing calculations.

7.4 Loans

Loan capital is strictly not 'capital' at all but rather a long-term creditor. It is the borrowed part of the long-term financing of the company – hence the term 'loan capital' – and is normally regarded as part of the total capital employed when calculating the 'return on capital employed' (ROCE).

Loan interest is charged in arriving at the profit, and is therefore tax deductible, whilst dividends are an appropriation of profit and are not tax deductible, being paid out of taxed profits and carrying a 'tax credit' in the hands of the shareholder.

Both interest and part of the capital borrowed have to be repaid periodically. The amount of interest paid depends upon the general level of interest rates and from where the money is borrowed. The time allowed for repayment is negotiated between the bank manager and customer. The longer the repayment time, the more interest has to be paid.

7.5 Term Loans

Loans can be taken out for varying lengths of time depending on the purpose for which they are required, which may be short, medium or long-term. What is short, medium or long-term will depend to a great extent on the nature of the business/industry eg, long-term in ship building 20 years, long-term in light engineering 10 years.

Short-term loans are usually granted by the clearing banks and merchant banks for a particular purpose. The capital and interest is usually repaid in instalments at regular intervals. The interest charges may be fixed or variable. Depending upon the amount and the size and track record of the company concerned, the bank may require security. Loans are financial products, and if a business/company needs one (short, medium or long), it may be most advantageous to shop around. There are many different loan offerings around, for example:

- unsecured;
- secured;
- fixed rates of interest;
- variable rates of interest;
- with 'repayment holidays', eg, no repayments for the first year.

A vast proportion of funds employed by manufacturing industry are now taken in the form of medium or long term loans, quite probably as a direct result of the matching process (eg, financing fixed assets). There are several sources from which this type of funding can be obtained. The principal ones are as follows:

- the clearing banks;
- merchant banks;
- finance houses;
- foreign banks;
- the EU.

The terms relating to interest charges and repayment vary considerably, providing the borrower with greater flexibility. Repayments can be scheduled in a number of ways, eg,:

(a) monthly, quarterly or half-yearly;
(b) no repayments at all for the first one or two years, ie, a 'repayment holiday';
(c) interest only with the capital being repaid at the end of the term.

Such loans may be secured or unsecured depending upon the company's track record, eg, profitability, size, credit worthiness and market expectations. The rates of interest charged are frequently linked to the LIBOR (London Inter-Bank Offered Rate). The company concerned may lose some degree of control over its affairs in that it may have to supply the financial institution concerned with information on a regular basis, eg, cash flows, investment plans, etc.

Long-terms loans are frequently in the form of debentures which may be simply described as 'a written acknowledgement of indebtedness, under covenants set out in a trust deed, which can be transferred or traded'.

Debentures are usually secured by charges which crystallise on default of payment of principal or interest under the covenants and terms of the debenture trust deed, but may take one of three forms:

- secured by a charge on specific assets – normally land and buildings, but sometimes equipment – and often, but not always, the asset whose purchase has been financed by the loan.
- secured by a floating charge – on all or a portion of the total assets. This is often expressed as a charge over the 'assets and undertaking' of the business.
- 'naked' debenture – unsecured by any charge.

A mortgage loan is similar to a debenture – save that it cannot be traded.

Project loans

These are for specific projects which may have their repayment profiles linked to the cash flows expected from the project. These are available from the 'money market' made up of accepting houses, UK and overseas banks. Call loans are available from the 'money market' and enable the company to repay tranches of the loan during its life and to redraw as required.

7.6 Borrowing from other sources

Whilst Banks can lend for most purposes money can also be borrowed from:

Insurance Companies who lend money to people who have insured their lives with them.

Building Societies who lend money (called a mortgage) to help buy a house / or some other asset.

Credit Card Companies who lend money to help buy household goods, electrical goods etc.

Hire Purchase Companies who lend money to help buy cars, household goods, etc.

Government (and EU) schemes come and go but may take the form of a loan guarantee scheme. This is a scheme in which the government guarantees a certain proportion of loans made by participating institutions.

7.7 The lending decision

As mentioned above, banks do extend credit to their individual and business customers via overdrafts and loans. However, before they do go ahead and authorise the lending they have to vet the application with great care and skill.

When customers come to borrow money the bank would have to establish:

(a) how much money is needed and how it is to be used?
(b) how the money is to be repaid?
(c) the credit worthiness of the individual or corporate customer.

7.8 Banks vetting applications for personal loans (including loans to new businesses)

Bankers need to find out quite a number of things which will help them come to a decision, and the following are of prime importance *(Bank Education Service)*:

(a) Character

Do you know enough about the customer?

Is the customer honest and trustworthy?

What has the customer's record with the Bank been like eg, how have they managed their current account?

(b) Purpose

What is the money to be used for?

Is the loan for starting a shop which sells something the customer knows very little about, eg, the local sweet shop owner buying a motor bike shop, or is the money to be used for buying an old car.

(c) Amount

How much is needed?

Is the amount asked for enough for the purpose?

Does the customer have any savings?

Is so, where? (It is usually expected that some of a customer's own money is used.)

In some instances eg, for the purchase of cars the law says that a customer must provide some of the money for the purchase. In these cases the Bank must always make sure that the minimum amount is provided by the customer.

(d) Repayment

For how long does the customer need the loan?

The longer a customer has the loan the more interest will need to be paid. Again the law may say that the loan has to be repaid within a certain time. If so the bank cannot lend for longer than the specified period.

(e) Capability

Will the customer be able to repay?

At the start it must be clear from where the money for repayment is to come. There are three things to find out from your records or by asking the customer:-

(i) How long and how successful has the customer been at work?

(ii) Is the customer thrifty or extravagant?

(iii) After paying all other bills, is there enough income left to repay the loan plus interest?

(f) Personal Resources

How much is being earned is obviously important, but there may be other things of value, eg, a house, life insurance, a car etc. Some of these suggest the customer is thoughtful about money eg, life insurance. Others suggest that the customer is fairly settled eg, a house and is unlikely to disappear very quickly after the loan has been given.

(g) Security

Is there something of value, just in case?

If the bank feels that this may be taking a risk they may ask for a 'security'. This is something of value and easy to sell or exchange for cash. It should be something that they could keep in the Bank's safe, so a car will not do. Good security could be the deeds of a house or life insurance policies.

Above all remember that as well as asking for a loan or overdraft the customer may be seeking advice. Your advice could be more valuable than lending the Bank's money.

Credit Scoring

Many banks have developed streamlined application forms which will enable them to process applications for personal loans with greater speed.

The above are guidelines used by Bank Managers. However, there are always many cases where one manager would say 'yes' to a request for a loan and another would say 'no'.

7.9 Advice from banks

Numerous reports and articles have over the years pointed to an 'information gap' as being responsible for firms having difficulty in obtaining finance from external sources. This obsession with the problems of raising funds from external sources, although very important, has arguably been at the expense of making firms more aware of their internal sources of capital. Firms not only need advice on how to obtain finance, they also need to know how to make the best possible use of it. It could well be the case, that nowadays there is such a wealth of information available that the real problem is a 'communication gap'. Thus, there is a great need for bankers to provide advice and communicate relevant information relating to both internal and external financing. Bankers are in a prime position to develop this ancillary advice service to meet the needs of their customers and to bridge the 'communication gap'. Banks have been instrumental in stimulating more interest in the use of budgetary control simply by requiring firms to produce cash flow forecasts in support of an application for an advance. Assistance given now to encourage firms to make better use of the finance they already employ can only prove to promote the banks' long-term success. If a banking customer can: (1) survive, (2) develop and grow, (3) become more efficient, and (4) manage more effectively, then the bank will also grow and prosper.

7.10 Activity

1. Why do lots of businesses look upon their overdrafts as a long-term source of funds? (8.3)

2. Which factors could lead the bank to require security for a loan or overdraft? (8.4)

3. Explain briefly the difference between a fixed charge and a floating charge (8.4)

4. Why are bankers in a good position to offer business advice? (8.8).

7.11 Solution

See the appropriate sections. It is however useful to pick out the key words. For example, in question 1 above the key words important to the answer are:

- flexibility – repaid as/when appropriate, easy to re-negotiate, quick to organise.
- long-term – actually used as long-term in practice.

- security – by fixed or floating charge.
- term loans – will not convert to term loans, because they are quite happy as they are.
- gearing – treatment can affect the way in which ratios are calculated / perceived.

7.12 Banks vetting loan applications from corporate / business customers

All of the above criteria mentioned in 7.8 would also apply to corporate applicants. However much more sophisticated vetting would need to take place. Banks would look at the following data/information:

- **Internal information**

  For existing customers banks do have a whole host of internal information eg, the customer's performance of internal information eg, the customer's performance in keeping within their overdraft, or keeping up with the payments on a previous loan.

- **Company / customer visits**

  Reports from staff on visits made in connection with other matters, or for the current application.

- **Financial performance and 'track record'**

  The bankers would look very carefully at published reports and accounts, and in particular:

  (a) Ratio analysis which reviews credit control, inventory control, liquidity, profitability, gearing and investor ratios, which are dealt with in greater detail later

  (b) The directors' report

  (c) The accounting policies which are being followed

  (d) Dates when fixed assets were revalued

  (e) Post balance sheet events

  (f) Assets already pledged as security

  (g) The level of gearing eg, is the company is already highly geared?

- **Trade press**

  Re-developments / information about the customer's products, prospects etc.

- **Risk assessments**

  Bankers do tend to be conservative in their outlook and come out with statements such as 'why should we risk our funds, if you are not going to risk yours?' They do not expect to or want to shoulder all the risk. They thus have to assess the risk of default and also whether or not they will require security. This could come via credit rating agencies.

- **Credit scoring**

  For certain types of loan it may be possible for the bank to use a rating scale to help them to arrive at a decision eg, loans for vehicles which are to be used in the business.

- **Independent advice**

  Banks may also be able to employ specialist advisors if the circumstances so dictate eg, for applicants from high-tech ventures, for very large lending proposals, for international lending etc.

7.13 Conclusion

Banks do extend credit to both individual customers and corporate / business customers by way of overdrafts and/or loans. In arriving at their lending decision they have to vet and review the applications in much the same way as any other credit control function / department. They too have to aim at keeping bad debts to a minimum and ensure that repayments are received on the due dates. They have to chase slow payers, re-schedule debts in certain cases and as a last resort call in overdrafts or start legal proceedings to have their customer wound up.

7.14 Activity

Dee and Doe wish to start a painting and decorating business. Dee would do all the painting and decorating, and Doe would keep the accounts and perform the administrative duties. Dee had worked part-time for one year with a relative, painting windows and door frames. Doe, aged 20, had successfully completed a Bec National Diploma in Business and Management Studies. Dee, now aged 21, has no formal qualifications apart from 4 GCSEs and 'A' level general studies at grade D. They both have balances of £3,000 in the building society and jointly £644 in the bank. They jointly own a house valued at £65,000.

Required

They have come to your bank and requested £45,000 to cover the start-up of their business. This should cover leasehold premises, £25,000 a vehicle £8,000, equipment £7,000 and £5,000 for working capital.

If you were the banker, explain with reasons whether or not you would give them this loan, and whether or not you would require security.

7.15 Solution

This is in effect a question with a catch. The answer is quite simple. Although they do have adequate security and a reasonable amount of savings, Dee does not have the experience which would be necessary to run this kind of business. If Dee is really keen then the banker should recommend that she receives relevant training first and also gains more experience eg, interior work etc. Thus, their proposal falls down on their capability to make a success of such a business.

7.16 Bank managers – 'old school or new breed'?

In recent times the banks have been subjected to a barrage of criticism for their failings in meeting the financial needs of small firms. It was in this context that a recent study held interviews with five bank managers from large northern city branches to ascertain what they felt about their own relationships with the small business sector in the UK. The interviews were designed to obtain the manager's view as opposed to the official view. It was, however, too much to expect managers to talk in general terms as their own experience and views depended very much on the attitudes, facilities and environments within their own banks.

It is extremely difficult to analyse in tabular form the responses of the managers to the various questions posed. The table does attempt to summarise the replies to certain key questions, but for a clearer understanding we must examine what the individual managers actually said.

Question		*Answer* *Mr A*	*Mr B*	*Mr C*	*Mr D*	*Mr E*
1	Are managers conservative by nature?	Yes	Yes and No	Yes	Yes	Yes and No
2	Is security essential for a new venture?	Yes	No, but	Yes and No	Yes	No
3	Should the banks have equity holdings in small companies?	No	Yes	Yes, but	Yes	Yes, but
4	Are terms loans adequately covered?	Yes	Yes	Yes	Yes	Yes
5	Have the banks too many schemes?	Yes	Yes	Yes	Yes	Yes

Conservatism

Although A said 'yes', he was convinced that in the south younger managers working in a more commercially vibrant environment could be less conservative. B did not agree about geographical location affecting conservatism, but did agree that age was an important factor. This was supported by C who said, 'You can't change the habits of 30 years', and E who believed that there was still a lot of 'deadwood' in the system.

- Are younger managers less conservative in their outlook?
- Can an old dog learn new tricks?
- Have the banks failed in the continuing education of their existing managers?

Education is and always will be a continuing process; a manager worth his salt should strive to keep abreast of current developments. This, however, is not enough: the manager's commitment should be matched by a commitment to continuing education by his/her employers.

Security

Managers appeared to be in agreement that security reflected commitment and provided an incentive on the part of an entrepreneur. B admitted that he would be worried about someone who was reluctant to put up security. It was apparent that banks are still risk averse by the various comments that were made, such as:

- D: Without a personal knowledge of customers, how can an advance be made without security?

- A: What they don't realise is that it is not our money. We have a responsibility to our depositors and shareholders.

It was also evident that change on this front is taking place. Although C considered that managers were risk averse out of the fear of failure, he sensed a more liberal attitude to risk being slowly accepted. E, however, was prepared to consider any viable proposition, security being the last consideration.

The wind of change

The interviews did reveal that slowly but surely the traditional conversative image of bank managers and attitudes to risk are changing. B pointed out that a 'new breed' of managers was beginning to emerge as a result of a more diverse and complex training system.

- C: The people at the top – and I mean London – are very determined but we are a large organisation and change takes time.

- D: If a banker doesn't occasionally back a loser he cannot possibly be operating in the right areas.

In addition, B stressed that in his view there was very little to choose between the main clearing banks in terms of facilities and schemes and that the principal differences were between individual bank managers. Bank managers are people, people are complex and are quite likely to response in various ways. This view was supported by the interviewees:

- C: If I'm having a bad day or I have too much work I'm inclined to say 'No'.
- D: I tend to regard it as my money and I don't like to lose it. Do we really want more small businesses?
- E: I don't need leaflets to tell me what to do.

Equity

Although the majority were in favour of equity holdings in small companies, they also pointed out that they had little or no experience of this and that in certain cases this form of support was dealt with by their venture capital subsidiaries.

Relationship with regional office and head office

Some of the managers expressed a contempt for the people at regional and head office and considered that their banks had become too bureaucratic and impersonal.

- C: I'm encouraged, from above, to go out and visit places and sit down with clients and give help, but it's often just a case of handing them a leaflet.

  The regional office often rejects the projects that I submit, but they don't know the customer as I do.

  The people over there are afraid of making a mistake when they are moving on in a year or two.

- D: We get thousands of new things passed down to us and quite often I only have time for a cursory glance.

  There is downward pressure caused by top level determination to become less security conscious at grass roots level.

  The interviews highlighted the difficulties of attempting to 'graft on' new functions to an existing organisational structure without tackling the serious personal and organisational problems that may ensue. The banks have, over the years, become rather like large oil tankers. They take a considerable amount of time to change direction. The banks have not been able to make the rapid transitions necessary to satisfy their critics. UK business needs to invest not just in new fixed assets, but in organisational efficiency.

  The major problems

  What do bank managers see as the major problems affecting small businesses?

  - A: There is a lack of professionalism, they are aware of how much they need now, but have no idea about future requirements.
  - B: The banks' services are quite adequate; their real problems arise as a result of bureaucratic controls, regulations and taxation.

    The accountants that they employ fail to introduce effective control systems.

More help for the small business?

A and C felt that more personal visits to new and existing customers, backed up by specialist advice, was a step in the right direction. When questioned about their own bank's advisory service the managers concerned admitted that they didn't know too much about that side of things. This indicates that there could well be a 'communication gap' and that the advisory service is not yet working in harmony with the branches.

There was general agreement between the managers that they were satisfied with their own bank's performance. However, E felt that the banks are still poor on the marketing side.

New Schemes

'Just what was needed to counteract the conservatism of certain managers', was how C described the Government Loan Guarantee Scheme. Although most of the managers welcomed this scheme there was unanimous agreement between them that there were far too many new schemes.

- C: You hear all about these wonderful schemes, but there are just too many to be able to know them in detail.

- D: Little did I know when I entered banking that I would be required to become an insurance agent, a computer manager, a travel agent and so forth.

  And E considered that there was no need for any more new schemes as any approaches from entrepreneurs could be satisfied by existing facilities.

Conclusions

Is this very small sample representative? If it is, then the banks should consider freeing their managers from trivia to enable them to use their time and talents in a more productive manner. Structural changes are necessary for improving organisational efficiency and improving morale.
Continuing professional education for existing managers whether they be 'old school' or 'new breed' is a prerequisite for improving the banks' performance in the long term. In a business environment of economic change and uncertainty the banks must be able to respond more quickly.

It is encouraging to find that the banks have already responded to these challenges. Some banks' managers are being freed from trivia, structural changes are taking place and the education and training of managers is certainly more intensive and demanding than it was, say, 10 years ago.

C strongly believed that the clearing banks were the only organisations capable of doing something to help the small business sector. The relationship between banker and customer is unique and has a vital part to play in bringing about an increase in the birthrate and a slowing down of the deathrate of small businesses. After all, the small firms born today could well be the large firms of tomorrow.

8 SUMMARY

8.1 The banker – customer relationship

The relationship is one of debtor/creditor. They may also have a contractual relationship eg, a loan contract or a mortgage contract.

8.2 Obligations

A banker must:

- repay amounts deposited on demand
- honour its customers' cheques
- provide a balance or statement on request
- not disclose confidential information
- use a professional level of care and skill

8.3 Cheques

The ways in which cheques are written and used are governed by legislation. Care has to be exercised by the customer when writing cheques and the bank when dealing with them. There are a number of circumstances where the bank cannot honour a cheque, for example if it's post dated, not signed, or if the words and figures for the amount differ.

8.4 Bank services

Banking services tend to grow all the time eg. telephone banking, the use of credit cards for business purposes, businesses using direct debits to collect amounts owing from debtors etc.

8.5 Bank / Bankers duties

A bank must:

- take reasonable care eg, check signatures

- honour cheques up to agreed overdraft limit

- not accept post-dated or incorrectly filled in cheques

- not cash a crossed cheque or pay a cheque crossed 'A/C Payee Only' into someone other than the payee's account

- give reasonable notice if the overdraft facility is to be amended, or an account is to be closed

- not release confidential information unless required to do so by the customer or by law.

8.6 Bank lending

Banks lend to individuals or business/other organisation via overdrafts and loans.

8.7 Lending to individuals / new businesses

This involves a careful review of:

- Character
- Amount

- Repayment
- Capability
- Personal resources
- Security

8.8 Vetting loan applications from corporate/business customers

In addition to the material mentioned in 8.7, this could also involve consideration of:

- Internal information
- Company / customer visits
- Financial performance analysis
- Trade press
- Risk assessments
- Credit scoring
- Independent advice

8.9 Bank managers - 'old school or new breed'

The final section in this area illustrates the point that bankers, are human and complex variables. Faced with the same information for the same lending decision they could come up with differing conclusions / recommendations.

9 SELF TEST QUESTIONS

9.1 List five duties of a bank/banker to its customer and provide a brief illustration of each (1.4)

9.2 In relation to cheques, what do the following component parts of the definition of a cheque mean?

- On demand (2.5)
- Sum certain (2.6)

9.3 Describe a special endorsement. (3.2)

9.4 Explain what a standing order is and what it can be used for. (6.2)

9.5 Describe the principal considerations / checks which would have to be made before making a large term loan available to an existing customer. (7.7 and 7.9).

6 THE WORK OF THE TREASURY DEPARTMENT

PATHFINDER INTRODUCTION

This chapter covers the following performance criteria and knowledge and understanding.

- The relationships between financial institutions (Element 14.2)
- Liquidity management (Elements 14.2, 14.3 & 14.4)
- Overdraft and loan facilities are arranged in anticipation of requirements and on the most favourable terms available
- Surplus funds are invested in marketable securities within defined financial authorisation limits
- The organisation's financial regulations and security procedures are observed.

Putting the chapter in context – learning objectives.

Management must strive to do the best they can with the limited resources which are placed at their disposal. They have to try to improve the productivity of the capital employed if they are going to survive and prosper. This is why nowadays treasury management, particularly in large organisations, is well established. In many cases its existence is more than justified by the contribution it makes towards *'the bottom line'* ie, profit. Although small and medium sized companies may not be able to have a separate treasury department they can still engage in many treasurership functions eg, investing surplus cash short-term.

The treasury function tends to be responsible for organising the firm's finances, credit control (ie, collecting cash from debtors) and the investment of surplus cash short-term (eg, on the money markets) for periods such as overnight, one week, one month etc. They may also arrange short-term borrowing eg, to sort out a shortage which has been identified by the cash budget. In a group they could be responsible for moving/transferring cash around the group. In cases where the company is involved in international trade, they could also be very involved with foreign exchange management.

In this chapter we review the essential features of the Treasury Department's function; the following chapters then look at two of its main responsibilities: raising finance in the short and medium term (chapter 7), and investing temporary cash surpluses (chapter 8).

At the end of this chapter you should have learned the following topics:

- the basic treasury functions, and how they fit in with the broader area of financial management
- the advantages and disadvantages of a centralised treasury department
- the meaning of, and finance options for, the cumulative capital requirement
- the different types of financial markets: primary/secondary; capital/money
- the development and purposes of parallel markets
- the nature and benefits of financial intermediaries.

1 THE TREASURY FUNCTION AND TREASURY PROCEDURES

1.1 Treasurership

The definition given in Chapter 1 is repeated here as a reminder:

Definition The function concerned with the provision and use of finance. It includes provision of capital, short-term borrowing, foreign currency management, banking, collections and money market investment.

1.2 Finance and Treasury activities: the broad picture

Financial management hinges on two key decision areas:- the investment decision-(what assets to invest in?) and the financial decision (having decided what to invest in, how can we pay for it?) Any financial decision should be aimed at a coherent objective and judged according to how well it meets that objective. Financial decisions should be judged according to whether, (and how much) they create value.

Investment decisions are essentially a search for projections which are worth more than they cost (ie, they create value).

In the case of financing decisions, the same guideline applies, using sources of finance that are worth more to the company than they cost. In a sense, this means trying to secure 'cheap' finance.

With investment decisions, finding value - creating opportunities is relatively straightforward. If the firm devotes resources to R & D and manages the process effectively, a stream of value-creating opportunities ought to emerge whereby the firm can exploit temporary product market imperfections—what marketing people call 'first-comer's advantages'.

With financing decisions this is more difficult. Financial markets are far more perfect than product markets and, given increasing globalisation, are becoming increasingly so. Providers of finance are increasingly able to price in the true risks of lending so that the structure of interest rates across the world's financial markets almost certainly reflects the risks inherent in different types of loan (and other methods of finance). This is a reflection of 'market efficiency' – an efficient financial market is one which fully incorporates the risk/return characteristics of different securities in their relative prices.

It is helpful to visualise the financial manager as operating at the interface of the firm's operations (ie, its investment projects) which drive demand for finance, and the financial markets which supply finances. His/her task is to provide the right amounts of finance, at the right cost at the right times, and to advise on the desirability of different courses of action.

The financial management function

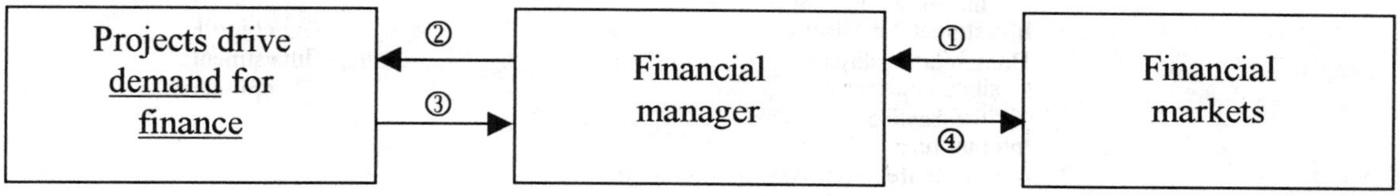

Arrow ① represents the flow of finance into the firm, arrow ②, the allocation of funds to projects, arrow ③, the return flow of cash from successful projects and arrow ④ the return of cash to investors as interest payments and dividends. In most firms, the amount returned to the market (flow ④) is less than the cash generated from operations, as firms wish to retain financial resources for re-investment.

Conclusion Essentially the task of treasury and finance is one of cash flow management—managing the flow of cash into, around and out of the firms to create value for the owners.

These are the broad functions of financial management. 'Treasury' is usually applied to a more specialised set of functions but within this overall framework.

1.3 Treasury activities

The activities of the treasury department have been stated as:

(a) Banking and exchange;
(b) Cash and currency management;

(c) Investment in short term assets;
(d) Risk and insurance; and
(e) Raising finance.

All the areas above are concerned with managing the liquidity of a business, which, as previously discussed, is essential to its survival and growth.

The finance function is typically structured as:

Head office finance department organisation

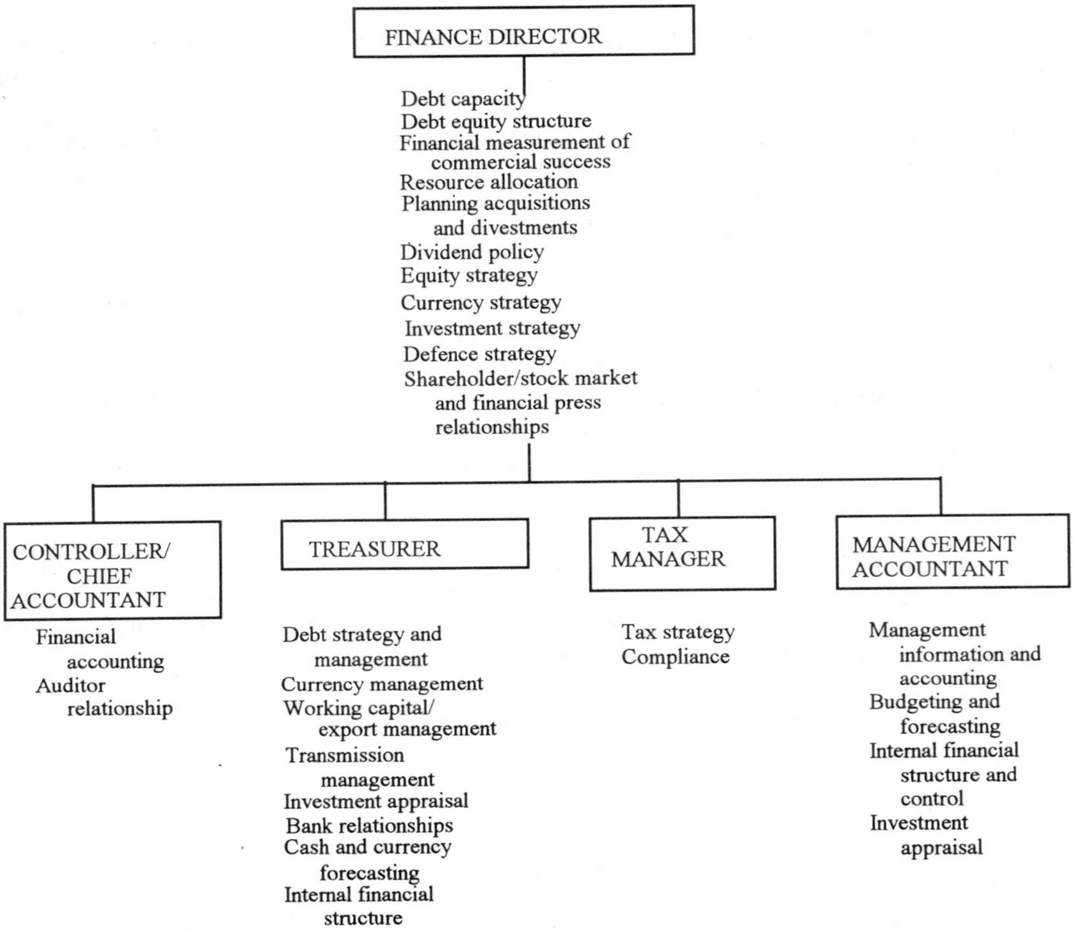

1.4 Reasons for the development of the treasurership (treasury) department

As indicated earlier, the functions carried out by the corporate treasurer have always existed, but have been absorbed within other finance functions. A number of reasons may be identified for the development of a separate treasurership department.

(a) Size and internationalisation of companies. These add to both the scale and the complexity of the treasury functions.

(b) Size and internationalisation of currency, debt and security markets. These make the operations of raising finance, handling transactions in multiple currencies and investing much more complex. They also present opportunities for greater gains.

(c) Sophistication of business practice. This process has been aided by modern communications, and as a result the treasurer is expected to take advantage of opportunities for making profits or minimising costs which did not exist a few years ago.

For these reasons, most large international corporations have moved towards setting up a separate treasurership (treasury) department.

1.5 The role of the treasurer

The treasurer reports to the finance director, with a specific emphasis on borrowing, cash and currency management and the investment of surplus funds. Surplus funds may be invested short-term eg, for overnight, one week or one month etc until required.

In addition, although the major responsibility is held by the finance director, the treasurer will have a direct input into the former's management of debt capacity, debt and equity structure, resource allocation, equity strategy and currency strategy.

Finally, often in common with the controller and management accountant, the treasurer will be involved in the investment appraisal process; and the finance director will often consult the treasurer in matters relating to the review of acquisitions and divestments, dividend policy and defence from takeover.

In summary, treasurers work closely with finance directors in key aspects of the latter's specific responsibilities, and with important decision-making responsibilities of their own. These responsibilities will vary slightly from group to group, but the underlying themes of borrowing, investment, cash and currency management will remain the same.

1.6 Establishing a treasurership department

Traditionally in the UK, the corporate treasurer, in common with other senior finance personnel, has been drawn from the ranks of qualified accountants. This contrasts with the USA, where only a minority of treasurers and finance directors are qualified accountants. However, even in the UK, the position is changing against the accounting profession, and more corporate treasurers are drawn from other sources eg, MBA and the corporate treasury department of multinational companies.

Treasurership departments are not large, since they are not involved in the detailed recording of transactions. They tend to rely heavily on new technology for information. Note that SMEs (small and medium sized enterprises) can also employ a treasury function eg, it could be carried out by the accountant.

1.7 The centralisation of treasury activities

The question arises in a large international group of whether treasury activities should be centralised or decentralised. If centralised, then each operating company holds only the minimum cash balance required for day to day operations, remitting the surplus to the centre for overall management. If decentralised, each operating company must appoint an officer responsible for that company's own treasury operations.

Advantages of centralisation

(a) No need for treasury skills to be duplicated throughout the group. One highly trained central department can assemble a highly skilled team, offering skills that could not be available if every company within the group had their own treasury.

(b) Necessary borrowings can be arranged in bulk, at keener interest rates than for smaller amounts. Similarly bulk deposits of surplus funds will attract higher rates of interest than smaller amounts.

(c) The group's foreign currency risk can be managed much more effectively from a centralised treasury since only they can appreciate the total exposure situation. A total hedging policy should be more efficiently carried out by a centralised office rather than each company doing their own hedging.

(d) Bank charges should be lower since a situation of carrying both balances and overdraft in the same currency should be eliminated.

Advantages of decentralisation

(a) Greater autonomy leads to greater motivation. Individual companies will manage their cash balances more attentively if they are responsible for them rather than simply remitting them up to head office.

(b) Local operating units should have a better feel for local conditions than head office and can respond more quickly to local developments.

2 PRINCIPLES OF FINANCIAL PLANNING AND STRATEGY

Definition Financial planning involves predicting the firm's demand for finance over time, and arranging to meet that demand at the right time and at minimum cost compatible with the firm's financial strategy.

2.1 Introduction

Most companies grow over time, some at a steady pace and others in fits and starts depending on how closely their activities are 'geared' to the overall economy. Growing firms face the need to finance higher levels of fixed assets and also working capital requirements. Fixed capital needs tend to be 'lumpy' ie, firms buy plant and equipment in discrete chunks (although replacement investment may have a smoother profile); working capital requirements tend to vary with seasonal factors, and with changes in policy towards debtors and creditors. The total financing need is called the Cumulative Capital Requirement (CCR), as shown in the diagram below.

The firm's cumulative capital requirement

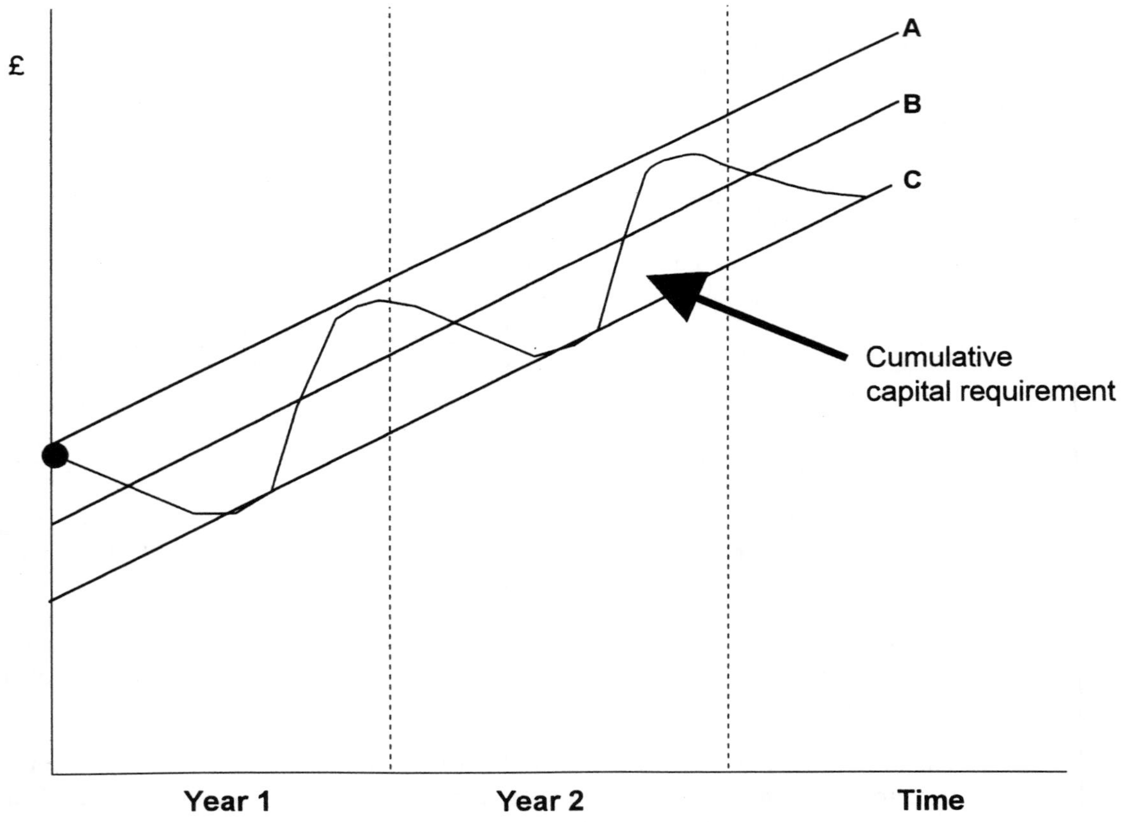

The diagram shows three possible long-term financing paths which firms might follow:

Path A-- always above the CCR. The firm has a permanent cash surplus ie, it is 'over-capitalised'. This is a very 'conservative' financing policy.

Path B— an intermediate strategy where the firm is in cash surplus for part of the year and can lend (ie, put money on deposit) but has to borrow at other times.

Path C— Always below the CCR. The firm is a permanent short-term borrower. This is a highly 'aggressive' policy, where the firm is 'under-capitalised'.

This picture of financing needs and policies is rather limited in what it shows. In particular it says nothing about the relationship between fixed and current assets and how they are financed by long- and short-term liabilities. To examine these issues, we need to look more closely at alternative financing strategies (see below), but first, an activity will provide sharper focus to this discussion.

2.2 Activity

The sales of Dorset plc for 1998 were £100,000. Sales for 1999 are expected to rise by 20% to £120,000. You are asked to advise on the additional financing required to support the higher level of sales. The summary balance sheet of the company as at 31 December 1998 is as follows:

	£		£
Shareholders funds:			
Ordinary shares	22,000	Fixed assets (net)	32,000
Retained earnings	15,000	Inventory	16,000
Debentures	10,000	Debtors	8,000
Creditors	11,000	Cash	2,000
	58,000		58,000

You may assume that except for ordinary shares, retained earnings, debentures and fixed assets, the balance sheet items vary directly with sales. Because of the fast growth policy of the company, they will need to spend about £15,000 on new capital investment and on replacement capital expenditures during 1999.

Dorset plc earnings in 1998 before interest and tax were 15% of sales. This was after deducting depreciation of £6,000. The depreciation charge for 1999 is expected to remain the same. The interest rate on the debentures is 10%, the corporation tax rate is 50%, and the company distributes, as dividends, 40% of its available earnings.

Required:

(i) Determine the increased net working capital required to meet the higher level of sales during 1999.

(ii) Determine the company's CCR for 1999.

(iii) Estimate how much new external finance Dorset plc is likely to require during 1999.

2.3 Activity solution

(i) Current net working capital needs (1998)

= (Stock + Debtor + Cash) – Creditors

= 16,000 + 8,000 + 2,000 – 11,000 = 15,000

1999: for 20% increase – amount they require = 18,000.

(ii) Total additional financing

= Fixed + working capital

= 15,000 + 3,000 = 18,000

(iii) Additional external finance

= Additional financing – cash flow

Cash flow

Assume: no accruals or pre-payments
no tax delay
no change in dividend policy

Then Cashflow = retained profits + depreciation

(NB - working capital increases eg, an increase in debtors which generates cash outflow, is already allowed for in the forecast above).

Forecast P & L

	£
Sales (100,000 × 120%)	120,000
COGS (85% of Sales)	(102,000)
Operating profit	18,000
Less:	
Interest (10% × 100,000)	(1,000)
Taxable profit	17,000
Corporation tax @ 50%	(8,500)
Profit after tax (PAT)	8,500
Dividend (40% × PAT)	3,400
Retained profit	5,100

Cash Flow

	£
Retained profit	5,100
Depreciation	6,000
	11,100
Predicted shortfall	6,900
Total financing needs	18,000

2.4 Twin dangers in financial planning

The key to successful financial planning is to meet the CCR by ensuring that sufficient capital is available at the right times and at the right cost. In doing this, there are two dangers to avoid:

- Having too much capital, which is wasteful and costly, because it requires servicing (ie, payment of interest or dividends) when it is not needed. This is called 'Over-capitalisation'.
- Having too little capital. This is the problem faced by rapidly growing companies who are unable to unwilling to raise additional long-term capital and who push short-term financing eg, bank overdrafts and trade credit, to the limits of creditors' tolerance. This invites the danger of inability to meet financial obligations and thus insolvency. This is called 'Under-capitalisation' or 'over-trading'.

Conclusion Over-capitalisation is wasteful but under-capitalisation poses the risk of financial failure.

2.5 Some common symptoms of over-trading

Over-trading companies may exhibit some or all of the following features:-

- rapid sales growth
- no increase in long-term finance, heavy use of working capital.
- sharp increase in trade-creditors
- sharp fall in cash balances/increase in overdraft
- sharp increase in gearing (allowing for short-term borrowing).
- sharp change in stocks (both falls and increases could indicate over-trading).
- sharp fall in profit margins (indicates cut-price offers to fuel growth)
- sharp increase in fixed-assets-to-turnover ratio (ie, more intensive use of capacity)
- sharp increase in debtors/debtor days.

Conclusion Over-trading firms are highly exposed to the dangers of unexpected demands on their liquidity.

2.6 Alternative financing strategies

Four possible strategies are considered below:

(1) <u>'The Golden Rule'—the matching principle</u>

It is generally considered prudent to follow the golden rule of finance, to match the maturity of finance to the life-time of the assets acquired with it ie, to finance long-term assets with long-term funds such as equity or long-term debt and to finance short-term assets such as stock and debtors with short-term methods of finance like bank overdraft and trade-creditors.

Conclusion The Golden Rule of financing is to finance long-term assets with long-term finance and short-term assets with short-term finance.

However, prudent as this is, not all firms adhere to this principle.

(2) <u>Assets permanence</u>

Some level of short-term assets will always appear in the accounts—in this sense, they are permanent and may be financed by permanent long-term funds. Assets permanence is shown in the CCR profile below (which for simplicity removes the growth trend).

Assets permanence

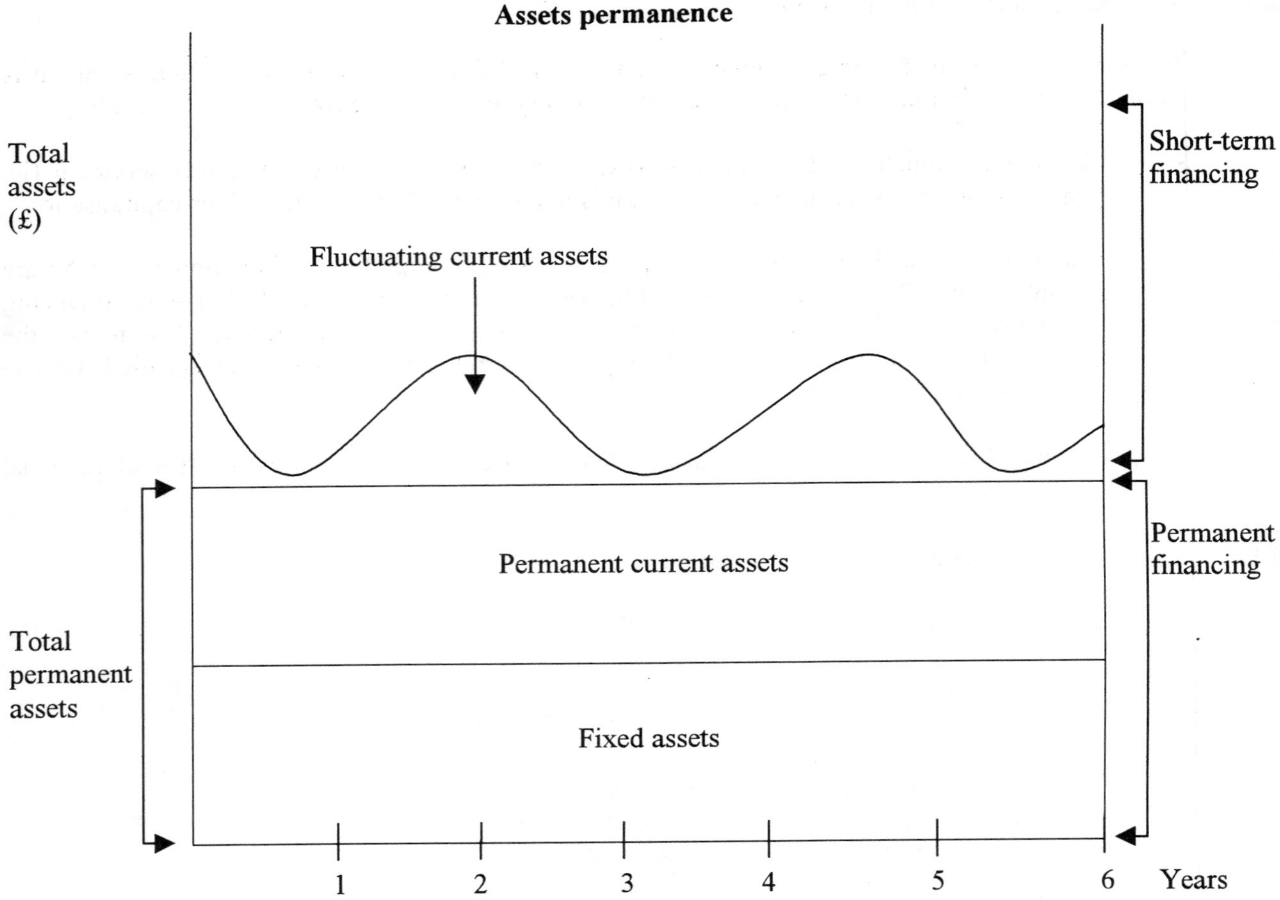

(3) Minimum short-term financing (conservative)

If the firm regards short-term financing as dangerous eg, because it can easily be withdrawn, it may want to maximise reliance on long-term finance. This is shown in the diagram below.

Conservative working capital policy

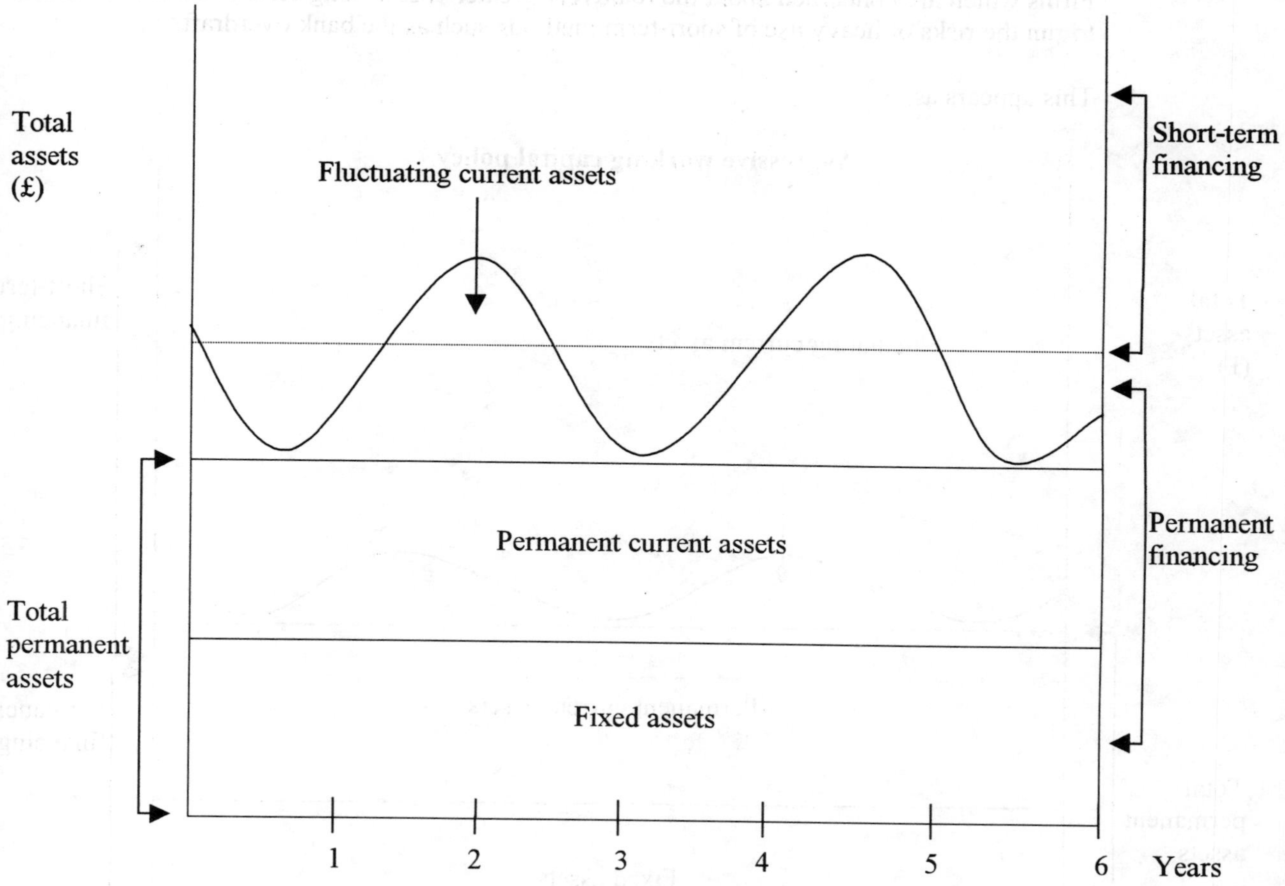

Conclusion A conservative financial policy involves very little, if any, use of short-term finance and hence cash surpluses.

(4) Minimum long-term financing (aggressive)

Firms which are concerned about the relatively greater cost of long-term finance may decide to run the risks of heavy use of short-term methods such as the bank overdraft.

This appears as:

Aggressive working capital policy

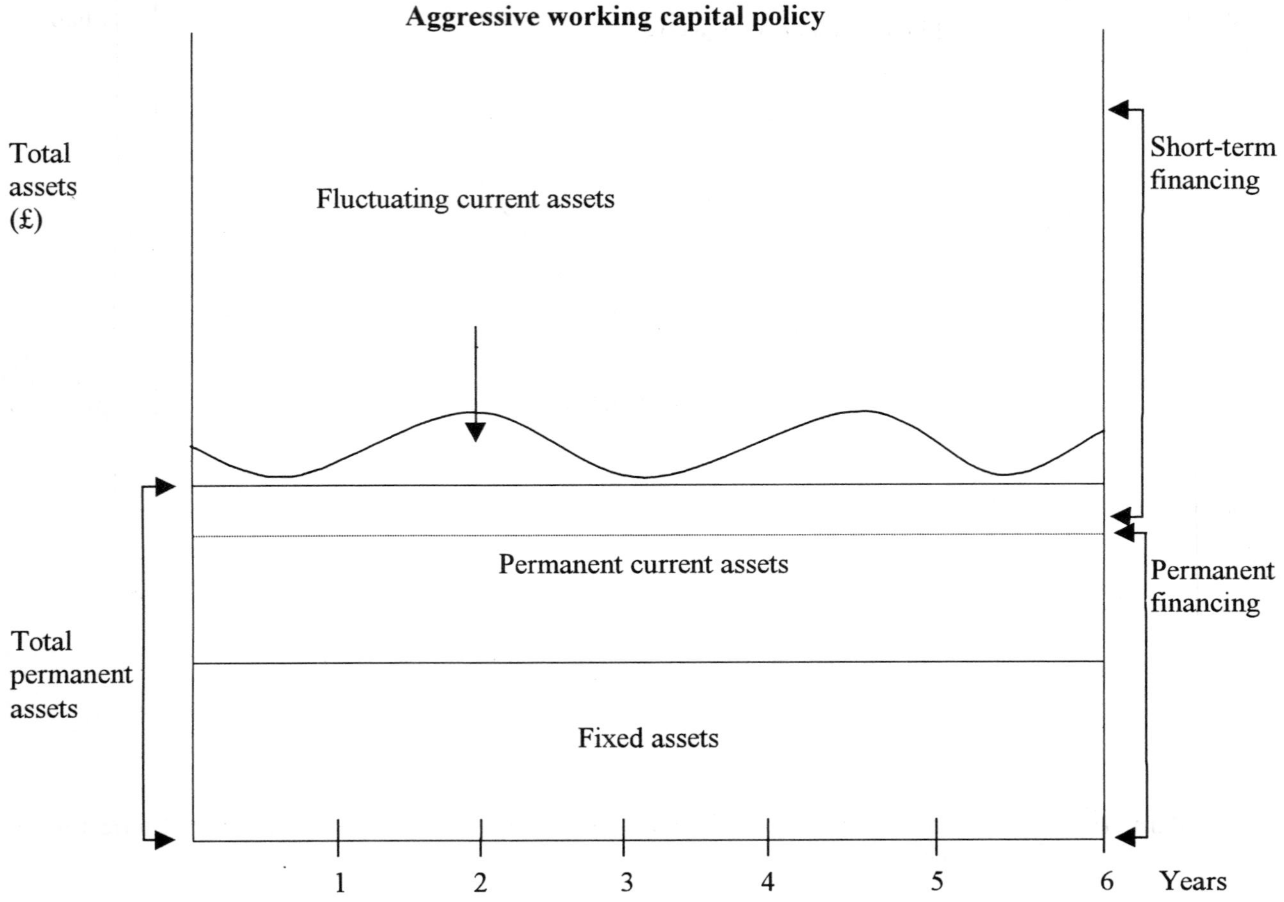

Conclusion An aggressive financial policy involves maximum use of short-term financing and hence very active management of working capital items, and a persistent cash deficit.

After an activity to consolidate these ideas, we will look in more detail at principles of managing short-term cash holdings and deficits.

2.7 Activity

The Treasurer of Ripley plc counterplates a change in financial policy. At present, Ripley's balance sheet shows that fixed assets are equal in value to total long-term debt and equity financing. It is proposed to take advantage of a recent fall in interest rates by replacing the long-term debt capital with an overdraft. In addition, the Treasurer wants to speed up debtor collection by offering early payment discounts to customers and to slow down payment to creditors.

As his assistant, write a brief memorandum to other Board members explaining the rationales of the old and new policies and pinpointing the factors to be considered in making such a switch of policy.

2.8 Activity solution

Memo to: Ripley plc main board members
From: An(n) Accountant
Subject: Alternative Financial Strategies

The present policy is a 'matching' one attempting to align the maturity of financial liabilities to the life of the assets acquired using it. It involves financing long-term assets with long-term finance such as equity or loan stock and financing short-term assets with short-term finance such as trade credit or bank overdrafts. This avoids the potential wastefulness of over-capitalisation whereby short-term assets are purchased with long-term finance ie, the company having to service finance not continuously invested in income-earning assets. It also avoids the dangers of under-capitalisation which entails exposure to finance being withdrawn when the company is not easily able to liquidate its assets. In practice, some short-term assets may be regarded as permanent and it may be thought sensible to finance these by long-term finance and the fluctuating remainder by short-term finance.

The proposed policy is an 'aggressive' one involving far heavier reliance on short-term finance, thus attempting to minimise long-term financing costs. This requires careful manipulation of the relationship between creditors and debtors (maximising trade creditors and minimising debtors), and highly efficient stock control and cash management. While it may offer financial savings, it exposes the company to the risks of illiquidation and hence possible failure to meet financial obligations. It also involves greater exposure to interest rate risk. The company should be mindful of the inverse relationship between interest rate changes and the value of its assets and liabilities.

Before adopting this policy, you should consider the following:

- How well do we forecast cash inflows and outflow? How volatile is our net cash flow? Are seasonal patterns evident?

- How efficiently do we manage our cash balances? Do we ever have excess cash holdings that we can reduce by active management?

- Will our information systems provide early warnings of illiquidity?

- Do we have any holdings of marketable securities that can be liquidated if we run into expected liquidity problems?

- How liquid are our fixed assets? Can any of these be converted into cash without unduly disrupting productive operations?

- Do we have any unused long- or short-term credit lines? These may have to be utilised if we meet liquidity problems.

- How will the stock market perceive our switch towards a more aggressive and less liquid financial policy?

3 FINANCIAL MARKETS

3.1 Introduction

The next two chapters of this unit look at ways of raising short- and medium-term finance and ways of investing short-term cash surpluses respectively. The emphasis, (for syllabus reasons) is thus on the short-term end of the spectrum of investment and financing options. However, the student should be also aware of the long-term methods of finance and the markets which deal with them. In the next sections, we therefore examine the nature of the financial markets used by corporate treasurers, the relationships between them and the key players in them.

3.2 What are financial markets?

Definition A financial market is a mechanism - sometimes a place, sometimes just a dealing network - which exists to bring together surplus and deficit units.

Specialist traders usually operate in these markets buying and selling financial claims on their own account to smooth over temporary excesses or shortages of funds. Two types of activity are usually conducted :

(a) **Primary markets,** which deal in new issues of loanable funds. These raise new finance for deficit units.

(b) **Secondary markets,** which do not provide new funds for deficit units but allow existing holders of financial claims to sell them to other investors.

Primary markets provide a focal point for borrowers and lenders to meet. The forces of supply and demand should ensure that funds find their way to their most productive uses.

Secondary markets allow holders of financial claims to realise their investment before the maturity date by selling them to other investors. They therefore increase the willingness of surplus units to invest their funds. A well-developed secondary market should also reduce the price volatility of securities, as regular trading in 'second-hand' securities should ensure smoother price changes. This should further encourage investors to supply funds to the primary market.

Conclusion In most advanced financial markets there are a vast array of institutions concerned with primary and secondary market functions. In some cases the institutions specialise in the provision of particular services, whereas in others, they can be described as financial conglomerates, whereby customers requiring a portfolio of services can be directed to different divisions within the same organisation.

The main financial markets in the UK are the capital markets and the money markets.

3.3 The capital markets

These are concerned with trading in financial claims with lives of more than one year. The bulk of this business is conducted on the London Stock Exchange, which includes the main market and the Alternative Investment Market. The major types of securities traded are as follows:

(i) Public sector securities, issued in the past to finance the budget deficit (properly known as the Public Sector Borrowing Requirement). Those issued by the central government are often known as gilt-edged securities

(ii) Stocks issued by the public authorities of overseas countries - this is sometimes known as sovereign debt

(iii) Company securities, both risk capital and fixed interest debt

(iv) Eurobonds

(v) Permanent Interest Bearing Bonds - issued by some building societies, and which are similar to gilt-edged securities.

Conclusion The capital market is the market for long-term funds ie, for deficit units wishing to finance their long-term activities.

3.4 The money markets

These are wholesale markets for funds, largely between financial institutions. No physical location exists, transactions being conducted by telephone or telex. On the discount markets discount houses borrow funds short-term (overnight or on demand) largely from the clearing banks and invest them in Treasury, Local Authority and Commercial Bills and various short-term securities. The parallel money markets trade in a range of unsecured financial claims the interest rates of which move closely together. The major participants are the banks, local authorities, building societies and industrial and commercial companies. This market also deals in Eurocurrency, ie, currency held on deposit or invested outside its country of origin.

Undoubtedly, London has become one of the world's major players in this sector. Probably the most important single explanation is the freedom with which relevant institutions have been able to operate over the last thirty years or so. There have been few if any attempts to prevent the free movement of funds either between the institutions themselves within the United Kingdom or between countries.

Conclusion The money markets exist to supply finance for short-term needs, and also to enable firms to make short-term investments.

3.5 Classifying sources of finance

To provide a framework for study of sources of finance, it is useful to classify them. The following classification used below relies on the capital market vs money market distinction.

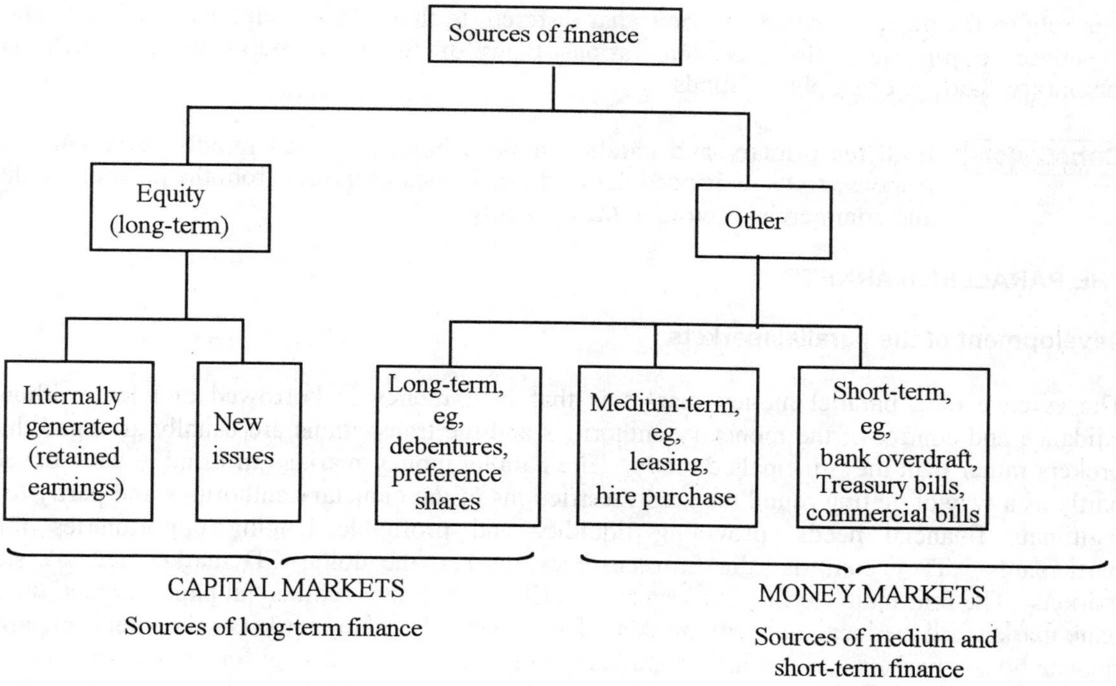

Definitions of long-term, medium-term and short-term are somewhat elastic but as a rough guide the following durations can be taken.

Short-term	Up to one year
Medium-term	1 year to 5 years
Long-term	5 years or more

3.5 The money market and money market instruments

The money market is a market mainly for short-term and very short-term loans, in both sterling and foreign currencies, though some longer-term transactions are also undertaken. In fact, it is not one single market but a number of different markets which closely inter-connect with each other. The main participants in these markets are the Bank of England, the commercial banks and the discount houses. Other participants include the finance houses, building societies, investment and unit trusts, local authorities, large companies, and some private individuals.

These markets can be further sub-divided into traditional and parallel markets.

The traditional markets comprise:

- the Bank of England;
- the discount houses; and
- the commercial banks.

The parallel markets comprise:

- the Eurocurrency market;
- the inter-bank market;
- the certificate of deposit market;
- the inter-company market;
- the local authority market.

The role of the parallel markets is somewhat different to that of the traditional markets. They are organised to provide a link between various types of financial intermediaries which have a temporary shortage or surplus of funds.

Conclusion Both the primary and parallel markets have expanded rapidly in recent years in response to the enhanced demand for financial services from the personal, industrial and commercial sectors of the economy.

4 THE PARALLEL MARKETS

4.1 Development of the parallel markets

The essence of a parallel money market is that in it money is borrowed and lent without the guidance and control of the monetary authorities and the transactions are usually arranged through brokers rather than the principals directly. The parallel money markets in London have developed partly as a way of getting round the credit restrictions of the monetary authorities and partly to meet legitimate financial needs, providing liquidity and profitable lending opportunities for the participants. They comprise the Euro-currency market, the dollar CD market and six sterling markets. The four main sterling markets are the CD market, the commercial paper market, the inter-bank market and the local authority market. The two other sterling markets - the inter-company and finance house markets - are of little significance in comparison with the four main markets. In the inter-company market the borrowers are companies and the lenders are companies and financial institutions. Normally only the top five hundred companies are involved. The minimum loan on the market is £50,000, with dealings in sums of £250,000 and larger; the period of loans is anything from three months to five years. In the finance house market, finance house and hire purchase organisations borrow from banks, other financial institutions, companies, and a few private individuals.

4.2 The sterling commercial paper market

An important additional credit instrument known as sterling commercial paper made its appearance in 1986. These are debt securities issued by major companies whose shares are listed on the Stock Exchange. They have a maturity from seven days up to five years. The minimum denomination is £100,000.

The introduction of sterling commercial paper has extended the financing options open to major industrial and commercial companies. They can now raise short-term finance in the money market on the strength of their own credit-worthiness as an alternative to bank borrowing or the raising of funds through bank acceptances such as commercial bills.

In practical terms these sterling commercial securities are simply certificates of deposit issued by a company rather than by a bank. In 1989 banks and building societies were given permission by the Bank of England to issue sterling commercial paper on their own behalf. They can do so under any description provided that the title used does not cause confusion with certificates of deposit.

5 FINANCIAL INTERMEDIARIES

5.1 Introduction

Definition The term 'intermediation' refers to the process whereby potential borrowers are brought together with potential lenders by a third party, the intermediary.

The variety and breadth of specialist services provided by financial intermediaries are distinguishing features of a developed financial system. First, we look at the broad functions of intermediaries and then we identify the most important ones in the UK system.

5.2 Why the financial system needs intermediaries

A financial intermediary is an institution which brings together units seeking funds with others wishing to invest temporarily surplus funds. Using their size and expertise, they offer important service to the financial system.

Maturity transformation

It would be difficult for individuals wishing to lend capital to find potential borrowers wishing to borrow for the same length of time. By pooling the funds of many individuals, the intermediary can extend loans of varying terms while using its liquidity to safeguard individuals' right to withdraw their capital.

Risk-spreading

An individual would find it difficult to assess the riskiness of potential borrowers, lacking both the time and resources to undertake a detailed credit evaluation. They would also be wary about over exposing themselves to risk by lending to small numbers or a (single) borrower. Pooling of funds allows the intermediary not only to specialise in credit risk assessment but also to spread the risk over a large number of clients.

Scale economies

Finding people wanting to borrow can be expensive and time-consuming so-called 'shoeleather costs'. An institution can utilise its size to exploit economies of scale in marketing to services to a broad range of potential customers.

Access to a managed investment portfolio

Some financial institutions, such as unit trusts and investment trust in the UK, allow investors access to well-diversified portfolios of securities. By pooling the funds of a large number of investors, they enable smaller investors to achieve a degree of diversification which they could not otherwise attain due to the transactions costs and the time necessary for active portfolio management. Investors receive returns in the form of regular dividends and capital value appreciation.

5.3 The major UK financial intermediaries

(a) Clearing banks

The familiar High Street banks provide a payment and cheque-clearing mechanism. They offer various accounts to investors and provide large amounts of short to medium-term loans to the business sector and the personal sector.

(b) Merchant banks

These concentrate on the wholesale end of deposit taking and lending. They also provide services to clients in the areas of investment advice, underwriting, advising on new issues, mergers and takeovers, etc. Many overseas banks operate offices in the UK and conduct similar business to the merchant banks.

(c) Savings banks

The National Savings Bank operates through the Post Office system and is used to collect funds from the small personal saver which are mainly invested in government securities. The Trustee Savings Bank used to fulfil a similar role but in the last few years has expanded its role until its operations more closely resemble those of the clearing banks, particularly since 1984 when it ceased its non-profit making role and obtained a stock market quotation. Its merger subsequently with Lloyds Bank further emphasised its primary clearing bank role.

(d) Building societies

These take deposits largely from the household sector and lend to individuals buying their own homes, though under recent legislation building societies can obtain up to 40% of their funding from the wholesale money markets. During the last two decades, the rate of growth of assets and deposits of the building society movement has been greater than that of the clearing banks, despite the fact that only a fraction of the societies' lending is to the industrial and commercial sector. The Building Societies Acts impose a limit on their lending to the non-personal sector, one reason why several former societies have ‘demutualised’ and converted into commercial banks eg, Alliance and Leicester.

(e) Finance companies

These come in three main varieties.

(i) Finance houses, providing medium-term instalment credit to the business and personal sector. These are usually owned by business sector firms or by other financial intermediaries. The trend is toward them offering services similar to the clearing banks.

(ii) Leasing companies, leasing capital equipment to the business sector. They are usually subsidiaries of other financial institutions.

(iii) Factoring companies, providing loans to companies secured on trade debtors, are usually bank subsidiaries. Other debt collection and credit control services are usually on offer.

(f) **Pension funds**

These collect funds from employers and employees and self-employed people to provide pensions on retirement or death. As their outgoings are relatively predictable they can afford to invest funds for long periods of time.

(g) **Insurance companies**

These use premium income from policyholders to invest mainly in long-term assets such as bonds, equities and property. Their outgoings from their long-term business (life assurance and pensions) and their short-term activities (fire, accident, motor etc) are once again relatively predictable and therefore they can afford to tie up a large proportion of their funds for a long period of time.

(h) **Investment and unit trusts**

Investment trusts are limited liability companies collecting funds by selling shares and bonds and investing the proceeds, mainly in the ordinary shares of other companies. Funds at their disposal are limited to the amount of securities in issue plus retained profits, hence they are often referred to as 'closed end funds'. 1997, however, witnessed a new type of investment vehicle appearing on the financial scene. This was the 'open-ended investment company' (OEIC), which, as the name implies, operates very similarly to an investment trust except that it has more flexibility in its sourcing of funds to invest. Unit trusts on the other hand, although investing in a similar way, find their funds vary according to whether investors are buying new units or cashing in old ones. All these investment vehicles offer substantial diversification opportunities to the personal investor, though insofar as investment trusts are concerned there are also institutional investors involved.

(j) **Others**

Many other intermediaries exist. For example, in recent years, there has been a large variety of different institutions established, each attempting to develop a particular niche in the financial market. Venture capital organisations and private equity funds, of which more will be discussed later, have grown especially rapidly. These institutions are concerned with the provision of risk capital to new and fledgling companies who are expected to achieve exemplary future growth, but, practice has shown, equally may fail to make an impact.

6 CHAPTER SUMMARY

This chapter has covered considerable ground and provided a foundation for understanding how companies can invest short-term cash surpluses and also raise short- and medium-term finance. We explained the nature of Treasury activities as a specialist area of financial management and then examined a variety of financial strategies. Treasury management needs to be conducted within a coherent financial strategy and planning framework with clearly specified and understood objectives. Financial strategy involves balancing long- and short-term assets and liabilities somewhere along a spectrum ranging from a 'conservative' to an 'aggressive' stance.

Whatever the financial strategy, the Treasurer must understand the operation of financial markets and identify the main depositories of surplus funds and vehicles for raising finance. We thus outlined the functions of the main financial markets and listed the main players (or intermediaries) and their functions.

In the next chapter, we look at ways in which a cash-short company can raise short- and medium-term finance, our main concern in this syllabus.

7 SELF-TEST EXERCISES

7.1 What are the two underlying financial decision areas? (1.2)

7.2 What are the main tasks of a modern Treasury department? (1.3)

7.3 What are the relative advantages and disadvantages of Treasury centralisation? (1.7)

7.4 Distinguish between 'over-' and 'under-capitalisation'. (2.4)

7.5 What is meant by the 'Golden Rule' of financing? (2.6)

7.6 Distinguish between 'aggressive' and 'conservative' financial strategies. (2.6)

7.7 Distinguish between the primary and secondary function of financial markets. (3.2)

7.8 Distinguish between the capital markets and the money markets. (3.3)

7.9 What is a parallel market? (4)

7.10 In what ways does a developed financial system benefit from the services of financial intermediaries? (5.2)

7 RAISING SHORT-TERM & MEDIUM-TERM FINANCE

PATHFINDER INTRODUCTION

This chapter covers the following performance criteria and knowledge and understanding.

- An understanding of bank overdrafts and loans; terms and conditions; legal relationship between bank and customer (Element 14.2)
- Types of marketable security (Bills of exchange, certificates of deposit, government securities, local authority short term loans); terms and conditions; risk (Element 14.2)
- Discounts for prompt payment (Element 14.3)
- Factoring arrangements (Element 14.4)
- Liquidity management (Elements 14.2, 14.3 & 14.4)
- Overdraft and loan facilities are aranged in anticipation of requirements and on the most favourable terms available (Element 14.2)

Putting the chapter in context – learning objectives.

The preparation of cash budgets and other cash flow monitoring procedures may highlight the need for additional finance to support the short and medium term operations of the business. This chapter looks at the various sources of such finance, outlining their characteristics and terms, and considering how appropriate they are for various business needs.

At the end of this chapter you should have learned the following topics.

- The nature and application of the main sources of short term finance:
  - trade credit (including costs of discounts foregone)
  - bank overdrafts and other short term bank loans
  - bill finance - bills of exchange, acceptance credits and commercial paper
  - factoring and invoice discounting
- The nature and application of the main sources of medium term finance:
  - term (bank) loans
  - hire purchase
  - leasing - finance and operating leases, sale and leaseback

1 SOURCES OF SHORT AND MEDIUM TERM FINANCE

1.1 Introduction

This chapter examines the nature and characteristics of alternative sources of finance ranging from very short-term facilities like trade credit to rather longer-term ones like bank loans and finance leasing. Generally, we classify these under the heading of short- and medium-term, although it should be recognised that the distinction is somewhat arbitrary. For example, lease finance can be used for varying time periods, ranging from the very short-term (operating leases) to as long as fifteen years, in the case of some finance leases. In addition, bank overdrafts are essentially short-term in nature but are often used continuously for lengthy periods.

1.2 Types of finance

The aim of this chapter is to evaluate the advantages and disadvantages of the following means of short- and medium-term finance:

Short-term

- Trade credit
- Bank finance
- Bills of Exchange and Acceptance Credits
- Factoring and invoice discounting

Medium-term

- Hire purchase
- Leasing
- Sale and leaseback

1.3 Finance from UK banks

Companies in the United Kingdom are more heavily reliant on short- and medium-term finance than typically is the case with American and continental companies. The explanation is largely historical, and relates to the relationship of the corporate sector with the banking system. Traditionally British banks were unwilling to provide finance other than to facilitate the continuing operation of the company. This precluded them from lending for longer than a year or two at most, whereas in most other countries the banks developed a different relationship, where they were prepared to provide funding for the long term expansion of the organisation. As such, then, it is not uncommon for these banks to take an equity stake in their client and additionally be willing to lend for periods in excess of ten years.

UK banks have not always enjoyed easy relationships with their clients. In recent years, banks have been criticised by small firm pressure groups over a variety of issues. For example, bank have been castigated for:

- reluctance to advance longer-term finance in the form of loans rather than overdrafts
- insisting on 'excessive' levels of security to back their lending
- reluctant to make equity investments in small firms
- the scale and range of their charges
- tardiness in passing on interest rate reductions to customers
- excessive haste in recalling funds when customers encounter trading difficulties.

However, attitudes are changing among UK banks. Not only have they had to face the pressures of globalisation and with it increasing competition, but some of their more traditional forms of lending have been somewhat unprofitable in recent decades.

Despite the problems, the banks remain the most important source of external finance for small and medium-sized firms. However, not only smaller firms tend to rely on shorter term finance – firms of all sizes utilise these sources to varying degrees. For example, most large companies arrange access to overdraft finance to tide them over temporary liquidity shortages.

1.4 When is short-term funding appropriate?

Definition Short-term finance is provided for a period of approximately less than one year.

The main short term assets of commercial organisations typically consist of cash and marketable investments, inventories (stocks of raw materials and semi-manufactured components) and debtors. For most companies, the level of internally generated cash resources is insufficient to provide for all these needs. There is the requirement, therefore, for external funding to be obtained.

In addition to the purchase of short term assets, there may be the need for a firm to obtain finance simply to maintain operations. This could arise because of a temporary shortfall in cashflow which may have arisen because customers have decided not to pay their bills on the mutually agreed date, or because the firm had not allowed for cost increases of certain raw materials or fuel.

As indicated in the introduction, finance to provide for these contingencies can be obtained from a number of sources, not just short term. The decision makers in the organisation will have to consider the most appropriate method to adopt. Recall the principle of matching. As a generalisation, short term assets should be financed with liabilities of similar maturity. The explanation for this is that such assets are likely to fluctuate considerably over even a limited period of time, and long term funding is unlikely to provide the flexibility necessary. It is virtually impossible to vary on a daily or weekly basis the extent of long term finance, whereas, as we shall see, this is not the case with liabilities having a much shorter duration.

Similarly it is normally not recommended that long term assets, like capital investment, should be financed with short term funding, since such finance can be called in at little or no notice. Capital assets are notoriously difficult to liquidate quickly, whereas this is not necessarily the situation with inventories and debtors.

It must be emphasised at this point that for the vast majority of firms reliance is placed on retained earnings - ie, those funds available to the firm after the payment of taxation and dividends from gross profits. Only a minority resort to significant external short-term finance.

Conclusion The circumstances justifying short-term borrowing are varied and complex and need careful consideration before a decision is made between short- and long-term finance.

2 TRADE CREDIT

Definition Trade credit is finance obtained from suppliers of goods and services over the period elapsing between delivery of goods (or provision of a service) and the subsequent settlement of the account by the recipient.

2.1 Introduction

Borrowing from creditors is an obvious way of obtaining funds. By delaying payment to creditors the company obtains the use of the funds owed for an extended period, during which the company can enjoy the goods/services provided without having to pay up.

However, trade credit taken within reasonable limits is vital for the smooth flow of production and trade; almost all industries have standard credit terms, which allow customers to pay after goods or services have been received.

For example, a manufacturer must buy raw materials and process them into finished goods before selling them. If he sells to the public, he may extend credit to his customers and if he sells to other traders, they will take trade credit. The time between purchasing the raw materials and receiving final payment can be very long indeed, and credit from his suppliers is vital if he is not to go out of business. It is also to his suppliers' benefit to allow credit, otherwise he would be unable to produce more goods until the first ones had been sold and demand for their product would be erratic and unpredictable.

2.2 Trade credit and the working capital cycle

For many firms, trade creditors, ie, amounts borrowed from suppliers, represent the major component of current liabilities. Together with current assets – cash, stock and debtors – current liabilities determine the firm's net working capital position ie, the net sum invested in working capital.

A firm's trade credit position is volatile as it depends on which of its suppliers are awaiting payment and for how much, factors which change continuously with the flow of business transactions. It is common to express the average trade credit period in days calculated as follows:

Definition Creditor days = (Trade Creditors/Credit Purchases) x 365

However, this only relates to the balance at the balance sheet date, and might have been 'window-dressed' by accelerated settlements just before drawing up the accounts. Ideally, it is expressed in terms of total purchases (but sometimes, based on cost of sales). The length of the trade credit period depends partly on competitive relationships among suppliers and partly on the firm's own working capital policy.

Conclusion Taking more trade credit shortens the cash conversion cycle.

2.2 Trade credit packages

As well as the length of the trade credit period, additional features of trade credit packages include the amount of credit which a company is allowed to obtain, whether interest is paid on overdue accounts, and whether discounts are offered for early payment.

A common way of expressing credit terms is as follows:

'2/10:net 30'

This means that the supplier will offer a 2% discount for early settlement, in this case, within ten days, otherwise, it expects payment of the invoice in full within 30 days. As shown below, not to take a discount is often an expensive option. For those tempted, firms should realise that a highly effective way of antagonising suppliers is to delay payment **and** attempt to claim the discount!

2.3 Activity

Interpret the following trade credit terms

'1.5/20:net 60'

2.4 Answer to activity

In this case, the supplier will offer a 1.5% discount for early settlement, ie, within twenty days, otherwise, it expects payment of the invoice in full within 60 days.

2.5 The costs of trade credit

Because trade credit represents temporary borrowing from suppliers until invoices are paid, it becomes an important method of financing investment in current assets. Firms may be tempted to view trade creditors as a cheap source of finance, especially as, in the UK, it is currently interest-free. Having a debtors collection period shorter than the trade collection period may be taken as a sign of efficient working capital management. However, trade credit is by no means free - it carries hidden costs.

Excessive delay in settling invoices can undermine the stability of the business in a number of ways. Existing suppliers may be unwilling to extend more credit until existing accounts are settled. They may start to attach lower priority to future orders placed by the culprit, they may raise prices in the future or simply not supply at all. In addition, if the firm acquires a reputation as a bad payer, its relationships with other suppliers may be soured.

Finally, by delaying payment of accounts due, the company may be passing up valuable discounts, thus effectively increasing the cost of goods sold. This is shown in the next activity.

Conclusion Exceeding the agreed credit terms extended by suppliers, however tempting, may jeopardise the very survival of the company.

2.6 Activity

Hawksworth plc is offered a discount of 2.5% on an invoice of £100,000 by a major supplier if it settles the account within fifteen days, rather than taking the normal credit period of 30 days. Hawksworth, which now has zero cash, can borrow from its bank at an interest rate of 15% pa. Should it borrow and take the discount, or take the full credit period?

2.7 Answer to activity

If Hawksworth takes the discount and pays on (but not before!) day 15, it will have to borrow (97.5% × £100,000) = £97,500 for an additional period of 15 days, since it would have to settle anyway after 30 days. If it waits until day 30, the cost of settling the bill is effectively the lost discount of £2,500. By advancing payment, Menston is borrowing £97,500 for 15 days in order to save £2,500, a return over 15 days of 2.56%. Expressed as an annual return on investment, this approximates to:

$$\frac{£2,500}{£97,500} \times \frac{365}{15} \times 100 = 62.4\%$$

(A more accurate solution can be obtained by compounding over the number of 15-day periods in a year [24.33] which gives the even higher rate of 85%). Either way, the return compares very favourably with the 15% cost of borrowing, so we advise Hawksworth to borrow to advance the payment.

2.8 Example

Penrith plc traditionally follows a highly aggressive working capital policy, with no long-term borrowing. Key details from its recently compiled accounts appear below:

	£m
Sales	12.00
Purchases	8.00
Gross profit	3.00
Earnings before interest and tax	2.00
Interest payments for the year	0.50
Debtors	0.40
Stocks	0.70
Trade creditors	1.50
Bank overdraft	3.00

A major supplier of Penrith, which accounts for 50% of its purchases, is highly concerned about Penrith's policy of taking extended trade credit. The supplier offers Penrith the opportunity to pay for supplies within 15 days in return for a discount on the invoiced value of 5%.

Penrith holds no cash but is able to borrow on overdraft from its bank at 12%.

Required

Recommend whether Penrith should accept the offer. Your answer should include the effects on:

- The working capital cycle
- Interest charges and interest cover
- Profit

2.9 Solution

The working capital cycle

At present, the working capital cycle is:

Debtor days:	£0.4m/£12m × 365	= 12 days
Stock days:	£0.7m/£9m × 365	= 28 days
(Cost of sales = £12 – 3)m = £9m)		
Creditor days:	£1.5m/£8m × 365	= 68 days
	Total	(28 days)

Clearly, Penrith is currently exceptionally efficient in its use of working capital. The proposed arrangement would shorten creditor days relating to half of cost of sales to 15 days. The effect is to lower the average to:

(½ × 68 days) + (½ × 15 days) = 41.5 days.

Overall, this will increase cycle time to:

[12 + 28 - 41.5 days] ie, to (1.5) days.

Interest charges and interest cover

At present, interest cover (earnings before interest and tax/interest) is:
- = £2m/£0.5m = 4.0 times,
which is not unduly low.

The advanced payment will raise interest costs but will generate savings via the discount. The discount applies to half of purchases ie. (½ × £8m x 5%) = £0.2m. The net advanced payment of (£4m - £0.2m) £3.8m will have to be financed for an extra (68 - 15) = 53 days, generating rather higher interest costs of:

[£3.8m x 12% × 53/365] = £66,214.

The interest cover slightly declines to:

[£2.0m + £0.2m]/(£0.50m + £0.066m] = 3.89 times.

Profit

Operating profit will rise due to the discount of £0.2m but at the level of profit before tax, this is partly offset by the extra interest of £0.066m ie, the net effect pre-tax is an increase of approximately £134,000.

Conclusion As Penrith has a very healthy working capital cycle, the interest cover is not significantly affected and the profits are increased by nearly 7%, it is recommended that the offer is accepted.

3 SHORT-TERM BANK FINANCE

3.1 Introduction

If trade credit is extended as a deliberate marketing ploy or if slow payment by customers becomes a problem, significantly extending the cash conversion cycle, firms may have to fall back on their banks for supplementary credit. Major commercial banks extend a variety of credit facilities, ranging from short-term overdrafts, or 'advances' to long-term loans of varying terms. The interest rate generally increases with the term of the advance, the actual rate being linked to the bank's base rate, which in turn depends on the base rate set by the Bank of England in conducting monetary policy.

Overdrafts are generally treated as short-term finance and loans as medium-term finance (see later).

3.2 Overdrafts

Definition An overdraft is a short-term credit facility extended by a bank which can be recalled on demand.

The best-known form of bank finance is the overdraft, a facility that may be available for specified short-term periods such as six months or a year. This facility also specifies a maximum amount which the firm can draw upon either via direct cash withdrawals or in payments by cheque to third parties. Interest is paid on the negative balance outstanding at any time rather than the maximum facility agreed. Compared to many other firms of finance, it is relatively inexpensive with the interest cost set at some 2-5 percentage points above base rate, although most banks also levy an arrangement fee, or commitment, of perhaps 1% of the maximum facility, in addition.

3.3 Activity

ABC plc negotiates an overdraft facility with its bank on the following terms.

Arrangement fee £100
Interest rate 3% above base rate
Transaction charges 30p when in credit, 60p when overdrawn (or if taking the account into the red).

During January, base rate was 7%, and rose to 8% for the whole of February. No interest is paid on positive balances. The transactions on ABC's account during that period were as follows

Jan 1 positive balance of £10,000
Jan 2 withdrawal of £15,000
Jan 16 deposit of £2,000
Feb 1 deposit of £12,000
Feb 14 withdrawal of £30,000
Feb 28 withdrawal of £10,000

How much does the bank charge ABC for this period?

3.4 Activity solution

Jan 2-16 15 days overdrawn by £5,000 @ 10%	=£20.55 (W)
2 transactions 60p + 90p	= £1.50
Jan 16-31 16 days overdrawn by £3,000 @ 10%	= £13.15
Feb 1 transaction	= £0.90
Feb 14 transaction	= £0.90
Feb 14 -28 14 days overdrawn by £9,000 @ 11%	= £37.98
Feb 28 transaction	= £0.90
Total	= £164.98

Working

$$£5000 \times \frac{15}{365} \times 0.1 = £20.55$$

3.5 Why overdrafts are required

From the bank's viewpoint the best reason for a company arranging an overdraft is to finance working capital, for example, investment in debtors. The overdraft is required to 'tide over' the firm until its customers pay. When they do, the overdraft is eliminated. In this sense, it is self-liquidating. Banks have few qualms about lending on overdraft to established, viable businesses. It is always worth reiterating the importance of working capital as the lifeblood of the firm in its role in financing the production cycle. Without adequate working capital the firm cannot purchase sufficient inputs to support production and is also severely exposed to the dangers of exceptional demands for cash and repayment of liabilities until customers pay. It is not lack of profits that triggers a business collapse but lack of ready cash or borrowing facilities. The next activity reinforces this message.

3.6 Activity

A firm begins the production cycle holding cash of £1,000 but needs £2,000 to support the production process which takes a month.

- Creditors will offer a month's credit
- Goods to the value of £5,000 are produced and sold to customers who are given two months' credit.

The working capital cycle is shown below

Requirements

(a) What is the cash deficit at point B, assuming the firm can utilise an overdraft?

(b) When does the firm make a profit?

(c) What is the cash deficit at point C, and thus, how big an overdraft is required?

(d) What is the cash holding (assuming no bad debts) at D?

(e) Distinguish between profit and cash flow.

Working capital cycle

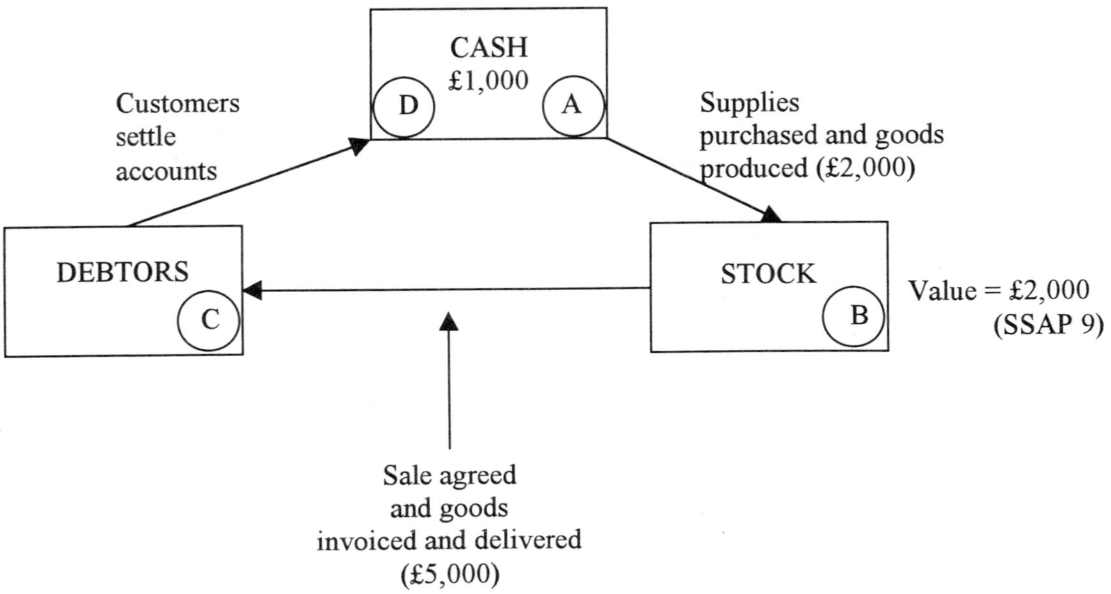

3.7 Activity solution

(a) At B, the firm needs to pay over the £2,000 to trade creditors, having purchased and used supplies (including labour inputs, presumably) of £2,000. The cash deficit will thus be £1,000 (remember, it started with cash of £1,000).

(b) Profit is normally recorded when a sale is agreed and the goods are invoiced and delivered, regardless of whether they have been paid for. So profit of (£5,000 - £2,000) = £3,000 is made as soon as stock is converted into debtors ie, at C.

(c) The cash deficit at C is still £1,000, representing the overdraft required.

(d) Once customers pay and the cash flows in, the dangers of illiquidity recede. The eventual cash holding at D is £4,000, allowing for the repayment of the overdraft.

(e) By the end of the sequence, cash has increased from £1,000 to £4,000, and the firm has made profits of £3,000 (ignoring non-cash items like depreciation of equipment), but along the way, there are significant imbalances between profit and cash and hence, times of serious exposure to abnormal demands for cash eg, what if the firm had to pay out £500 for an unplanned repair to equipment? Or it had a VAT bill to pay?

This example exhibits the notion of 'swing'. When customers pay, the overdraft account swings back into surplus, ie, from minus £1,000 to plus £4,000 – it swings by £5,000, the proceeds of the sales. Accounts which are permanently overdrawn are said to have a hard core deficit. The hard core is the minimum amount by which the account is overdrawn. Such accounts do swing, but only from larger deficits to smaller ones. A rising hard core in an overdraft is grounds for concern. It may suggest chronic lack of profitability, in which case the bank would take steps to ensure the company reduced it. Alternatively, it may be a reflection of business expansion, in which case, the bank may insist that the overdraft be converted into a medium-term loan to avoid the risks of undercapitalisation.

Conclusion A 'self-liquidating' overdraft is one that is eliminated by the customer's receipts from sales ie, collection from debtors.

3.8 Use and abuse of overdrafts

In principle, overdrafts are repayable at very short notice, even on demand, although unless the company abuses the terms of the facility, by exceeding the agreed overdraft limit, the overdraft is unlikely to be called in. Besides, it is rarely in the best interests of a bank suddenly to do this, as it could exert such severe financial pressure on the client as to force it into liquidation. Nevertheless, the bank retains the right to appoint a receiver if the client defaults on the debt. In practice, well-behaved clients can roll forward overdrafts from period to period. As a result, the overdraft effectively becomes a form of medium-term finance. Even in these cases, it is wise policy not to use the overdraft to acquire long-term assets which would be difficult to liquidate at short notice if the bank did suddenly decide to call in the debt.

Conclusion For many firms with hard core overdrafts, this effectively becomes medium-term finance, although this depends on the bank's compliance.

3.9 Securing an overdraft

To protect against risk of loss, the bank will usually demand that the overdraft be secured against company assets ie, in the event of default, the receiver will re-imburse the bank out of the proceeds of selling these assets. Security can be in two forms: a 'fixed charge', where the overdraft is secured against a specific asset, or a 'floating charge' which offers security over all of the company's assets. Banks prefer to secure overdrafts against high quality assets, ie, those with a ready and stable second-hand market. For trading companies, overdrafts are often secured against the inventory which the company purchases with the funds borrowed. In this respect, the overdraft is 'self-liquidating' – it can be reduced as the company sells goods and banks the proceeds.

Alternatively, and more to the liking of most bankers, overdrafts are secured against property. However, this created problems in the recession of the early 1990s, when the unprecedented collapse of property market prices often reduced the value of assets upon which overdrafts were secured below the balance outstanding. Many banks made major provisions against the increasing likelihood of bad debts. In addition, they incurred much ill-will by allegedly recalling overdrafts prematurely, thus exacerbating the liquidity difficulties of their clients, already seriously affected by falling sales. Many critics accused the banks of being excessively 'trigger-happy' in this respect, forcing many essentially sound companies out of business.

Conclusion Overdrafts have to be treated with care. Whilst they are relatively inexpensive to operate they can pose severe dangers, especially to firms in volatile trading environments.

4 USING THE MONEY MARKET: BILL FINANCE

4.1 Introduction

The term 'bill finance' covers several variants, including bills of exchange, acceptance credits and commercial paper.

Definition A bill of exchange is an unconditional order to pay a certain amount of money at a specified date (typically in three month's time ie, 91 days).

A bill may be a requirement to pay on demand (sight bill) or some time in the future (term bill). The bill is drawn on the party which is ordered to pay, the drawee, and the payee is the recipient of funds.

Conclusion The requirement to pay is unconditional and, if duly authorised, the bill is almost good as cash.

4.2 Bills of exchange

A bill is often likened to a post-dated cheque or an IOU, as it represents a commitment to pay out a specific sum of money after a specified period of time. Bills are traded on the money market, which specialises in providing funds repayable over periods of less than a year. The major players in the money market are the commercial banks who lend to each other, often overnight, to cover temporary cash shortages, at the London Inter-Bank Offered Rate (LIBOR), and to the Discount Houses.

There are two main types of Bill that a company can utilise to raise finance, a trade bill (Bill of Exchange) and a bank bill (Acceptance Credit). The first is easier to understand.

4.3 Trade bills

These bills of exchange are generally trade-related, connected to specific trading transactions. They began many decades ago to assist merchants, often trading overseas, to bridge the gap between acquiring goods for sale and subsequently receiving payment from customers. The trader purchasing goods draws up a bill stating a promise to pay at some future date, and then conveys the bill to the supplier of the goods. The supplier may then hold the bill to maturity or sell it in the market, perhaps to a Discount House. The terms of the bill will include an implicit interest charge (see below).

4.4 How trade bills work

It is useful to show how they operate with a structured example. The system is fairly complex, so there follows a simplified description, illustrated by Figure 1.

(a) The first transaction to take place is that a supplier sends goods to a customer, who sends a bill of exchange back to the supplier. Assume that the promise is to pay £100 in three months' time.

(b) This gives the supplier a little more security than if he had no bill at all, but is no guarantee that the customer will honour the debt. To give more security, the supplier may insist that the customer gets the bill 'accepted'.

Definition A bill is accepted when a third party or Accepting House such as a bank, guarantees to honour the bill if the customer defaults.

The customer will have to pay a fee to the bank for accepting (guaranteeing) his bill.

(c) The supplier could just wait for three months and then collect the £100 from the customer, or from the accepting bank if the customer defaults. Alternatively, he can use the bill to obtain money immediately by selling it, just like any other asset.

The supplier would go to a bank or 'discount house' and 'discount' the bill.

Definition Selling a bill to a third party at less than its face value is called 'discounting' the bill. Discount houses are involved in buying discounted bills, both those of the government and of private sector firms.

For example, the supplier might sell the bill to a discount house for £98 (ie, at a discount to its true value).

(d) When the three months are up, the discount house will go to the customer and present the bill for payment. If the customer defaults, the accepting bank will pay the discount house.

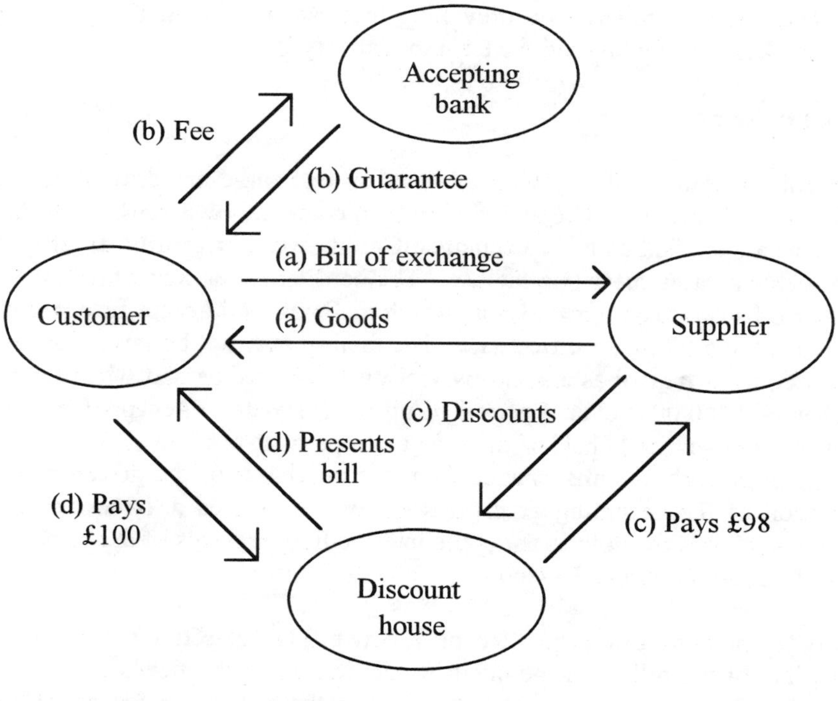

Figure 1 Using bills of exchange

Note that the discount house has effectively earned £2 (=£100 - £98) 'interest' on a three-month loan of £98. It gave the supplier £98 at the beginning of the period and then, after three months, received payment of £100 from the supplier.

4.5 Example - the cost of bill finance

A trader wishes to acquire goods to the value of £1m. He draws up a Bill of Exchange, which is accepted by his bank for a fee of £20,000. The bill promises to pay £1m in three months time. The bill is then sent to the supplier of goods who immediately sells it to a Discount House which pays out £975,000, ie, a discount of £25,000. If the Discount House holds the bill to maturity, it earns a profit of £25,000. This is equivalent to an interest rate of £25,000/£975,000 = 2.56% over three months, or in annual terms:

$$(1.0256)^4 - 1 = 1.1064 - 1 = 0.1064 \text{ ie, } 10.64\%.$$

Because the amount of the discount would otherwise have been received by the supplier of goods had he waited, this is the cost of using the money market to advance payment. If the trader can borrow at a lower rate, then it will pay him to wait until maturity. This is unlikely due to the generally lower creditworthiness of traders compared to money market operators.

Conclusion Bills of exchange do not pay interest in the normal way. The interest payment is implicit in the discount to face value at which the bill is traded.

If the bill discounter can borrow at less than the implied rate, it can make a profit. If interest rates fall, the profit margin widens. Alternatively, the Discount House may sell the bill on the money market, its value rising as it nears maturity. The ultimate holder will present the bill to the bank which assumes responsibility for payment. By this time, the trader has sold his goods at a profit and is in funds.

Term bills of exchange are drawn up for periods of between 60 and 180 days, for values of a minimum of £75,000, reflecting interest rates based on LIBOR, as adjusted for the riskiness of the companies concerned, and their credit ratings.

Conclusion The discount depends on prevailing interest rate levels, the yield required by the purchaser of the bill and the term to maturity.

4.6 Acceptance credits (bank bills)

These are often called 'Bank Bills'. Whereas Bills of Exchange are drawn on the purchaser of goods by a supplier, an Acceptance Credit is drawn by a company on a bank ie, the bank accepts the obligation to pay at a specified time. Acceptance Credits were originally developed by merchant banks but all large banks now offer this facility. The bank grants a credit facility whereby a client company can draw bills (up to an agreed limit) which the bank will accept ie, agree to honour when presented for payment at a future specified date. The facility may not be immediately utilised by the client company but can be treated as a stand-by facility to be used as and when required, usually in minimum tranches of £250,000, over a period of up to five years. Accepted bills are sold on the discount market by the bank on behalf of the client company at a relatively 'fine' or low discount. The company thus effectively obtains finance from the purchaser of the discounted bills, using the name and reputation of the accepting bank as security. It is thus a somewhat roundabout way whereby one company lends to another, using the intermediary services of the bank. Bank bills have a period to maturity of 30, 60, 90 or 180 days.

At the maturity date, the bank can either 'accept' a new bill (ie, effectively roll over the old one) or receive the full value of the bill from the client's account, using the funds to pay the bearer of the bill. The cost to the client is the amount of discount on the bill plus a fee payable to the bank of around 0.5%. Banks may require security for such facilities, the nature and type of which depends on the size and credit standing of the client.

Acceptance Credits have become increasingly popular in recent years. Among their advantages are the following:

- the 'interest' cost is relatively low, often below that of an overdraft, because the bills are backed by a bank.

- the cost involved with the bill is known when it is discounted, and is not affected by subsequent interest rate changes, allowing greater accuracy in cash budgeting.

- Acceptance credits can be negotiated for longer periods than overdrafts, thus offering more security to the borrower.

- Unlike traditional Bills of Exchange they are not tied to specific transactions.

However, they are only available to large companies with sound credit ratings, and they lack the flexibility of overdrafts, which can be reduced if the firm wishes to lower interest costs.

Conclusion Bank bills are a means whereby larger firms can mobilise the creditworthiness of their bankers to arrange immediate finance, or simply standby credit facilities.

4.7 Commercial paper

Definition Commercial paper is a bill of exchange that does not require acceptance.

Bills of exchange require acceptance ie, a guarantee of payment by a bank. Companies which are highly creditworthy (eg, Sainsburys and Tesco now operate banking facilities in their own rights) do not need this imprimatur. Hence, they can issue bills which have not been accepted, thus saving the acceptance fee. Commercial paper are promissory notes, or certificates issued usually by a Blue Chip company, which incorporate a promise to pay a fixed amount at a specific date. Like other bills, these can be traded at a discount, reflecting the return required by the purchaser.

5 FACTORING AND INVOICE DISCOUNTING

5.1 Introduction

Definition A factor is a financial institution that accelerates the cash conversion cycle for client companies, allowing them to gain access to debtors more quickly than if they waited for the normal trade credit period to elapse.

Some companies realise that, although it is necessary to extend trade credit to customers for competitive reasons, they need payment earlier than agreed in order to assist their own cash flow. Factors, mainly subsidiaries of the major banks, such as Griffin Factors Ltd, owned by Midland Bank, one of the 37 members of the Factors and Discounters Association, (FDA) exist to help such companies. Emanating from the USA, factoring in the UK has increased greatly in importance over the past decade or so, with FDA members handling about £50 billion of clients' turnover and adding over £3.75 billion of liquidity to clients in 1997.

Factoring is most suitable for small and medium-sized firms which often cannot afford sophisticated credit and sales accounting systems, and for firms which are expanding rapidly. These often have substantial working capital investment which can be made more liquid ie, turned into cash by factoring debts. Factoring is also useful in relation to overseas debtors. In 1997, international factoring accounted for about £2.5 billion of client turnover, and 5% of the total factoring activity.

Conclusion Factoring is primarily designed to allow companies to accelerate cash flow, thus enhancing liquidity, although finance can be provided.

Factors provide two main types of service, factoring proper and invoice discounting.

5.2 Types of factoring facility

Factoring involves raising cash based on the security of the company's debtors, thus accelerating payment from customers. A factor provides three main services - sales administration, credit protection and provision of finance. Factors tend to make an initial charge, equivalent to interest, payable for any cash advance, and a factoring charge, which is essentially a commission to allow the factor to earn a profit on the deal. The package of charges depends on the type of factoring facility provided.

5.3 Sales administration

A factor assumes the various functions of sales ledger administration, ranging from recording sales details to sending out invoices and reminders, and collecting payment. The benefits for the client are the cost savings from reducing in-house administration and access to a more efficient, specialist debtor management team. This is particularly valuable to a young fast-growing company, which may outgrow its administration system and otherwise be exposed to the liquidity risks of over-trading. The fee for such an administration service would lie in the range of 0.5% to 2.5% of the value of turnover handled.

5.4 Credit protection

The factor may also provide a credit evaluation service for clients, analysing customer characteristics before deciding on their credit-worthiness. When all risks are borne by the factor, the service is termed 'without recourse' ie, the factor has no 'come-back' or recourse to the client if customers default. Under this system, the factor would require total control of credit approval, monitoring of customers' payments and attempts to ensure payment.

These first two facilities are offered in service factoring.

5.5 Service factoring: how it works

The diagram below shows how service factoring operates. Payment to the client is based on the industry average settlement date.

Service factoring

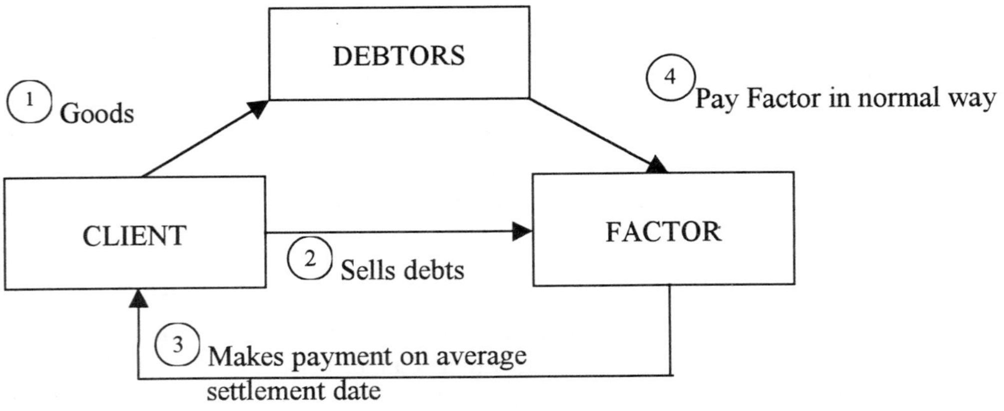

5.6 Activity

Ewden is a medium-sized company producing a range of engineering products which it sells to wholesale distributors. Recently, its sales have begun to rise rapidly due to economic recovery. However, it is concerned about its liquidity position and is looking ways of improving cash flow.

Its sales are £16 million pa, and average debtors are £2.6 million (representing 59 days worth of sales).

One way of speeding up collection from debtors is to use a factor. The factor will operate on a service-only basis, administering and collecting payment from Ewden's customers. This is expected to generate administrative savings of £100,000 pa and, hopefully, will also shorten the debtor days to an average of 45. The factor will make a service charge of 1.5% of Ewden's turnover. Ewden can borrow at an interest rate of 18% pa.

Determine the relative costs and benefits of using the factor.

5.7 Activity solution

Reduction in debtor days = (59 - 45)	=	14 days
Reduction in debtors = $\frac{14}{365} \times$ £16m	=	£613,699
Interest saving = (18% × £613,999)	=	£110,466
Administrative savings	=	£100,000
Service charge = (1.5% × £16m)	=	£240,000

Net cost = (£240,000) + £100,000 + £110,466 = (£29,534)

Ewden will have to balance this cost against the security offered by greater liquidity. The cost of using the factor depends on the factor successfully lowering Ewden's debtor days. Should the factor retain these cash flow benefits for himself, rather than passing them on to Ewden, the net cost of the factoring option will rise.

5.8 Provision of finance – finance factoring

Definition Finance factoring is where the factor makes a cash advance to the client, as well as conducting administration services.

A factor will also advance funds to a client, based on a proportion, usually 80%, of approved ie, reliable, invoices. For example, a company with sales on 30-day credit terms from reliable customers of, say, £500,000 per month, would receive an advance of 80% ie, £400,000 each month. The interest rate would be related to the bank's base rate, probably slightly above the cost of an overdraft. The client would receive the balance of the payment less interest and an administration charge, perhaps equal to 0.5% of turnover.

The following diagram show how this operates.

Finance factoring

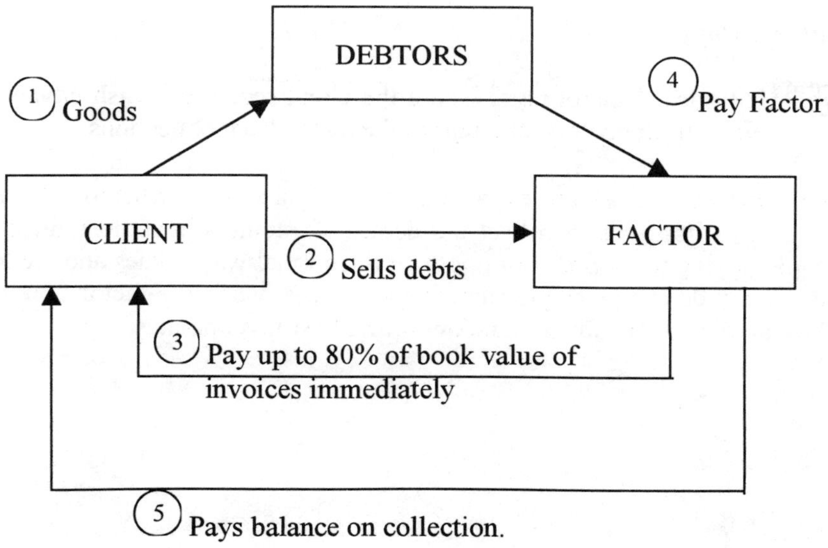

5.9 Problems with Factoring

Although factors provide valuable services, companies are sometimes wary about using them. A possible problem with factoring is that the intervention of the factor between the factor's client and the debtor company could endanger trading relationships and damage goodwill. For this reason, some clients prefer to retain responsibility for collection of problem debtors. This is known as 'with recourse' factoring whereby the factor will call upon his client to reimburse the funds advanced on an invoice relating to a delinquent account. The possible difficulties over collection of payment have been mentioned. On top of this, widespread knowledge that a company is using a factor could damage goodwill in another way - it may arouse fears that the company is beset by cash flow problems, raising fears about its viability. If so, its suppliers may impose more stringent payment terms, thus negating the benefits provided by the factor.

Conclusion Using a factor can create problems with customers who may resent being chased for payment by a third party, and may also question the supplier's financial stability.

5.10 Activity

A company's sales ledger totals £125,000, representing three months' sales. A factor will operate the ledger on a non-recourse basis for 2% of turnover. There is a danger of loss of business if it is generally known that the firm is using a factor : sales will fall by an estimated £15,000 pa. Using the factor would generate administration savings of £20,000pa. Bad debts currently run at 3% of turnover. Is it worth using the factor?

5.11 Activity solution

Annual cost of using the factor:		
Fee 2% × [(£125,000 × 12/3) - £15,000]	=	£9,700
Loss in sales × 97%	=	£14,550
		(£24,250)
Annual benefits of using the factor:		
Admin savings	=	£20,000
Bad debts saved:		
3% × [£125,000 × 12/3) - £15,000]	=	£14,550
		£34, 550

Net saving from using the factor = £10,300 (although this solution ignores interest costs).

5.12 Undisclosed factoring

Definition Undisclosed factoring is where the client receives a cash advance but continues to collect from debtors, and repays the factor from collections.

Goodwill problems can be addressed by undisclosed factoring, whereby the factoring company appoints its client as its agent to collect the debts. Customers have no indication that a factor is involved, simply paying the supplier of goods in the normal way. Sales and credit control appear to still reside in the hands of the supplier but 'behind the scenes', the factor is releasing cash against the outstanding invoices. The diagram below shows how this operates.

Undisclosed factoring

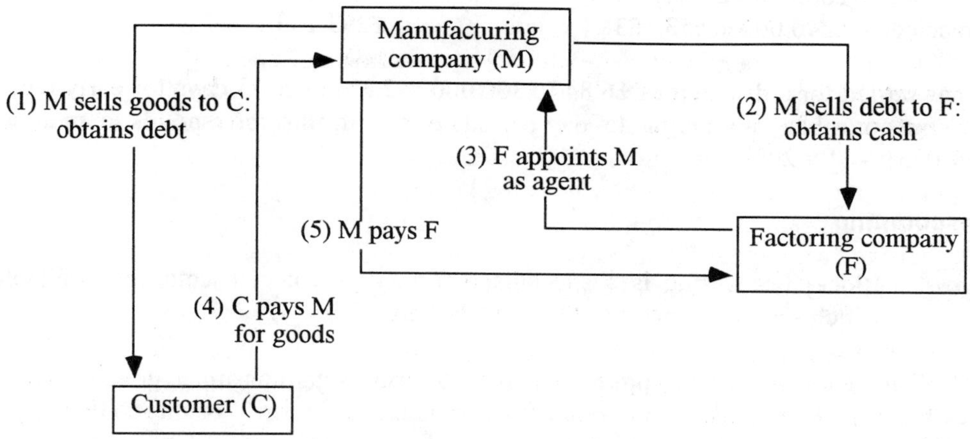

5.13 Invoice discounting

A less comprehensive form of factoring is invoice discounting.

Definition Invoice discounting is a method of raising finance against the security of debtors without using the ancillary services of the factor such as sales administration.

A company seeking merely to improve its cash flow is likely to use an invoice discounting facility. This involves the purchase of selected invoices, sometimes just one, by the discounter. The discounter will advance immediate cash up to 80% of face value. He assumes no responsibility for the administration of the accounts receivable, nor the collection of the debts. The service is totally confidential, the client's debtors being unaware of the existence of the discounter. It is therefore equivalent to the financing service provided by a factor, although restricted to a narrower range of invoices.

Administration charges for this service are around 0.5-1% of a client's turnover. It is more risky than factoring since the client retains control over its credit policy. Consequently, such facilities are usually confined to established companies with turnovers above £1m. Interest costs are usually in the range 3-6% above base rate, although larger companies and those which arrange credit insurance may receive keener terms.

5.14 How invoice discounting works - example

At the beginning of August, Baildon plc sells goods for a total value of £300,000 to regular customers but decides that it requires payment earlier than the agreed 30-day credit period for these invoices. A discounter agrees to finance 80% of their face value, ie, £240,000. Interest is 13% p.a. The invoices were due for payment in early September, but were subsequently settled in mid-September, exactly 45 days after the initial transactions. The service charge is 1%. A special account is set up with a bank, into which all payments are made. The sequence of cash flows is:

August:
 Baildon receives cash advance of £240,000
Mid-September:
 Customers pay up £300,000
 Invoice discounter receives the full £300,000
Mid-September:
 Baildon receives the balance payable receivable less charges ie:

Service fee = 1% × £300,000	=	£3,000
Interest = 13% × £240,000 × 45/365	=	£3,847
Total charges	=	£6,847

Net receipts	= (20% × £300,000 - £6,847)	
	= £60,000 - £6,847	= £53,153
Total receipts	= £240,000 + £53,153	= £293,153

Baildon has settled for a discount of £6,847/£300,000 = 2.3% over 45 days for early receipt of 80% of the accounts payable. With eight 45–day periods in a year, this corresponds to an annual interest rate of $[(1.023)^8 - 1] = 20\%$.

5.15 Block discounting

Definition Block discounting is a specialised form of invoice discounting available to firms which sell consumer durables on HP terms.

A variant of invoice discounting applies where a company sells consumer goods on hire purchase terms (see below). If desired, it can obtain finance using the security of these HP debts. It sells a block of HP contracts to a finance house, in return for an immediate advance of, say 75% of the outstanding debt. The advance is repaid over the average unexpired term of the HP agreements using the repayments made by the original HP customers.

5.16 Activity

Distinguish between factoring and invoice discounting, explaining the benefits which companies obtain from each.

5.17 Activity solution

Factoring and invoice discounting are two ways in which a company can obtain speedier payment in respect of sales made to customers. The shorter working capital cycle will quicken the rate of cash flow and in turn enable the company to reduce its reliance on other, perhaps less dependable, sources of short-term finance, such as bank overdrafts.

Factoring is the service provided by a financial institution which will lend the firm up to around 80% of the value of its debtors. The factor will then administer the sales accounts and undertake the collection of the debts. The remaining 20% or so of the value of debtors will, be paid over to the client company either when all of the invoices have been settled or after some agreed time period, net of administration fees and interest charges. The service charge will vary between 0.5%-2.5% of turnover, and the interest charge will typically be in the range of 1-3% above base rate.

There is a distinction between 'non-recourse' factoring, whereby bad debts are the responsibility of the factor, as opposed to 'with recourse' factoring under which bad debts remain the liability of the client company. An additional fee, typically, 0.5% of turnover, will be required for the factor to provide protection against bad debts.

Sometimes, for reasons of goodwill, a company with a need to quicken its cash flow may not wish to reveal that it has enlisted the aid of a factor, preferring to retain the role as debt collector. In this case, it may utilise invoice discounting, a less comprehensive service which involves the financial institution purchasing selected invoices from the client at a discount. The interest cost of this provision of finance is reflected in the discount. For example, if a bundle of invoices with an average maturity of two months were sold at a discount of 2%, the effective interest cost would be $(1.02)^6 - 1 = 12.6\%$ (approximately). The administration of the customer accounts remains with the company which settles the debt to the invoice discounter out of the payments duly collected from its customers.

Thus, the main additional benefit provided by full service-and-finance factoring is the saving in administrative costs from not having to operate the credit management function. The factor, perhaps by utilising information about customers obtained from operating the sales accounts of other firms, may also be a more efficient collector of debt than the client company, although there may be adverse goodwill implications.

6 USING MEDIUM-TERM FINANCE

6.1 Introduction

Definition Medium-term finance is that obtained by borrowing organisations for a period of between approximately one to five years.

Much of the supply of such finance emanates from similar sources to short term funding, but there are a number of critical differences as will be described later in this section.

6.2 When is medium-term financing appropriate?

Much of a firm's working capital requirements will be met by the type of funding discussed in the previous sections. However, evidence suggests that a proportion of the working capital of many industrial organisations is rather constant in nature and amount over considerable periods of time. This is particularly the case with inventories. It would be inappropriate for companies to run down their stocks to minimal levels for the fear of incurring stock-out costs associated with the non-delivery of the finished product to customers. In these circumstances it might be sensible to finance these assets with the use of medium-term funding, given the danger of inability to refinance short term borrowing if need be. As indicated earlier there can be no guarantee that such finance will always be available. Reference was made in chapter 4 that one way in which the government can reduce the money supply is by open market operations, the effect of which, as a result of the banks needing to maintain their liquidity, could be increased reluctance on their part to offer short term finance.

Medium term finance may also be required to enable capital projects to be implemented, at least those with an expected payoff within a five year time horizon. In recent years, many of the larger public companies have been engaged in extensive restructuring exercises involving medium term funding. An example of this has been the practice of companies in buying back their own shares in the market with the use of bank loans. This is deliberate strategy to increase their debt-equity ratios.

7 TERM LOANS

Definition Bank loans for periods above a year are called term loans.

7.1 Introduction

We noted above the UK banks' traditional reluctance to lend on a long-term basis, mainly because the bulk of their deposit liabilities are short-term. In the event of unexpectedly high demand by the public for cash, banks could be vulnerable to failure if unable to quickly recall advances from borrowers. Indeed, this low exposure to default risk is generally regarded as the reason why there have been so few banking collapses in the UK this century.

However, for various reasons, not least criticism by a series of official reports on the financial system and the advent of intensive competition from London branches of overseas banks, the main UK banks are now far more willing to lend longer-term. Nevertheless, the matching principle still applies - banks prefer to see customers using medium-term loans to acquire assets which have a medium term lifetime.

7.2 Loan costs and conditions

Term loans can be more expensive than overdrafts if, as is usual, the interest is applied to the initial loan. The rate may be fixed for the duration of the loan or floating, tied to some key interest rate like the London Inter Bank Offered Rate (LIBOR) ie, the rate at which the large banks lend to each other on the short-term money market. The rate set may be 2-5 percentage points above the key rate, depending on the credit-rating of the client and the quality of the assets offered as security. Generally, the larger the firm, the more likely it is be able to obtain variable rate finance, and thus benefit from interest rate declines. Should rates increase, it has the flexibility of the opportunity of repaying part or all of the loan.

Banks generally prefer to offer fixed rate finance because the repayments are more predictable but competition (which is stiffer among banks seeking business from large firms) may force them to offer variable rate loans. As well as the interest costs, there is often an arrangement fee to pay 'up front'.

Conclusion Variable rate loans offer flexibility but can be more expensive if interest rates rise.

In order to monitor the financial health of the company, the bank will insist on a timely flow of information from the company - at a minimum, its annual accounts, but usually, regular management accounts which track the company's operating performance, perhaps on a monthly basis. In addition, the bank will attach restrictive conditions, or 'covenants', to the loan agreement. If these are violated, the bank may recall the loan. These can take various forms eg, setting a minimum level of liquidity, setting a maximum gearing ratio or even prohibiting the company from further borrowing. There is a covenant attached to British Steel's debt preventing its tangible fixed assets from falling below a stipulated level.

Conclusion Monitoring of the loan is conducted by scrutiny of company financial statements and control is exercised by covenants which specify the operating and financial rules which the company must observe.

7.3 Tailor-made loans and repayment profiles

Tailor-made facilities are available to some firms with repayment terms designed to suit their expected cash flow profiles. Sometimes, the bank may grant a 'grace period' at the outset of the loan when no capital is repayable and interest may be charged at a relatively low, but increasing rate. This is particularly suitable for a small, developing company trying to establish itself. Similarly, a 'balloon' loan is where increasing amounts of capital are repaid towards the end of the loan period, while a 'bullet' loan is where no capital is repaid until the very end of the loan period.

Conclusion Some firms may have special needs due to particular trading conditions, which banks can accommodate by customised loans.

Most loans are arranged on the amortisation principle, (rather like a mortgage) whereby the principal plus interest of the loan is steadily repaid over the term of the loan, at regular intervals, perhaps monthly or quarterly. Interest may be charged on the initial amount of the loan or on a reducing balance basis, which is generally cheaper.

7.4 Activity

Contrast the cost and amortisation profiles of a £12,000 three-year term loan at a fixed 10% pa interest, arranged

(i) on a reducing balance basis, and
(ii) with interest charged on the initial loan.

All payments are made at year ends.

7.5 Activity solution

(i) The reducing balance case

$$\text{Annual repayment} = \frac{\text{Initial loan}}{\text{3 year annuity factor at 10\%}} = \frac{12{,}000}{2.487} = £4{,}825$$

Year	Opening Balance £	Interest £	Total debt £	Repayment £	Closing balance £
1	12,000	1,200	13,200	4,825	8,375
2	8,375	837	9,212	4,825	4,387
3	4,387	438	4,825	4,825	0
	Total interest	2,475			

(ii) Interest on initial loan

Opening balance + interest = £12,000 × 3 (1 + 10%) = £15,600

$$\text{Annual repayment} = \frac{£15600}{3} = £5{,}200$$

Year	Opening Balance £	Repayment £	Closing Balance £
1	15,600	5,200	10,400
2	10,400	5,200	5,200
3	5,200	5,200	0

Total interest cost = £3,600 ie, higher by £1,225.

8 HIRE PURCHASE

Definition Hire purchase (HP) is a means of acquiring durables where the user makes an initial payment and agrees to pay a series of (usually) monthly charges over a specified period, at the end of which legal title passes to the user.

8.1 Introduction

When a company is unable to obtain a medium-term bank loan, it may use hire purchase (HP) to acquire equipment. HP by companies is similar to HP by consumers of durables such as TVs. The equipment is purchased initially by a finance house, most of whom are subsidiaries of commercial banks, and members of the Finance and Leasing Association (FLA). The hirer usually makes a down-payment and then signs a commitment to a series of (usually) monthly hire charges over a specified period, at the end of which the legal title to the good passes to the user. The hire charge contains two elements, an interest charge to reflect the borrowing of the capital involved, and also a capital repayment element. Because of the way interest is calculated, HP can be very expensive, but may a useful fall-back when no other source is available.

8.2 Costs and benefits of HP

Major advantages of HP are that it avoids a major cash outlay at the outset of the project and the asset immediately becomes available for use, although the user assumes all the responsibilities of maintenance and insurance. However, if the user fails to fulfil the payment schedule, the owner can repossess the asset. In this event, the user loses all title and obtains no credit for payments already made. HP tends to be used by smaller and riskier firms. Because of the default risk, the contract period is always less than the asset life so that in a re-possession, the owner knows that he will hold a saleable asset with unexpired working life. In longer-term HP contracts, the owner runs risk of technological progress outdating the asset and reducing its marketability. As a result of these factors, HP is often expensive.

Conclusion To safeguard against the perceived risk of default, providers of HP finance require downpayments and write contracts for terms less than the asset life in order to ensure a resale value above the outstanding loan.

8.3 How HP works - example

BMB Builders wants to obtain an earthmover using HP. It contacts a manufacturer who arranges an HP contract with a finance house. The finance house buys the asset, which has an expected lifetime of four years, for £120,000 and arranges the following terms:

- The asset will be purchased over three years.
- A down-payment of £20,000 is required.
- Interest is charged at 16% on the initial loan (£100,000)
- Capital will be repaid in three equal instalments.

8.5 Activity

Note that even though the balance outstanding declines over the three year period, interest is applied to the initial loan of £100,000. Work out the monthly payments on this contract.

8.6 Activity solution

Interest = 16% × £100,000 = £16,000pa
Capital = £100,000/3 = £33,333pa

Total £49,333pa (or £4,111 monthly)

Because the interest is paid in this way, the true interest rate is roughly double the quoted rate. The annual interest charge of £16,000, applied to the average capital outstanding of £50,000, yields an effective interest rate of £16,000/£50,000 = 32%

8.7 Tax treatment of HP

An advantage of HP is that the user qualifies for tax relief both on the interest element in the repayment profile and also a writing down allowance (WDA) on the capital expenditure component (25% reducing balance), based on the total cash price of the asset. The profile of tax relief for the BMB Builders example is shown below. It assumes tax is paid at 30%, with no delay, and that the asset has a sale value of £20,000 after three years.

Tax relief on BMB Builder's HP contract (£)

Year	*Interest*	*WDA**	*Total*	*Tax saving*
1	16,000	30,000	46,000	13,800
2	16,000	22,500	38,500	11,550
3	16,000	47,500	63,500	19,050
			Total	44,400

The Writing Down Allowance is applied to the full cash price. In the final year, the undepreciated balance, (£120,000 - £52,500 = £67,500) less the resale value of £20,000, is fully written off for tax purposes (balancing allowance). Repayments of capital are not tax-allowable.

It should be stressed that tax relief is only of value to profitable companies with taxable capacity. Many of the smaller-sized and higher risk companies (often start-ups) which use HP are unable to exploit the tax breaks, making HP a very expensive form of finance.

(*Note* that similar tax breaks are available when using a bank loan).

Conclusion Although HP is usually more expensive than bank loans, the additional cost can be defrayed by exploiting tax breaks.

8.8 Activity

What is the total cost over time of the HP contract if BMB Builders is:

(i) a tax-paying company?
(ii) a non-taxpayer?

8.9 Activity solution

(i) A tax-payer will have to pay out a gross amount of 36 months × monthly instalment = 36 × £4,111 = £148,000 = capital cost of £120,000 plus interest of 3 × £16,000. Against this is set the resale value of £20,000 and tax savings of £44,400. The net cost is thus:

[£148,000 - £20,000 - £44,400] = £83,600

(ii) The non-tax-payer receives no tax savings so the total net cost is [£148,000 - £20,000] = £128,000.

8.10 Variants of hire purchase

A number of other medium-term financing arrangements exhibit some features in common with HP. These are plant hire, contract hire and instalment credit.

(i) **Plant hire**

Plant hire is a term used in the construction industry, although similar hire arrangements can be found in other industries.

It is possible to obtain the use of certain types of durable goods eg, plant and machinery, by hiring them instead of purchasing them. By so doing, hirers do not have to pay in advance for the service the goods will render during their effective life. They are relieved of the burden, and of many of the risks, of financing them.

Where goods are available either for purchase or hire, intending users must decide which they prefer. If they have not, or cannot obtain the necessary finance to buy, they may be compelled to hire. However, if they can afford to buy, the decision may depend on whether their need is purely temporary (and if so, whether it would be cheaper to hire than to buy and re-sell), and whether they are prepared to take the risk of a fall in prices and deprive themselves of the chance of buying cheaper later on. There is also the question of maintenance and repairs, which the supplier may be better able to provide than the hirer.

(ii) **Contract hire**

A further form of hiring and renting assets, is contract hire, which is particularly applicable to private cars and small commercial vehicles. Motor dealers offer comprehensive hiring systems which cover the supply, servicing, replacement and licensing of such vehicles. Many finance companies offer a vehicle-hiring system without the facility of servicing, etc.

(iii) **Instalment credit**

Instalment credit relates to the payment for goods by instalments and is thus similar to hire purchase, except that the ownership of the goods passes to the buyer immediately on delivery ie, there is no hire element. Therefore, the seller cannot recover the goods in the event of default by the buyer unless the loan is specifically secured on the asset.

An instalment credit agreement can be spread over five years and, unlike a bank overdraft, there is no possibility of early enforced repayment. Although instalment credit is relatively expensive, it is widely used as it provides a second line of credit behind the bank overdraft which can then be used to meet any unexpected problem that arises. For taxation purposes, it is considered that the whole of the expenditure on plant and equipment has been incurred when the first instalment has been paid.

9 LEASING

9.1 Introduction

Leasing has increased significantly in popularity since it was introduced to the UK in the 1960's. It appeals to companies who may wish to avoid the often significant up-front cost of outright purchase. It is similar in many ways to HP except that no down-payment is required, although the rentals may be paid in advance, and ownership of the asset does not revert to the user when the contract is completed.

9.2 How a lease works

Definition The intending user of the asset is the lessee, and the provider of the asset is the lessor.

Most leasing activity is undertaken by banking and similar institutions, such as Forward Trust Group, a subsidiary of Midland Bank. Some manufacturers, such as IBM and Philips Electronics, also operate leasing companies to market their products. A company wishing to use an asset (the **lessee**), for example, an airline wishing to lease an aircraft, will approach the leasing specialist (the **lessor**) with its requirements. The deal will involve the lessor purchasing the plane, and arranging to rent it out to the lessee in return for a pre-specified series of rental payments over a specific time period.

At the expiration of the lease contract, the two parties may negotiate a '**secondary lease**', or the owner may otherwise dispose of the asset. For long-life assets, the lessor may ignore the resale value of the asset when setting the rentals, it being too distant in time to forecast accurately. Instead, he may agree to reimburse the lessee with a proportion, often over 90% (but never 100%) of the resale value. Such agreements are known as '**rebate clauses**'. Secondary leases are often undertaken at nominal or 'peppercorn' rentals to reflect their bonus nature - the owner will already have received back his outlay plus target profit if the contract has run its full term.

9.3 Activity

McCaffrey Pleat Aviation (MPA) is approached by a client to lease a new aircraft. The required outlay is £10 million. The term of the lease is ten years. If MPA requires a return on capital of 15%, what annual rental will it apply? Give your answer using simple interest.

9.4 Activity solution

MPA wishes to recover its outlay plus a 10% annual return on capital ie, a total of £10m plus (10% × £10m × 10) = £10m + £10m = £20m. Hence, the required rental will be £2m pa.

9.5 Types of lease

Where the agreed term of the lease approximates to the expected lifetime of the asset, the lessee is clearly using the lease arrangement as an alternative form of finance to outright acquisition. As a result, he avoids having to incur the perhaps substantial outlay required at the outset of the project. Hence, the type of lease described so far is called a **finance lease** or **capital lease**, or a **full-payout lease**.

9.6 Operating leases

However, not all forms of lease operate over long time periods. The user may not wish to incur the long-term contractual liability to pay rentals, especially if he wishes only to obtain the use of the asset to perform a specific job (eg) drilling equipment to bore out a specific oil well. Lessors are willing to rent out equipment to such firms on the basis of an operating lease. This is usually job-specific and can be easily cancelled, whereas cancellation of a finance lease usually involves financial penalties so severe that termination is rarely worthwhile. The lessor will obviously hope to arrange a series of such contracts in order to recover his capital outlay and to achieve a profit. For this reason, the operating lease is called a part-payout lease. Unlike the finance lease, where the user bears the full risks both of 'downtime' (inability to use the asset), and also of obsolescence, the owner incurs the brunt of these risks. To compensate for the risk of having a yard full of idle, rusting equipment, the lessor will apply a rental which is higher per unit of time than that for financial lease, thus incorporating a risk premium.

Operating leases have another advantage for lessees. They are usually negotiated on a 'maintenance and insurance' basis, whereby the owner will undertake to insure and service the asset. This is normally the responsibility of the user in the case of the finance lease, although the owner may actually perform the servicing functions for a fee. The suitability of the operating lease for short-term projects explains its popularity in the construction industry under the guise of plant hire, and for assets with a rapid rate of technological advance such as photocopiers and computers.

9.7 Finance versus operating leases

The following table summarises the differences between finance leases and operating leases.

	Finance lease	*Operating lease*
1	One lease exists for the whole useful life of the asset.	The lease period is less than the useful life of the asset. The lessor relies on subsequent leasing or eventual sale of the asset to cover his capital outlay and show a profit
2	The lessor does not usually deal directly in this type of asset.	The lessor may very well carry on a trade in this type of asset.
3	The lessor does not retain the risks or rewards of ownership.	The lessor is normally responsible for repairs and maintenance.
4	The lease agreement cannot be cancelled. The lessee has a liability for all payments.	The lease can sometimes be cancelled at short notice.
5	The substance of the transaction is the purchase of the asset by the lessee financed by a loan from the lessor ie, it is effectively a source of medium- to long-term debt finance.	The substance of the transaction is the short-term rental of an asset.

Conclusion Finance leases are contracted for a term (roughly) equal to the asset's life, while operating leases are for more short-term ie, job-specific.

10 FINANCE LEASES

10.1 Introduction

Definition A finance lease is contracted for a fixed term and avoids the need to lay out large amounts of capital when an asset is acquired.

Until 1984, UK companies were able to disguise their true indebtedness by undertaking financial leases. Neither the asset acquired nor the contractual liability incurred had to appear on the Balance Sheet, although the rental payment obligation had to be stated in the notes to the accounts. To ensure that balance sheets give a truer picture of a company's asset/liability position, in 1984, the Accounting Standards Committee introduced SSAP21 'Accounting for Leases and Hire Purchase' which clarified the definition of a finance lease and issued instructions on how to account for one.

Since the period of a finance lease usually matches the expected lifetime of an asset, SSAP21 defined a finance lease as one 'that transfers substantially all the risks and rewards of ownership to the lessee'. It assumes that such a transfer takes place if at the start of the lease, the present value of the lease amounts to 90% or more of the fair value of the asset (normally its cash price).

Leases are also treated as financial leases if they meet one or more of the following criteria:

(1) At the end of the lease period, the lessee is given the option to buy the asset at a price below its anticipated market value.
(2) The lease period is no less than 75% of the estimated working life of the asset.
(3) Ownership of the asset can be transferred to the lessee at the end of the lease.

It should be noted that if at the termination of a finance lease, the ownership of the asset does pass from lessor to lessee, all previously exploited tax benefits will be clawed back by the Inland Revenue.

10.2 The accounting treatment of a finance lease

The standard lays down detailed rules for the accounting treatment of a finance lease.

- The fair value is capitalised as a fixed asset in the balance sheet and is depreciated over its useful life (or lease term, if shorter).
- Rental payments are treated as comprising two elements: a finance charge and a capital repayment. The finance charge is written off over the lease period at a constant periodic rate.
- The obligation to pay the capital element of the future rentals is recorded as a long-term creditor in the balance sheet. At the outset of the lease period, the capital element should equal the cash value of the asset.
- Every year, the appropriate finance charge is set against the profit and loss account.

Conclusion There are stringent rules governing the accounting and tax treatment of a finance lease.

10.3 The tax treatment of lease rentals

Tax relief in a finance lease used to be based on the rental payment. In 1991, the UK tax authorities brought the tax treatment of leases into line with SSAP21. This dictates that finance leases be stated on the balance sheet and depreciated accordingly. For leases taken out after April 1991, the Inland Revenue requires a separate treatment for the implicit finance charge and the implicit capital charge. The former depends on the interest rate implicit in the least contract, and is tax-allowable in full in the relevant accounting period. The capital repayment element is derived by spreading the total capital charge – normally the asset's cash price – over its useful life. In other words the depreciation charge in the accounts becomes the tax-allowable figure, dependent on the method of depreciation used and its acceptability to the Inland Revenue.

11 SALE AND LEASE-BACK (SAL)

11.1

Definition Sale and leaseback is the sale of an asset to a third party, typically a financial institution, who then leases back the asset to the original owner on the payment of regular instalments.

11.2 The characteristics of SAL

Strictly speaking, SAL is long-term finance, but is mentioned here as it has several features in common with leasing, as the name implies.

Such a financing strategy has been adopted by football clubs and local authorities as well as commercial companies. At least one local authority has sold some of its parking meters to a bank and then, for a periodic rental, has leased them back. Unlike parking meters, however, the main characteristics of assets more usually involved in this sort of transaction, is that they are likely to appreciate in value, such as land and property. Perhaps a more typical transaction would be for a supermarket to build a new 'superstore', say costing £30 million. Immediately on completion, it is sold to an insurance company, and then leased back for an agreed period of time for a pre-determined fee, perhaps with a 'rent' review every five years. The monies received by the store operator can then be used to finance the development of further enterprises. In this way, a relatively small initial amount of funds can be used to create a larger empire over a few years. SAL was an important mechanism whereby Tesco financed its recent growth.

Clearly there are downsides of this operation to the user of the asset. Title transfers to the purchaser of the asset, so that any capital appreciation will not benefit the original creator of the asset. Moreover, at the end of the contract with the purchaser, the user will have to find alternative premises or other relevant assets to replace the initial ones. The costs, legal and other, can be quite substantial on a transaction of this sort. The trading company will naturally have to consider whether the financial benefits associated with receiving the cash from the sale of the asset are sufficient to justify the periodic payment required under the lease agreement.

In some SAL agreements, there is a clause entitling the lessee to regain ownership of the asset, sometimes in the form of a first option to buy the asset when the financial institution decides to sell in order to realise accrued capital gains.

11.3 Activity

Sainscos wants to raise £10m capital to finance the building of a new megastore in virgin territory. In order to exploit this temporary market opportunity, it plans to sell existing property and lease it back.

The sales from the megastore will be £50m pa at an operating profit margin of 7%. Legal and other fees connected with the disposal will be £0.5m and store rental payments will be £0.5m pa. Ignoring tax, assess whether this a viable proposition for Sainscos.

11.4 Activity solution

Annual benefit = operating profit margin = 7% × £50m = £3.5m. Annual rental = £0.5m, hence annual benefit = £3.0m. This will recoup the legal fees well within one year. Beyond this, it is all (taxable) profit. But remember that Sainsco is foregoing the capital appreciation in the site value.

Conclusion SAL is an important means for an asset-rich company seeking investment capital to raise finance in the pursuit of strategic development. However, it can be used by any organisation wishing to quickly raise finance for a variety of purposes. The key thing to remember is that the vendor is exchanging future capital value for cash and liquidity now.

11.5 Activity

Briefly explain the main features of:

- Sale-and- leaseback
- Hire Purchase
- Financial leasing

11.6 Activity solution

Sale-and-leaseback (SAL)

SAL is an arrangement whereby a firm sells an asset, usually land or a building, to a financial institution and simultaneously enters an agreement to lease the property back from the purchaser. The seller receives the purchase price almost at once, but is committed to a series of rental payments over an agreed period, long enough for the purchaser to recoup his initial outlay plus an element of profit. The main advantage to the vendor is the rapidity with which otherwise illiquid assets can be converted into cash, and it is therefore suitable for capital-rationed companies who are eager to finance expansion programmes before perceived market opportunities evaporate.

The main disadvantage for the vendor of the asset is the loss of participation in any capital appreciation. A further disadvantage is the reduction in the balance sheet value of **owned** assets and hence possible reduction in the company's future capacity to borrow.

Hire Purchase (HP)

In an HP contract, equipment is purchased on behalf of the intended user by a finance house, usually a subsidiary of a bank. The user pays a periodic hire charge, commonly monthly. This includes both an interest element on the initial outlay plus recovery of capital. The ownership of the asset passes to the user at the end of the contract period, unless the user defaults on the payment schedule, in which case the owner can re-possess the asset. To ensure that the asset is worth re-possessing, the hire period is always set at less than the expected useful life of the asset. A feature of an HP contract is that the user ie, future owner, can claim capital allowances on the initial cost of the asset.

Financial Leasing

A finance lease is a contract where equipment is purchased by a leasing company, often a subsidiary of a bank, for long-term hire. The hire period corresponds to the expected lifetime of the asset, and, in most cases, the ownership of the asset does not pass to the user. In the UK, capital allowances are available to the purchaser, and may be passed on to the user in the form of a reduced rental charge. If the owner does relinquish ownership, these capital allowances are clawed back by the tax authorities. In the UK, both the leased asset and the corresponding stream of rental liabilities have to appear on the user's balance sheet. As a result, finance leasing cannot be used to disguise gearing but it is helpful to the capital-rationed firm, and also considerably cheaper than HP.

12 CHAPTER SUMMARY

Firms in temporary financial deficit have a wide selection of sources of both short- and medium-terms finance. The methods described here are the most important ones but the reader should remember that the financial services sector is ever ingenious in devising new ways of accommodating the financial requirements of companies and other organisations, often in response to monetary policy restrictions. The reader should also realise that with the advent of the Euro and a more integrated European financial market, new opportunities to borrow and in new forms are likely to emerge. Finally, (for syllabus reasons) we have said nothing in this chapter about raising long-term finance, although it was identified as an important element of financial planning in the previous chapter.

13 SELF-TEST QUESTIONS

13.1 When is use of short-term finance most appropriate? (1.4)

13.2 What are the dangers of abusing trade credit offered by suppliers? (2.5)

13.3 In what sense is a bank overdraft a 'self-liquidating' form of finance? (3.7)

13.4 How does a Bill of Exchange provide finance? (4.4)

13.5 What is a Bank Bill? (4.6)

13.6 What services are provided by a factor? (5.2, 5.3, 5.4 5.8)

13.7 How can a client of a factor avoid the goodwill problems associated with factoring? (5.12)

13.8 In what ways can a bank charge interest on a bank loan? (7.2)

13.9 How does a Hire Purchase contract work? (8.3)

13.10 Explain the differences between operating and finance leases. (9.5, 9.6)

8 INVESTING SURPLUS CASH

PATHFINDER INTRODUCTION

This chapter covers the following performance criteria and knowledge and understanding.

- Types of marketable security (Bills of exchange, certificates of deposit, government securities, local authority short term loans); terms and conditions; risks (Element 14.2)
- Managing risk and exposure (Element 14.2)
- Liquidity management (Elements 14.2, 14.3 & 14.4)
- Surplus funds are invested in marketable securities within defined financial authorisation limits (Element 14.2)
- Account is taken of trends in the economic and financial environment in managing cash balances (Element 14.2)
- An adequate level of liquidity is maintained in line with cash forecasts (Element 14.2).

Putting the chapter in context – learning objectives.

This chapter examines ways in which a company may invest a cash surplus in the short-to medium term. It begins by establishing the general principles underlying an investment strategy and emphasises the need to obtain both an appropriate balance between risk and return and also between cash and less-liquid assts. Some simple models of cash management are also presented. The specific depositories of temporarily surplus funds examined are:

(i) Bank deposits
(ii) Certificates of deposit
(iii) Government Stock
(iv) Local Authority stock
(v) Other Fixed Interest securities
(vi) Foreign currency holdings.

It should be remembered that some of the items examined in Chapter 7 as sources of finance for cash-short companies also represent ways of investing cash for cash-rich companies eg, Bills of Exchange and commercial paper.

The chapter concludes with a mini study-case to test some of the principles established in the chapter.

At the end of this chapter you should have learned the following topics:

- the key objectives in the investment of short term cash surpluses – liquidity, safety and profitability
- the risk-return trade-off
- cash management models – Baumol and Miller-Orr
- the relationship between market price of fixed interest stocks and interest rates
- the nature and applicability of the various depositories of short and medium term funds as listed above.

1 SHORT-TERM INVESTMENT PORTFOLIOS

1.1 Introduction

Definition In this section, surplus cash is defined as liquid balances held by a business which are neither needed to finance current business operations nor held permanently for short-term investment. Their availability is temporary, awaiting employment either in existing operations or in new investment opportunities (whether already identified or not).

Short-term investment opportunities present themselves when cash surpluses arise. The company's attitude to risk and working capital management will determine the planned cash holdings. An aggressive working capital policy will plan to minimise funds held, with deficits met by borrowing. A conservative policy will set aside cash in an investment portfolio, which can be drawn upon when the need arises.

In Chapter 1 we introduced the basic principles of short term investment; this chapter deals with the practical aspects of the management of a portfolio of such investments.

1.2 How does surplus cash arise?

As a reminder, surplus cash can become available in the following ways:

(a) Overfunding; (arising from excessive long term finance raising)
(b) A reduction in operating or other assets; (eg, from seasonal trade or business decline)
(c) A surplus of retained earnings over the increase in net assets employed;
(d) Improved credit control;
(e) The sale of surplus fixed assets or surplus obsolete stocks;
(f) The nature of the business eg, journal subscriptions received by the publisher of the journal.

1.3 Objectives in the investment of surplus cash

The objectives are categorised as follows:

(a) **Liquidity**: the cash must be available for use when needed.

(b) **Safety**: no risk of loss must be taken, as the cash will be needed for later, more important, business uses.

(c) **Profitability**: subject to the liquidity and safety objectives mentioned above, the aim is to earn the highest possible after tax returns.

Each of these objectives raises problems which will be explored now.

1.4 Liquidity

This problem is at first sight simple enough. If a company knows that it will need the funds in three days (or weeks or months), it simply invests them for just that period at the best rate available, taking safety into account. The solution is to match the maturity of the investment with the period for which the funds are surplus.

There are however, complications.

(a) The exact duration of the surplus period is not always known. It is of course known if the cash is needed to meet a loan instalment, a large tax payment or a dividend, but it will not be known if the need is unidentified, or depends on the build-up of inventory (stock), the progress of construction work, or the hammering out of an acquisition deal.

(b) It will be seen below that the maturity of investments can also depend on the view taken of future trends in interest rates.

(c) The options are extended (and therefore complicated) by the possibility of borrowing to bridge the gap between the time when the cash is needed and the subsequent date on which the investment matures.

(d) Finally, an investment may not need to be held until maturity if either an earlier withdrawal is permitted by the terms of the instrument without excessive penalty, or if there is a secondary market and its disposal in that market causes no excessive loss.

1.5 Safety

Safety means no risk of loss. Superficially, this again looks simple. The concept certainly includes the absence of credit risk. For example, not depositing with a bank which might conceivably fail within the maturity period and thus fail to repay the amount deposited.

But suppose that a company is holding the surplus cash with the express purpose of paying for a new capital asset like a freehold factory, the ultimate cost of which depends on building costs. It has not yet negotiated a fixed money price for it, and construction contractors are unwilling to accept a price which is not subject to a cost escalation clause. It is interested in any investment instrument which will (after tax) maintain its purchasing power against domestic price inflation. In that case a safer instrument might be an index-linked gilt-edged bond with a maturity date about the expected date of the capital payment.

Again, suppose the surplus cash is held specifically against a payment due in a foreign currency like the D-mark. For example, against a deferred credit payment for a capital asset bought from a German supplier. In that case, the only riskless investment would be one denominated in DM. This may give a lower nominal return, but its DM value would not be exposed to exchange rate fluctuations. Moreover, in practice it would pay to ask the German supplier to quote for a discounted immediate cash price and compare the after-tax saving on this with the after-tax return on the most favourable D-mark investment.

So safety is not necessarily to be defined as the certainty to get the original investment repaid at 100% of its original *sterling* money value. This may be correct, but if the purpose for which the surplus cash is held is not itself fixed in sterling, then other criteria of safety may apply.

1.6 Profitability

Once more, this objective looks deceptively simple at first: go for the highest rate of return subject to the overriding criteria of safety and liquidity. However, here there are added complications such as:

(a) Fixed or variable rates?
(b) What maturity?
(c) Timing of interest receipts.
(d) Tax effects.
(e) Use of other currencies.
(f) Difficulties in forecasting available funds.
(g) Ascertaining the most favourable rates.

These questions can be answered by an approach similar to that explained above. These aspects will be considered further in the following sections.

Conclusion The company's strategy for investing short-to-medium cash surpluses should be governed by the three principles of safety, liquidity and profitability.

2 ASSESSING RISK: THE RISK RETURN TRADE-OFF

Definition The risk-return trade-off is the relationship between prospective returns on an investment and the risk incurred by the investor.

2.1 Introduction

Any developed financial system will establish a clear relationship between the rate of return offered (and required) on different types of investment and their respective risks. The yield on short-term government stock usually establishes the benchmark yield among securities traded on the market because it is regarded as risk-free. Other securities have to offer an extra yield or 'risk premium' as compensation for the risk they carry. The riskiest securities of all are ordinary shares because there is no obligation for the company to pay a dividend, and in the event of insolvency, the ordinary shareholder, being last in line, stands to receive nothing (conversely, the risk to the company is low because failure to pay a return ie, the dividend, will not result in legal action, as would apply in the case of corporate bonds).

A typical risk return trade-off is shown below (although the relationship is unlikely to be linear.)

The risk-return trade-off

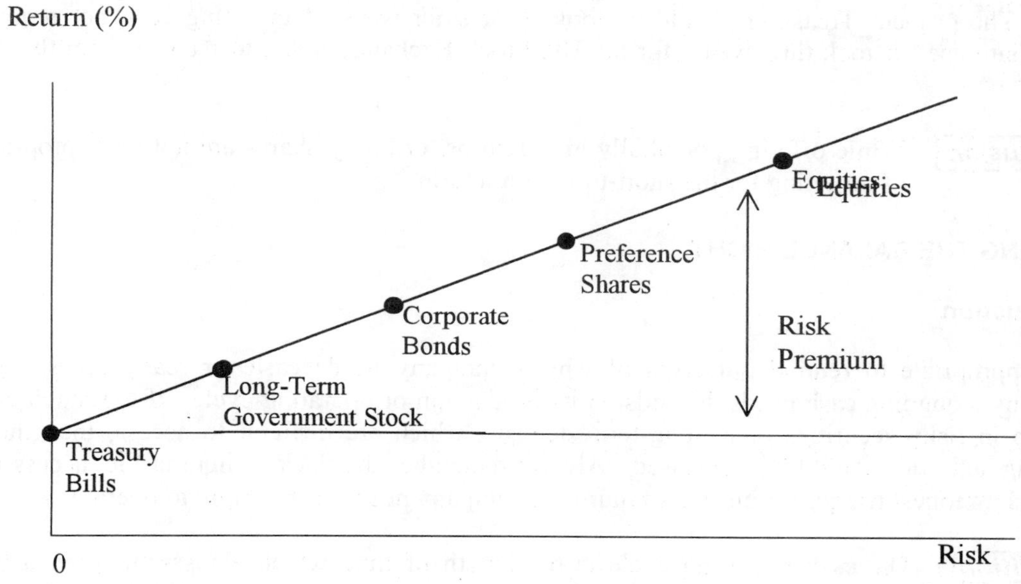

2.2 Types of return

Returns on investment come in two broad forms. A regular interest or dividend payment, paid annually or semi-annually (sometimes more frequently with short-term deposits), and capital appreciation. With ordinary shares, the bulk of the return is in the form of capital gain, while government stocks offers the bulk of their returns in the form of interest payments.

2.3 Types of risk

There are two broad types of risk

(i) **Risk of default**—failure to pay interest when due, or failure to repay the capital at the required redemption date. This is the main risk for fixed interest securities.

(ii) **Variability in returns**—some securities eg, ordinary shares, can experience considerable volatility in both their market values and also their periodic payments to investors. As noted, companies are not legally obliged to make dividend payments to ordinary shareholders, while extraneous events, such as the Asian crisis in 1998, can cause sharp falls in share prices. Sources of variability in share prices are usually split into two categories:

(a) *Systematic risk*—variability in returns due to changes in general economic and political conditions which impact on all securities.

(b) *Unsystematic risk*—this variability is caused by factors specific to the individual company such as the loss of a key contract or embezzlement by the finance director.

2.4 Beta values

Unsystematic risk can be diversified away by forming a portfolio of shares, but the investor is still left facing systematic risk factors. Companies differ in their degrees of systematic risk – they have different exposures to changes in general market conditions, as measured by their Beta coefficients. Broadly, this measures the extent to which variations in the return for the shares of one company are related to variations in the stock market as a whole.

A Beta above one signifies an 'aggressive' security whose returns (in both directions) exceed those on the market as a whole, and a Beta below one signifies a 'defensive' security. The Beta values of companies which are actively traded on the Stock Exchange tend to cluster around one, so even the shares of 'Blue Chip' companies such as Marks and Spencer and Diageo are subject to potentially sharp swings in value.

For this reason, ordinary shares are not regarded as a suitable depository for temporary surpluses of cash. The prudent Treasurer should be looking at safer ways of investing cash not required for immediate use. It took three years for the UK Stock Exchange index to recover from the crash of 1987.

Conclusion While offering potentially high returns, ordinary shares are not an appropriate way of investing for the short-to-medium term.

3 GETTING THE BALANCE RIGHT

3.1 Introduction

It is appropriate to remind ourselves of why a company needs cash, or ready access to it. A company's ongoing cash needs depends on its production or operating cycle. If too much capital is tied up in risky securities or in long-term deposits which are difficult to access, then the firm's ongoing activities could be jeopardised. Always remember that lack of liquidity ie, access to cash, is the commonest trigger for business failure. A company needs cash simply to operate.

Definition The cash operating cycle is the length of time which elapses between a business paying for its raw materials and the business's customers paying for the goods made from the raw materials. It equals the debtors' collection period plus the length of time for which stocks are held, less the creditors' payment period.

3.2 Activity

A company generally pays its suppliers six weeks after receiving an invoice, while its debtors usually pay within four weeks of invoicing. Raw materials stocks are held for a week before processing, which takes three weeks, begins. Finished goods stay in stock for an average of two weeks.

How long is the company's operating cycle?

3.3 Activity solution

The operating cycle equals debtors' collection period plus raw materials' stock-holding period and processing time plus finished goods' stock-holding period less the creditors' payment period

$= 4 + 1 + 3 + 2 - 6 = 4$ weeks

3.4 The Baumol cash management model

A number of different mathematical models have been developed for managing everyday cash balances, based on the Economic Order Quantity approach of inventory control such as the Baumol model.

Baumol's model suggests that a fixed cost can be identified with each time cash is raised and a variable cost can be estimated as the opportunity cost of lost interest of holding cash per time period. Holding too little cash results in frequent raising of finance with the associated fixed costs each time; holding too much cash results in a large variable cost of lost interest. A formula can then be used to estimate the optimum amount of cash to raise.

3.5 Activity

Bramham plc, which currently has negligible cash holdings, expects to have to make a series of cash payments totalling £1.5m (P) over the forthcoming year. These will become due at a steady rate, and can be met by making periodic sales from existing holdings of short-term securities. According to Bramham's financial advisers, the most likely average percentage rate of return (i) on these securities is 12% over the forthcoming year, although this estimate is highly uncertain. Whenever Bramham sells securities, it incurs a transaction fee (T) of £25, and places the proceeds on short term deposit at 5% per annum interest until needed. The following formula specifies the optimal amount of cash raised (Q) for each sale of securities.

$$Q = \sqrt{\frac{2 \times P \times T}{i}}$$

Required

(i) What is the optimal number of times Bramham should sell securities?
(ii) What are the costs resulting from this policy?
(iii) How would you criticise this approach?

3.6 Activity solution

(i) Optimal proceeds per sale: $Q = \sqrt{\frac{2 \times £1.5m \times £25}{0.12}} = £25,000$

Number of sales: = £1.5m/£25,000 = 60

(ii) As well as cash transaction costs, this policy involves an opportunity cost in terms of the foregone returns from holding securities. This second element is partly offset by interest earnings on the average cash balance held.

Transaction costs	=	60 × £25	=	£1,500
Average cash balance	=	£25,000/2 = £12,500		
Holding cost:	=	£12,500 × 12%	=	£1,500
Interest on short-term deposits:				
Av. cash balance × 5%	=	£12,500 × 5%	=	(£625)
Total management costs				£2,375

(iii) Some limitations of this simple model are:

- It assumes a steady run-down in cash holdings between successive security sales. In reality, the pattern of cash holdings is likely to be far more erratic, with exceptional demands for cash punctuated by periods of excessive liquidity. However, the period between sales is short enough and the transaction cost low enough to allow flexibility in cash management.

- It allows for no buffer stock of cash. In reality, security sales are unlikely to be made when cash balances drop to zero, but when they fall to a level deemed to be the safe minimum.

- It uses a 'highly uncertain' estimate of the return from the portfolio. Bramham should investigate the implications of assuming alternative (higher and lower) rates, and perhaps determine a 'break-even rate', at which the two policies are equally attractive. In this example, the actual rate would have to be well above 12% to achieve this result.

- There may be economies in bulk-selling of securities, although exploiting these would increase the holding cost.

3.7 The Miller-Orr model

The model takes into account uncertainty and both receipts and payments of cash. It is best explained with reference to the following diagram:

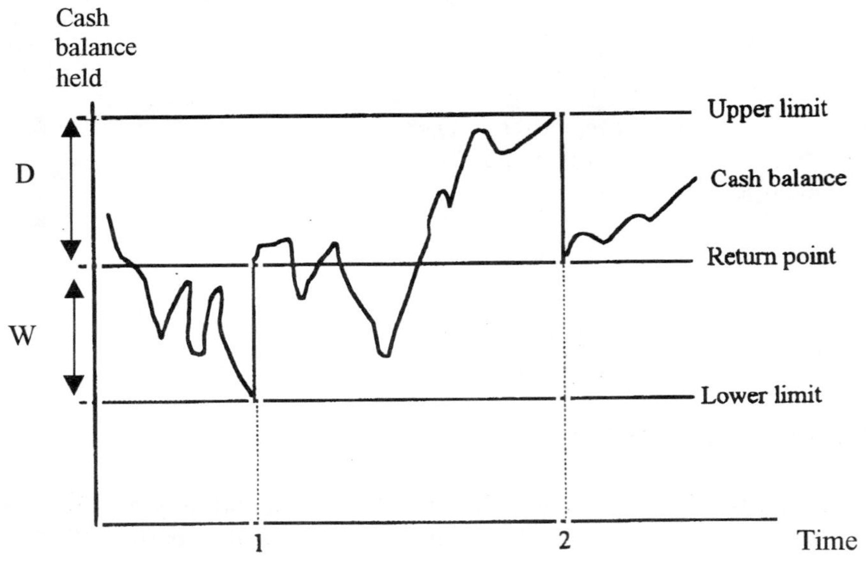

All cash receipts and payments are met from the cash balance and, as can be seen from the diagram, the cash balance of the firm is allowed to wander freely between two limits. The lower limit has to be specified by the firm and the upper limit is calculated by the model (which is outside the syllabus). If the cash balance on any day goes outside these limits action must be taken.

At point 1 the cash balance reaches the lower limit and must be replenished in some way eg, by the sale of marketable securities or withdrawal from a deposit account. The size of this withdrawal is indicated on the diagram (W), and it is the distance between the return point (calculated by the model) and the lower limit.

At point 2 the cash balance reaches the upper limit and an amount (D) must be invested in marketable securities or placed in a deposit account. Again, this is calculated by the model as the distance between the upper limit and the return point.

4 BANK DEPOSITS

4.1 Introduction

All of the so-called commercial banks offer deposit facilities to companies, in addition to traditional cheque-clearing facilities. It is not the general rule to pay interest on cheque accounts. In order to qualify for interest, the company will have to set up a separate account into which to deposit excessive cash balances. Deposits may be made at the company's own initiative or it may be possible to arrange a 'sweep' system whereby if the positive balance on the cheque account rises above a specified ceiling, the bank will automatically transfer the excess into the deposit account. The reverse may apply when there is downward pressure on the cheque account balance. Withdrawals from deposit accounts usually require a period of notice, typically seven days. Interest rates are usually tiered, rising with the amount on deposit.

4.2 Achieving higher returns

For larger sums of money, the bank may offer Treasury account facilities whereby money can be deposited on the money market for varying periods, usually upwards of seven days. The interest rate is usually higher than an orthodox deposit account. The rate of interest is likely to increase both with the amount invested and with the term of the deposit.

Some 'fringe' banks may offer slightly higher interest rates to depositors but as ever, the investor should question the risk-return relationship. If an above average return is offered, this usually indicates an above average degree of risk. Possibly, the institution is less tightly regulated than 'mainstream' UK banks or it is investing in risky assets, eg, unsecured loans. It is worth remembering that under the Deposit Protection Scheme, depositors are only protected from insolvency of the deposit-taking institution up to 90% of the first £20,000 of deposits. It is hardly worth risking millions for the sake of an extra ¼% interest.

Conclusion The first 'home' for temporary liquidity surpluses will be bank deposits, but the rewards are directly related to the amount deposited and the period of notice of withdrawal required.

5 CERTIFICATES OF DEPOSIT (CDs)

Definition A CD is a negotiable instrument issued by a financial institution which certifies the existence of, and access to, a deposit of funds

5.1 Introduction

An attractive way of 'parking' unwanted cash is to make a deposit for any time, but usually between three months and five years, in a financial institution, usually a bank, which issues a CD as proof of title to the funds involved. The interest rate on a CD is usually a little higher than on instant access deposits. The minimum amount which can be deposited is £50,000, and the commonest term is for six months. The appeal for the bank is that it can rely on continuous use of the funds for lending purposes for a specified period of time. As well as the higher interest rate, the appeal for the depositor is the fact that there is an active market in CDs. They are particularly attractive for investors for whom anonymity is important, as they are payable to the bearer with no need to prove identity, at the end of the specified term.

5.2 Trading CDs

The market for CDs closely resembles the market for Bills of Exchange (examined in the previous chapter). CDs are an attractive investment for Discount Houses, especially if they have only a few months to maturity. If the original depositor requires cash before the full term, it only requires a telephone call to a Discount House to agree a price and delivery terms in order to convert the CD into cash. A CD may change hands several times before the maturity date. The price at which it is traded will normally increase as the maturity date approaches, but at any one time, will reflect prevailing interest rates. Unlike ordinary shares, there is no stamp duty payable on the transaction – all fees and costs (including the trader's profit margin) are reflected in the current price.

Conclusion The appeal of a CD to the depositor is the relatively high interest rate and the liquidity implicit in the knowledge that there is an active second-hand market.

6 GOVERNMENT STOCK

Definition Government stock, or gilt-edged securities ('gilts') range from short-term securities ie, Treasury Bills, to long-dated and irredeemable stock. These are effectively free of risk.

6.1 Introduction

Securities issued by the Government are virtually risk-free. The interest payment is guaranteed by the stability of the Government and its monetary authorities. The only real source of risk is the rate of inflation undermining the real return on these securities.

Government securities come in several forms, as outlined below.

6.2 Treasury Bills

These are mainly 91-day Bills which are issued to finance the Government's short-term funding needs and also to fine-tune the money supply, given that these securities count towards the liquid assets of the banking system. The yield on Treasury Bills used to be taken as the benchmark rate of interest ie, the price at which Treasury Bills were sold indicated the Bank's view of what interest rates ought to be. Now that interest rates are set by the Monetary Policy Committee, the emphasis is rather different – Treasury Bills are now sold at an interest rate consistent with the MPC's decisions on interest rates.

Use of the term 'interest rate' is something of a misnomer. Treasury Bills do not carry interest as such. They are issued at a discount to their face value ie, the amount which the Bank of England promises to repay, and the investor receives his return in the form of a capital appreciation. In this respect, they can be viewed as the equivalent of commercial Bills of Exchange, although less risky.

Note that when yields on Treasury Bills are quoted in the financial press, these are always equivalent annual or 'annualised' yields

6.3 Activity

The Bank of England issues a block of 91-day Treasury Bills, each having face value of £10,000, at a price of £9,800. What is the implicit annual rate of return, or yield, on these Bills, if held to maturity?

6.4 Solution

The holder will make a capital gain of £200 on an investment of £9,800 over three months. This represents an annualised return of roughly:

$$\left(\frac{£200}{£9{,}800} \times \frac{365}{91}\right) = 8.19\% \text{ p.a.}$$

These would be worth buying if the investors can raise finance at an interest rate of less than 8.19%.

Strictly the true answer is found by compounding over four periods, ie,

$$\left[\left(\frac{£200}{£9{,}800}\right) + 1\right]^4 - 1 = 8.41\%$$

More sophisticated treasurers will look more closely at this true rate.

6.5 Fixed interest stocks

Securities issued for longer periods carry entitlement to receive interest. These stocks are usually classified as follows:

Short-dated ('shorts') – with lifetime up to 5 years
Medium-dated ('mediums') – with lifetime between 10 and 15 years
Long-dated ('longs') – with lifetime beyond 15 years

All are issued through, and traded on, the Stock Exchange.

The current market prices of these are quoted daily in the financial press. The Financial Times of 13th August 1998 revealed the following examples:

	Interest Yield	Redemption Yield	Market Price
Short-Dated Treasury 6pc 1999	6.06	7.09	99xd
Medium-Dated Treasury 10pc 2004	8.40	6.03	119
Long-Dated Exchequer 12pc 2013-17	7.31	5.67	$164^{3}/_{16}$

The short-dated stock will be redeemed at its nominal value in 1999, its market price is currently £99 per £100 nominal value (ex dividend).

The interest payable on this stock is called the 'coupon rate' which is 6% ie, holders of the stock receive (6% × £100) = £6 interest per £100 nominal stock. Most government stocks pay interest twice a year, although any buyer of this Treasury 6pc is too late to qualify for an interest payment as the market price is quoted 'xd' ie, ex-dividend, which means without the interest payment included. Given the nearness to maturity of this stock, it appears that the only return which a purchaser would receive would be capital appreciation of £1.

6.6 Interest rates and market values

The medium-dated stock is repayable in 2005, and is currently selling at a price above par value. The long-dated stock also sells above par value. In both these cases, people who hold to maturity will realise a capital loss. In each case, the market price is above the par value because the coupon rate of interest exceeds the going market rate of interest, making each of these two stocks appear relatively attractive. Roughly speaking the market value and the par value of fixed-interest securities are linked by the following formula:

$$\text{Market price} = \text{Par value} \times \frac{\text{Coupon rate}}{\text{Going market rate}}$$

However, this expression only 'works' for a small category of government stocks, those which are perpetual, or irredeemable, such as 3½% War Loan. However, this formula does yield the following guidelines:

Conclusion When interest rates rise, the market value of government stock falls and vice versa.

This means that the treasurer must take a view on the likely future course of interest rates—if they rise, he could find himself nursing a capital loss.

The relationship between interest rates and the prices of government stock is explained in more detail in the next section.

6.7 Activity

The government issued 5% irredeemable stock in 1995. What is the market price per £100 of stock when:

(i) interest rates are 10%
(ii) interest rates are 5%
(iii) interest rates are 20%

6.8 Activity solution

(i) market price = £100 × $5\%/10\%$ = £50

(ii) market price = £100 × $5\%/5\%$ = £100

(iii) market price = £100 × $5\%/20\%$ = £25

6.9 Bond yields

It is important that Treasurers fully understand the relationship between interest rates in the market and the price of government and other stock. Consider this example.

A bond priced at £85 per £100 of stock, offers a coupon rate of 7% and is redeemable in five years at par. What is the yield on this stock?

There are several measures of yield, viz:

(i) The interest yield or running yield is simply:
Interest/market price = £7/£85 = 8.23%

(ii) Redemption yield.
With five years life to maturity, someone who buys it for £85 will receive a capital gain in redemption of £15. Averaged over five years, this represents an additional gain of £3 per annum. Based on the purchase price of £85, this raises the yield to redemption to roughly:

8.23% + £3/£85 – 8.23% + 3.522% = 11.75%

However, this is only a crude approximation to the true redemption yield which depends on the precise timing of the investor's income flows. For example, assume he buys the stock now, having just missed out on the interest payment, thus anticipating five future annual interest payments plus the redemption payment of £100 at the end of the fifth year. The yield to maturity is the solution R in the following expression:

$$\pounds 85 = \frac{\pounds 7}{(1+R)} = \frac{\pounds 7}{(1+R)^2} + \ldots\ldots\ldots + \frac{(\pounds 7 + \pounds 100)}{(1+R)^5}$$

(You can solve this using the IRR function on a spreadsheet, or by trial and error). The precise solution is 10.9%. As above, this would be offset by the investor's tax liability. As this figure is gross-of-tax, it is also called the Gross Redemption Yield. The same principles apply in calculating yields on all government securities.

6.10 Activity

Work out the flat, crude redemption and true gross redemption yields on the following bond which is to be redeemed at par (100) at the end of two further years.

Market price = £10x xd
coupon rate = 12%
All payments are at year-ends.

6.11 Solution

(i) Flat yield = £12/£105 = 11.43%
(ii) crude redemption yield –
[average capital loss/£105] + 11.43%
= £2.50) / £105 + 11.43% = (2.38%) + 11.43% = 9.05%
(iii) The true yield, R, is found from the expression

$$£105 = \frac{£12}{(1 + R)} + \frac{£12 + £100}{(1 + R)^2}$$

Conclusion If the market price of government stock is currently above its par value, the investor will incur a capital loss if he holds to maturity (and vice versa).

If you now return to the table which gives the information about yields on government stock, the meaning of the terms interest yield and redemption yield should now be clear.

7 LOCAL AUTHORITY STOCK

Definition Local Authority stock is issued by borough and county councils with the ultimate backing of the government.

7.1 Introduction

Local authority debt instruments can be issued with a period to maturity ranging from as little as two days to ten or fifteen years. The longer-term stock is often issued to finance infrastructure investment and the shorter stock to meet short-term liquidity problems which are endemic in the local authority sector. The most popular local authority bonds are called 'yearlings' which have a maturity of one year and six days and are issued in minimum denominations of £1,000. They carry a fixed- semi-annual interest coupon with the yield set slightly in excess of that currently available on gilt-edged stock. All local authority debt is guaranteed by the government and is thus very similar in most respects to government stock. As there remains in some quarters the slight suspicion of default or delay in payment, the small risk premium is required. The market is much thinner than for government stock which provides an additional reason for a premium.

Longer dated stocks also offer semi-annual interest payments and have a similar maturity profile to government stocks, even including a handful of irredeemables. Two examples of local authority stocks listed in the Financial Times (14 August 1998) are:

	Interest Yield	Redemption Yield	Price
Birmingham 11½% 2012	9.54%	6.68%	£120½
Liverpool 3½% irredeemable	6.25%	--	£56

Conclusion Local authority securities offer slightly higher yields than government stock because the market is less liquid and the security of a local authority is not regarded quite so highly as that of central government.

8 OTHER FIXED INTEREST SECURITIES

This section considers longer-term forms of investment, but all with a ready market ie, they possess liquidity.

8.1 Corporate loan stock (corporate bonds)

Companies which have a stock market quotation are also allowed to issue loan stock which can be traded on the stock Exchange in the same way as ordinary shares. These come in several forms.

(i) **Debentures**

Debentures are secured on the company's assets ie, in the event of default, the creditor can enforce the sale of the assets concerned in order to obtain repayment of the loan and interest owing. Some debentures are secured on specific assets eg, a plot of land (a mortgage debenture) and others carry a 'floating charge', being secured on assets in general. Like government stock, these have a par value, a coupon rate and a specified redemption rate and their value varies inversely with market interest rates. However, because the risk of default is greater with companies, the interest rate payable ie, the yield demanded by the market exceeds that on government stock. Clearly, companies vary in their credit-worthiness so a range of yields will be available at any one time—A FT-SE company's debentures will offer a lower yield than a Stock Exchange 'minnow'.

(ii) **Unsecured loan stock**

These are similar to debentures in all respects except one—as the name suggests, they are not secured on company assets. If the borrower defaults, creditors cannot enforce asset sales to obtain repayment. In effect, they represent an act of faith, ie, confidence on the part of the market in the company's continued ability to make the interest payments. In this they are 'secured' on the company's future earning power. They are sometimes called 'junior' securities because they rank behind secured loan stock in the queue for repayment, (this term also applies to some secured stock, issued sometime after other loans—date of issue usually confers seniority or precedence for repayment).

(iii) **Convertibles**

A convertible starts life as loan stock (which may or may not be secured) with the usual characteristics, but it carries the right for the holder to convert into ordinary shares at some future date. This ability to convert is usually on attractive terms, offering the prospect of a capital gain, for this reason they can be issued at a relatively low interest rate.

Arcadia plc (formerly the Burton Group) issued 8% Convertible Bonds redeemable between 1996 and 2001, but carrying the right to convert into ordinary shares at any time during 1995-6 at a price of £2.34 per share. Beyond this date, the company could redeem the stock at par with 60 days' notice. (This is called a 'call option').

8.2 Corporate preference shares

Many quoted companies also issue preference shares. They represent part of shareholders' funds but do not carry the full set of rights attaching to ordinary shares eg, no right to vote. The return on a preference share is usually fixed, rather like that on debentures, but there is no legal obligation to pay it. Preference shares may be:

Cumulative If the preference divided is missed one year, it can be carried forward and paid in a future year.

Participating If company profits exceed a specified level, the preference shareholders may be paid an additional dividend.

Convertible They may be convertible into ordinary shares.

Redeemable Unlike ordinary shares, they may be repayable at par at some (often unspecified) future date.

Clearly the risk attending to preference shares is rather higher than on corporate loan stock, although they may have unexpected bonuses. For example, in the event of a take-over bid, they may assume voting rights and sharply rise in price.

8.3 Permanent-Interest Bearing Securities (PIBS)

These are securities issued by some building societies to raise long-term funds to back their lending activities. Like corporate debt and preference shares, they are traded on the Stock Exchange. They carry rather higher yields than government stock and many corporate loan stocks. They are irredeemable and rank behind other creditors and shareholders in the Society concerned. Nor do they qualify for compensation under the Building Society Investor Protection Scheme.

An example of a PIBS is the Bradford and Bingley Building Society 13% which can be dealt in multiples of 10,000 units. The issue size was £60m and dividends are paid at the coupon rate in April and October. On July 24th 1998, its market price was £184.75, reflecting a flat yield of 7.01%.

Some PIBS have larger dealing sizes eg, the PIBS of the demutualised societies have dealing multiples of 50,000 but some are as low as 1,000 (eg, Birmingham and Midshires). A curiosity of PIBS is that dealings are transacted at the quoted price plus or minus daily accrued interest. Barclays Capital supplies an up-to-date listing of prices and interest accruals.

The market prices of PIBS are subject to similar influences as other fixed interest securities ie, there is an inverse relationship between interest rates and their market values.

Conclusion Like government stock, the market price of other fixed-interest bearing securities rises and falls inversely with going market rates of interest.

9 FOREIGN CURRENCY DEPOSITS

9.1 Introduction

If the company is involved in overseas trade, then some proportion of its liquid funds might sensibly be held in the form of foreign currency. For example, if the company expects to have to meet an obligation in Canadian dollars (C$) in a few months time, it may be prudent to build up a holding of C$. While this would cause no cash cost, it would involve an opportunity cost. If the C$ does depreciate, the required quantity could have been acquired more cheaply at the time of the transaction by using the spot market, ie, the market for immediate delivery.

9.2 Using the forward market

Some companies prefer to hedge against the risk of adverse foreign exchange rate movements by using the forward market, the market for future delivery. If people in general expect the C$ to appreciate in the future, this will normally be reflected in the forward rate of exchange ie, the rate applicable for future delivery of currency.

For example, imagine a trader wants to have C$2m in three months. Today's spot rate is C$2.45 per £1 and the quotation in the forward market is C$2.40 per £1. If the trader buys C$ now the cost is $^{2m}/_{2.45}$ = £816,327. If he uses the forward market, the cost is $^{C\$2m}/_{2.40}$ = £833,333 but by doing this, he is protected against a sharper appreciation of the C$. Using the forward market is a way of locking-in today's rate. In this example, he retains use of the sterling which can be invested over the three month period until it is required to pay for the delivery of C$.

9.3 Warning signs

There are two signs to watch for when attempting to manage foreign currency in this sort of situation:

(1) If the forward rate is higher than the spot eg,
C$ spot 2.40 per £1
C$ forward 2.45 per £1

this means people expect the C$ to depreciate against sterling, and thus it may be better to buy on the spot market in 3 months time..

(2) If the interest rate applicable to sterling deposits exceeds that applicable to deposits in C$, this means that sterling is expected to depreciate versus the C$.

In theory, any interest rate differential should exactly offset the difference between the spot and forward rates. This is called Interest Rate Parity (IRP). This almost always holds, due to the actions of speculators who react to short-term discrepancies by moving 'hot money' from one centre to another until the scope for making profit disappears. This is called arbitrage.

9.4 Is it sensible to predict exchange rates?

In practice, exchange rate movements that occur often dwarf the spot-forward differential. Exchange rate changes can occur for a variety of reasons eg, speculation, changes in government policy, etc, factors which are largely unpredictable. If the company feels it can predict future exchange rate movements, then it may wish to take a 'position' (ie, hold currency which it expects to strengthen versus sterling.)

However, predicting currency movements is a dangerous game, best left to experts. Moreover, even the forecasting record of the experts is not impressive. The magazine 'Corporate Finance' publishes a list of foreign exchange rate forecasts made by various banks. In August 1998, of 26 banks surveyed, the mean prediction for the three month Dollar/Sterling rate (the 'Cable rate') was US$1.64 per £1, but forecasts ranged from 1.68 (2.4% above the average) to 1.58 (3.7% below the average). The commonest forecast was also 1.64, selected by nine banks.

The 12 month forecasts averaged 1.60 over a range of 1.50 – 1.71.

Conclusion If the 'experts' get it wrong, you probably will too.

For those prepared to speculate, the following advice might apply when expecting to make a **payment** in a foreign currency (FC)

You expect the FC to:	Action
strengthen vs £	Hold currency
weaken vs £	Delay purchase

Arguably, trading and manufacturing companies should not be speculating in foreign currency. Use of the forward market is generally considered to be the most prudent policy to adopt. However, if the firm expects to have obligations in a variety of currencies, holding a 'currency cocktail' may offer protection if there is no consistent pattern in the way other currencies move against sterling.

9.5 The example of British Steel

The table below shows the foreign currency (FX) holdings of British Steel at its 1998 year end (March 28).

	£m	%
Swedish Kronor	2	3
Deutschmarks	25	34
Guilders (Netherlands)	6	8
US Dollars	18	24
Canadian Dollars	8	10
French Francs	12	16
Others	4	5
	74	100

However, it should be noted that FX holdings were only 7% of its total holdings of cash and short-term investments of £1,043m.

Conclusion If there are expected liabilities in different currencies, holding liquid FX assets has a role, but these holdings should not be excessive.

9.6 Activity

Monkton plc, which relies on imported components from the USA, is concerned about the risk of its overseas liabilities. It has to pay in US dollars and does not hedge currency risk, accepting invoices at the prevailing spot rate, which is currently US$1.45:£. It is considering hedging its US dollar liabilities on the forward markets. Its bank has offered to sell dollars at a fixed rate of US$1.55:£1. Monkton's advisers estimate the following changes of various sterling/dollar rates of exchange prevailing over the forthcoming year:

Dollars per £	*Probability*
1.60	0.1
1.50	0.2
1.45	0.4
1.40	0.2
1.30	0.1

Required

(i) Work out the sterling cost of an import bill of US$1m at each possible exchange rate.

(ii) Briefly discuss whether Monkton should hedge the foreign currency risk associated with its overseas sales.

9.7 Activity solution

(i) Sterling cost of meeting import bill of US$1m

Dollars per £	*Sterling cost*
1.60	625,000
1.50	666,666
1.45	689,655
1.40	714,286
1.30	769,231

The sterling cost can range from 9.4% below the central value to 11.5% above it. These sorts of variations can seriously undermine the profitability of overseas traders.

(ii) In theory, foreign exchange earnings should not be hedged, as the chances of an adverse movement are equal to those of a favourable one, so that in the long-term, importers like Monkton should break even. This can be inferred from the figures above – there is an equal chance (30%) of the dollar depreciating as of appreciating.

However, failure to hedge can leave firms exposed to the risk of erratically large adverse currency movements, perhaps large enough to bankrupt the smaller firm. So although the perceived risks in the long-term are roughly symmetrical, many companies deem it prudent to hedge at least some part of their overseas earnings, especially those relating to major contracts.

In this case, Monkton might be advised to hold a proportion of the expected dollar liabilities in dollar form. Even better, if it receives any payments in dollars, these can be left on deposit unconverted in order to meet the liabilities as they emerge.

10 MINI CASE-STUDY

GZ plc trades mainly in the UK but plans to expand in the US either by acquisition or joint venture within the next year or so. It has built up a portfolio of investments as shown in the table below, the aim of which is to provide funds for its US investment programme.

Type of security	*Value (£m)*	*Average return in 1998*
3–month Treasury Bills	5.5	7%
Local Authority Bonds	2.5	7.5%
UK government stock	4.0	7.9%
UK equities	7.0	12%
US equities	15.0	14%
Total	34.0m	

The return on the UK stock market during 1998 was 9% overall, and on the US market, 11%.

Critically evaluate GZ's investment portfolio.

10.1 Answer to mini case-study

- The paramount aim of this portfolio should be medium-term liquidity to provide investment funds (unless alternative forms of finance are available). The fixed interest element totals just £12m out of a total portfolio of £34m (ie, 35%).

- The fixed interest component is subject to interest rate risk, the extent of this depending on nearness to maturity. The Treasury Bills do not exhibit great dangers here, but the local authority bonds and government stock have some time to maturity, during which their capital values could be undermined by interest rate increases. As the date of investment approaches, GZ should be moving more of its funds into the short-dated fixed interest securities. To remove the risk of capital loss, the maturity dates of the investments should ideally have been aligned with the date when the money is needed.

- There is arguably too high a proportion in equities (65%). The return on both categories of equity exceeded the average in 1998 which suggests a greater degree of volatility than the market as a whole. This could signify excessive exposure to the risk of a falling stock market.

- The high proportion of US equities (68% of the equities, 44% of the total) makes some sense. By holding investments denominated in the currency of the country of intended investment, exposure to adverse foreign exchange rate movements is reduced. However, there remains the risk of a downturn in the US stock markets. Possibly a better solution might be to hold short-dated US government debt.

11 SUMMARY OF CHAPTER

This chapter has examined the other side of the coin examined in chapter 7, ie, the ways in which a company can invest a cash surplus in the short to medium term. The essential principles are to examine the liquidity, safety and profitably of any investment, bearing in mind the concept of the risk-return trade-off. If the return looks high, the risk almost certainly is also. The keynote to investing for the short-to medium-term is access–it is not prudent to lock up money that may shortly be needed, for example to finance an investment project. Our stance here is that investment in equities is normally inappropriate for short-term purposes, and so the prudent treasurer should look to highly liquid investments like bank deposits and easily marketable securities traded on the money market.

If an element of risk can be tolerated then he or she may consider government, local authority or commercial stock.

Foreign currency investment carries special risks and should be linked in closely with the pattern of the company's trading relationships.

12 SELF-TEST QUESTIONS

12.1 How does surplus cash arise? (1.2)

12.2 What are the three key principles in short-term investment management. (1.3)

12.3 What is meant by the risk-return trade-off? (2.1)

12.4 Why are equities considered an inappropriate vehicle for short-term investment? (2.4)

12.5 Outline the Baumol cash management model, and its limitations. (3.4, 3.5, 3.6)

12.6 In what sense do Treasury Bills pay interest? (6.2)

12.7 What is the relationship between the market value of government securities and market rates of interest? (6.6)

12.8 Why do corporate bonds offer higher yields than government securities? (8.1)

12.9 What are the dangers of holding foreign currency deposits? (9.1)

12.10 What is the function of the forward market for foreign exchange? (9.2, 9.3)

9 BASIC LAW OF CONTRACT

PATHFINDER INTRODUCTION

This chapter covers the following performance criteria and knowledge and understanding.

- Legal issues: basic contract; terms and conditions of contracts relating to the granting of credit (Element 14.3)
- Legal issues: remedies for breach of contract (Element 14.4)

Putting the chapter in context – learning objectives.

When a business accepts an order from a customer, it has entered into a contract. This brings certain obligations on both parties, and it is important that the people involved in managing the sale are aware of these obligations. This chapter starts by examining the elements of a valid contract, and then considers the possible remedies available if either party fails to meet its terms – ie, is in breach of contract.

At the end of this chapter you should have learned the following topics.

- the elements comprising a legally binding contract
  - offer and acceptance
  - intention to create legal relations
  - consideration
  - capacity
  - form
- the special terms enforced by the Sale of Goods Act 1979
- the possible remedies available for breach of contract:
  - damages
  - action for the price
  - specific performance
  - injunction
  - *quantum meruit*

1 WHAT IS A CONTRACT?

1.1 Definition

Definition A contract is an agreement between two or more parties which is enforceable by the law.

Although all contracts are agreements, not all agreements are contracts. This is because some agreements we might make are not enforceable at law. For example if two friends agree to go out to dinner together this is not a contract: neither could sue the other in court should one of them back out.

1.2 Outline of contract law

Is there a contract? The answer to this question lies in the rules relating to **formation** of a contract. In order for a legally binding contract to exist the following elements must be satisfied.

- **Agreement ie, offer and acceptance**

  There must be an offer by one party which the other accepts without qualification. For example, if John offers to sell his car for £500 to Bill by word of mouth and Bill verbally accepts, then a contract exists, provided the other essential elements are satisfied.

- **An intention to create legal relations**

  The agreement must be intended to be subject to an action in a court of law if a dispute arises between the parties, as opposed to a mere domestic or social arrangement such as agreeing to dine at a restaurant with a friend.

- **Consideration**

  This means that each party to the contract must suffer a loss or detriment, in return for the benefit received. For example, in a contract of sale the buyer acquires the goods and pays the price, whilst the seller receives the price in return for the goods handed over. The law enforces bargains made by the parties, not gratuitous promises.

- **Capacity**

  Each party must have the legal power to bind himself contractually to the agreement concluded. For example, the Crown, corporations, persons under the age of eighteen (minors) and persons of unsound mind or under the influence of drink have limitations on their power to contract.

- **Form**

  Some contracts are required to be made in a particular form such as writing. For most contracts, however, there is no special requirement and an oral agreement is just as much binding in law as a written agreement.

2 THE OFFER

Definition An offer is a definite and unequivocal statement of willingness to be bound by contract.

2.1 Form of the offer

(a) The offeror can make the offer expressly. This is where a person makes the offer orally or in writing.

(b) The offeror can make the offer impliedly (ie, by conduct). This is where a person's behaviour implies the offer. An example of this would be a person filling his tank with petrol, at a petrol station. It is implicit in his behaviour that he is offering to buy the petrol.

In order to be valid the offer must have certain elements. Without these elements the offer does not legally exist and so cannot be accepted.

2.2 Requirements of an offer

The requirements of a valid offer are set out below.

(a) **Definite and unequivocal**

The offer must be a definite and unequivocal statement of willingness to be bound in contract. It cannot be vague or uncertain in its interpretation. So, an offer to sell someone a particular car for £5,000 will be an offer. But a statement that a person will sell: "... one of my cars for about £5,000" will not be an offer.

(b) **Clear intention to be bound**

There must be a clear intention of present willingness to be bound by the offer. The offeror must not merely be negotiating. All the offeree has to do is to accept the terms as laid down by the offeror and the contract will be complete.

2.3 Persons to whom an offer may be made

The offer can be made to a particular person, to a class of persons or even to the whole world.

An example of an offer made to the whole world arose in the leading case of **Carlill v Carbolic Smoke Ball Co [1893]**

Facts: the manufacturers of a medicinal 'smoke ball' advertised in a newspaper that anyone who bought and used the ball properly and nevertheless contracted influenza would be paid a £100 reward. Mrs Carlill used the ball as directed and did catch 'flu. The manufacturers claimed that they did not have to pay her the £100 as an offer could not be made to the whole world.

Held: that an offer could be made to the whole world, that the wording of the advert amounted to such an offer, and that Mrs Carlill had accepted it by properly using the smoke ball.

Another example of an offer to the world at large is a more typical advert for reward, say when someone has lost their cat and they offer a financial incentive for the finder to return it.

2.4 Communication of the offer

The offer must actually reach the person to whom it was made. In other words the offeree must know of it. An offer will not be valid unless the offeror has clearly communicated it to the offeree and that person is aware of it.

2.5 Termination of an offer

The offer must be 'open' (ie still in force) when the offeree accepts it. It is important to note that when an offer has been terminated it can no longer be accepted.

(a) **Revocation of offer**

One of the most important ways in which an offer can be terminated is by revocation by the offeror.

(i) An offer can be revoked at any time before it has been accepted by the offeree. The revocation may be by express words or it may be implied from the offeror's conduct. The critical thing to note is that the revocation will not take effect until the revocation has been received and clearly understood by the offeree. Until then, it remains open, and can be accepted.

Example

Facts: an offer was posted by Alan in Cardiff on 1 October. It was received by Barry in New York on 11 October. He at once cabled an acceptance (effectively accepting on this date). In the meantime Alan had changed his mind and had sent a letter of revocation from Cardiff on 8 October. This letter of revocation reached New York on 15 October. The question before the court was whether the offer had been accepted or revoked.

Held: the revocation was not complete until it had been communicated to the offeree. This was on the 15 October. In the meantime, however, the offer had been accepted. As a result, the revocation was ineffective and the contract did exist. Alan was therefore liable under the contract.

(ii) The rule that an offer can be revoked at any time before acceptance applies even though the offeror has stated that he will keep the offer open for a stated time.

Example

Facts: Grant offered to buy Routledge's horse and gave him six weeks to decide whether or not to accept. Before the six weeks had elapsed, Grant withdrew his offer.

Held: in the absence of Routledge already having accepted, Grant was entitled to revoke his offer.

(b) **Rejection of an offer - Counter offer**

An offer can be terminated by a rejection. This is the action of the offeree turning down the offer. This is either outright, by the offeree stating that he will not accept it, or by a counter-offer.

Definition A counter-offer is an offer made in response to an offer.

An example of a counter-offer is where the offeree offers a lower price or in any other way barters with the offeror. This is imposing conditions on the acceptance and, as we will see, an acceptance must be unconditional. This counter-offer, in the same way as an outright rejection, terminates the original offer.

Example

Facts: Wrench offered to sell Hyde a farm for £1,000. Hyde made a counter-offer, by offering £950. Wrench rejected this. Later Hyde came back and said that he now accepted the original offer of £1,000. Wrench rejected it.

Held: Hyde could no longer accept the original offer. It had been terminated by the counter-offer and was no longer capable of acceptance. His 'acceptance' was merely a fresh offer which Wrench was free to turn down.

Note that a mere request for further details does not constitute a counter-offer.

Example

Facts: M offered, in writing, to sell a quantity of iron to S at a given price. S replied querying delivery times.

Held: M could not treat the query as a counter-offer. S had not intended to prejudice M's position, just to establish the parameters of the deal. Therefore M's offer was still open.

(c) **Lapse of an offer**

An offer can also be terminated by **lapse**.

If the offer is stated only to be open for a specific time period it will end after the expiration of this time. If there is no specific period of time mentioned by the offeror the offer will lapse after a reasonable length of time. If there is a dispute about the time period the court will decide what is reasonable. It is a question of fact to be decided in each case.

2.6 Activity

Gail offers to sell Clare her dog for £10 and says she will keep the offer open for two days. Clare is not sure and wants to check with her husband first. Before the two days have elapsed Gail sells the dog and tells Clare.

Advise Clare.

2.7 Activity solution

Clare cannot accept Gail's offer to sell the dog because the offer has been terminated by an effective revocation.

3 SITUATIONS WHERE THERE IS NO OFFER

3.1 Introduction

It is vital to decide whether or not the facts amount to an offer. Not all statements amount to an offer and only an offer can be accepted, so leading to a contract. It is vital to distinguish the offer from the other possibilities.

3.2 Invitation to treat

Definition An invitation to treat is not an offer in itself but is an invitation to others to make an offer.

Thus A may tell B that A has a car to sell for about £3,000 and will invite B to make an offer. Note that A has not made an offer and B cannot therefore accept by agreeing to pay £3,000. B has to make an offer (thus becoming the offeror) and it is up to A to accept or not as he sees fit.

An invitation to treat is often the starting point of the negotiations.

Example - Shop displays

Facts: statute requires that the sale of certain pharmaceuticals must be carried out under the supervision of a qualified pharmacist. Boots operated a store where the drugs were sold on a self-service basis and the customers paid at a cash desk for the goods they had selected. A pharmacist was present at the cash desk but not at the shelves where the goods were displayed with a price tag. The Pharmaceutical Society claimed that the statute was being contravened.

Held: the display of goods in a shop was not an offer but an invitation to treat. It was the customer who made the offer and Boots could either accept or reject this offer at the cash desk (in the presence of a qualified pharmacist). The act constituting the acceptance is the ringing up of the price on the till by the cashier and at that moment a binding contract of sale is made.

4 ACCEPTANCE

4.1 Definition

Definition Acceptance is the unconditional assent to all the terms of the offer.

We have already seen that if an offeree attempts to change the terms of the offer or qualify it in any way it will terminate the offer and be classed as a counter-offer. It is only when the offeree has accepted the offer unconditionally that the parties can be said to be in agreement. This complete agreement about the terms and conditions of the contract is fundamental in English contract law.

Remember that not all enquiries about the terms of the contract will amount to a counter-offer by the offeree. The offeree may only be enquiring about delivery times or other less essential terms of the contract. Only that which amounts to a complete rejection of the terms suggested by the offeror will terminate the offer, rendering it incapable of acceptance. However, an enquiry about the price will almost certainly be a counter-offer. It depends upon the facts of the question and what the parties consider are the conditions (or fundamental terms) of the contract.

The acceptance must also not be 'subject to contract'. This phrase is frequently used in the buying and selling of land. The phrase 'subject to contract' denotes that the parties have reached a degree of agreement but there will be no binding commitment until they enter into a formal contract, usually in writing.

4.2 Form of acceptance

(a) Any form of acceptance is valid whether it be oral, written or merely inferred from the conduct of the parties.

(b) An offeror may stipulate a mode or method of acceptance.

If he makes his stipulation mandatory (eg, by stating that acceptance **must** be in writing) then no other form of acceptance would be valid.

If he makes his stipulation as a request any other equally advantageous form of acceptance is valid.

(c) An offeror is not allowed to stipulate that silence shall amount to acceptance.

4.3 Communication of acceptance

Acceptance is not effective until and unless it is communicated to the offeror.

4.4 Activity

Will a contract exist in the following situations?

(1) Jules offers Sam a room in his hotel for £50.00 but insists that Sam accepts by midday the next day in writing. Sam drives round to Jules' hotel the next day but because of heavy traffic does not arrive until 2.00pm to pass over his letter of acceptance.

(2) Susie offers Alan her pony for £500. She says that she will assume Alan accepts if she hears nothing from him by Saturday. Alan, who does not wish to accept, does not reply.

(3) Tim sends for some shoes from a mail order company but the company has run out of shoes in his size. They return his money.

4.5 Activity solution

(1) No. The offer is terminated by lapse - passage of stipulated time.

(2) No. The offeror cannot stipulate that silence shall constitute acceptance.

(3) No. The mail order catalogue (or advertisement if this is what Tim responded to) is an invitation to treat. Tim's sending away is an offer. The company's sending back of his money is a rejection of his offer.

5 NATURE OF CONSIDERATION

5.1 The basic rule

Every simple contract must be supported by consideration.

5.2 Definition of consideration

Consideration implies that there must be an exchange; one person does something **because** the other person does something. A simple everyday example is where a person purchases a drink from a vending machine. One party inserts the money into the machine and in **exchange** for this receives the canned drink. Both parties are receiving a benefit (the person inserting the money, takes the canned drink, and the vending machine company takes the money), and simultaneously they are each being detrimented. The purchaser is losing the purchase price and the drinks company the can that has been vended.

5.3 Consideration need not be adequate but must be valuable

In law, the parties to a contract are free to conclude their bargain on whatever terms they think are appropriate. The courts will not question the adequacy of the consideration agreed upon by balancing the respective promises or acts of the parties to ascertain whether the agreement is fair in an objective or commercial sense, but they must be satisfied that there is something of real value provided by the parties. As long as the parties are of equal bargaining power and there is no duress they will not investigate the motives behind the transaction or check the consideration given.

Valuable consideration means money or money's worth, that is to say something upon which a monetary value can be placed such as rendering a service.

The consideration provided must be valuable in the sense that it must have some value, however slight. Thus a promise to convey a house to a widow on her promise to pay £1 per year rent and keep the house in repair was binding; the promise to pay £1 per year and keep the house in repair was valuable consideration.

5.4 Activity

Explain whether Paul is required by the law of contract to fulfil his promise if he promises to sell an expensive car to Arthur for £10.

5.5 Activity solution

Consideration must be valuable but need not be adequate. The word 'valuable' means that the consideration must be of some economic or monetary value, such as a motor car and money. 'Need not be adequate' means that the consideration given by each party does not have to match in value. Thus £10 in return for an expensive car is consideration even though inadequate. Accordingly Paul is bound by his promise to Arthur.

6 INTENTION TO CREATE LEGAL RELATIONS

6.1 Introduction

Some agreements are not intended to be legally enforceable, their nature being such that a reasonable man viewing the words and conduct of the parties objectively would not conclude that they intended to create legal relations. For example, a reasonable man would not expect an enforceable legal obligation to spring from a mere social engagement, such as an invitation to lunch, despite the presence of all the other essential elements necessary to create a binding agreement.

6.2 Domestic and social arrangements

In domestic and social arrangements there is a presumption that there was no intention that the agreement be legally binding. Arrangements in a domestic or social context include agreements made between members of a family and between friends. A presumption means that the plaintiff in the action need not prove certain matters on a balance of probabilities; the court presumes that they exist.

7 CONTRACTS FOR THE SALE OF GOODS

7.1 Introduction

The Sale of Goods Act 1979 (SOGA 1979), amended by a further piece of legislation, the Sale and Supply of Goods Act 1994, sets out some terms relating specifically to the sale of goods. The Act covers the sale of tangible, movable items in return for a money consideration, the price. This is one of the most practical areas of this contract law section.

One of the main purposes of SOGA 1979 is the protection of buyers from unscrupulous sellers.

7.2 Implied terms

SOGA 1979 contains three main implied terms. This means that they are inherent in any contract for the sale of goods, and do not have to be included in the contract itself, whether written or verbal.

7.3 Implied term as to title

There is an implied term that the seller of the goods has the right to sell. He only has this right if he owns the goods. If it transpires that the seller did not have the right to sell, the buyer can demand his money back.

Example

Facts: Rowland bought a car from Divall, but then discovered that it had been stolen some months earlier. Rowland then had to return it to the true owner. He could then sue Divall, for breach of the implied term as to title, even though Divall was not aware of the problem at the time of the sale.

7.4 Implied term as to description

There is an implied term that where goods are sold by description, they will correspond to their description. For example, if a purchaser buys a bar of chocolate described as milk, and then discovers on unwrapping it that it is in fact plain, he can reject the contract and demand his money back.

7.5 Implied terms as to satisfactory quality and fitness for purpose

The implied term as to satisfactory quality is designed to protect the consumer from shoddy goods and faulty workmanship. For example if a purchaser buys a pair of shoes, there is an implied term that they will not fall apart after a reasonable period of wear.

The implied term as to fitness for purpose is designed to protect against goods which do not do what they are supposed to do, ie, against unsuitable goods. For example, if a purchaser buys a football which does not bounce, it is not fit for its purpose. Often, a seller is in breach of both implied terms over the sale of the same item, as by implication if goods are not fit for their purpose, they may not be of satisfactory quality.

Example

Facts: Frost bought some milk which, unknown to the seller was contaminated. After drinking the milk Frost became ill.

Held: The seller was in breach of both terms, as the milk was not of satisfactory quality, and was not fit for its purpose, ie, being drunk.

These two terms, however, only relate to situations when the seller is selling in the course of a business to a buyer who is not acting in the course of a business (ie, a consumer). Purchasers buying in a shop will be protected by these terms, but purchasers buying at a car boot sale, or in response to a private advertisement in a newspaper, will not. For these purchasers, the basic rule is *caveat emptor*, or let the buyer beware.

Conclusion If you buy faulty goods at a jumble sale, you will have no recourse against the seller of the goods or the organiser of the sale.

7.6 Activity

Jane buys a video camera from Stan, who has advertised it for sale in the 'small ads' column of the local newspaper. The camera never works properly, and after a few weeks ceases working altogether. Jane wants her money back from Stan.

Advise Jane.

7.7 Activity Solution

Jane cannot reclaim her money. The implied condition as to satisfactory quality in SGA 1979 only applies where a business sells to a consumer. Stan is not selling in the course of a business.

7.8 Exclusion of Implied Terms

Sometimes, businesses try to exclude liability for breaches of contracts, so that they will not be liable to pay damages should there be a breach. You have probably seen notices along the lines of 'The company accepts no responsibility for any loss or damage suffered'.

The Unfair Contract Terms Act 1977 (UCTA 1977) restricts the extent to which this can legally happen in a contract for the sale of goods. In a consumer sale (ie, where a business sells to a consumer) it is not possible to exclude liability for any of the implied terms discussed above. In a business to business sale, such exclusions must be reasonable.

It is never legal to exclude liability for the implied condition as to title, regardless of the nature or identity of the buyer and seller.

Example

Sarah buys a coat from a department store. A notice at the counter says that goods will not be exchanged for any reason. When she gets home, Sarah finds that some of the buttons are missing.

Regardless of the notice, Sarah will be able to claim a refund for the coat, as the clause excluding liability is not valid.

You may have seen notices on products which you have bought which set out the rights of the buyer and seller, for example to a 'full refund within 21 days if not completely satisfied'. Such notices are almost always accompanied by the phrase 'This does not affect your statutory rights'. This means that your rights under the implied terms of the Sale of Goods Act are protected, even if they seem to be contradicted by the additional terms set out by the seller.

7.9 Activity

Mark buys some wellington boots from Outdoor Outfitters Ltd, and wears them to go fishing. He discovers that they leak. When he takes them back to the shop, the sales assistant says that no refund can be given as Mark has obviously used them for something other than their proper purpose, and in any event Outdoor Outfitters Ltd does not accept responsibility for any faults in its products.

Advise Mark as to whether he is entitled to a refund.

7.10 Activity Solution

Mark is entitled to a refund. The shop is in breach of the implied terms of fitness for purpose, as it is reasonable to assume that wellington boots are for the purpose of standing in water. This term cannot be excluded in a consumer sale, so Outdoor Outfitters' exclusion clause is not valid.

8 CONTRACT : REMEDIES

8.1 Introduction

The preceding sections considered whether or not a contract has been breached. This section considers the remedies available for breach of contract comprising monetary remedies (eg, damages and an action for the price) and, where a monetary remedy would be inadequate, the court orders of specific performance and injunction.

This section also covers limitation of action.

8.2 Summary of remedies

In appropriate cases the party who has suffered a breach of contract may have any of the following remedies:

(a) damages;
(b) action for the price;
(c) specific performance;
(d) injunction;
(e) *quantum meruit*;

9 DAMAGES

9.1 Aim of damages

The aim of damages in contract is usually to put the injured party into the position he would have been in if the contract had been properly performed - often referred to as *bargain loss*. Thus in a contract for the sale of goods where the seller has failed to deliver goods, the buyer's measure of damages will be the difference between the agreed contract price and the price the buyer needed to pay in order to get the goods elsewhere, ie, the prevailing market price. However, in some cases the courts award 'reliance losses', that is posses incurred in trying to perform the contract prior to the breach.

Damages are compensatory; they are not usually intended to be punitive. Thus damages are not usually affected by the motive or intention behind the breach of contract - whether good or bad.

9.2 Liquidated damages and penalty clauses

The parties may agree a sum to be paid in the event of breach or may not discuss it at all.

(a) Where the contract does not make any provision for damages the court will determine the damages payable on the basis of the principles set out in paras 3 and 4. They are **unliquidated damages.**

(b) Where a contract provides for the payment of a fixed sum on breach, it may either be a **liquidated damages clause** or a **penalty clause.** It is crucial to differentiate these as the results are different.

Definition **Liquidated damages**: if the clause is a **genuine attempt at estimating the loss** in advance of the breach it is a **liquidated damages clause** and will be valid and **enforceable** by either party to the contract. Thus, if the actual damages suffered by the innocent party are greater than the damages provided for, he can only claim the liquidated amount.

Cellulose Acetate Silk Co v Widnes Foundry [1933]

Facts: a contract for the building of a factory contained a clause providing for payment of a fixed sum in compensation for each day's delay in completion of the work. The work was finished late and the plaintiffs suffered losses considerably greater than those envisaged when the contract was made.

Held: the plaintiffs were entitled only to the contract rate of damages: that figure had represented a genuine estimate of loss when it was inserted in the contract.

Definition **Penalty clauses**: where the clause is expressed to force a party to perform his obligations under the contract, it will be *penal*, and the clause will be of **no effect** (ie, the person will have to prove the loss suffered and the damages will be unliquidated damages assessed in accordance with the rules set out in paras 3 and 4).

Whether a clause is a penalty or for liquidated damages is a question of construction of the contract; certainly the name that the contract gives to the clause is not conclusive.

10 UNLIQUIDATED DAMAGES

10.1 Calculation of unliquidated damages

Damages is the common law remedy and is available as of right for every breach of contract.

Two questions arise when the court is assessing a claim for unliquidated damages:

(a) What losses should be included in the claim? - remoteness of damage.
(b) What level of damages will compensate the party claiming? - measure of damages.

10.2 Remoteness of damage

The basic rule is that damages are awarded to put the innocent party in the same position that he would have been in had the contract been properly performed. Thus damages are awarded for loss of bargain. However, some losses, albeit flowing from the breach, are nevertheless too remote and not recoverable.

Consider, for example, the following situation. A builder agrees to build a factory by a certain date. If erection of a new factory is delayed, the manufacturer may lose profits on his trade for the period of delay; he may have to buy products (which he could have made) in order to fulfil contracts to supply customers; he may have to pay interest charges on capital invested in raw materials which he cannot use or pay wages to employees for whom he has no work. Which of these indirect losses and expenses (loosely called **consequential loss**) can he recover from the builder as damages for breach of contract in failing to complete the factory on time?

Hadley v Baxendale [1854]

Facts: a carrier was given a mill-shaft to deliver to a plant manufacturer as a model for making a new shaft. The carrier delayed in delivery and, unknown to him, the mill stood idle during the period of delay.

Held: he was not liable for the loss of profit and the rule was formulated as follows: **the loss should be such as may fairly and reasonably be considered either arising naturally, ie, according to the usual course of things, from the breach of contract, or such as may reasonably be supposed to have been in the contemplation of both parties at the time they made the contract as the probable result of the breach of it.**

So there are two types of loss for which damages may be recovered:

(a) that which arises naturally in the usual course of things - **general damages;** sometimes known as 'normal loss'; and

(b) that which does not occur naturally in the usual course of things but both parties could foresee, when the contract was made, as the likely result of breach - **special damages;** sometimes known as 'abnormal loss'.

10.3 Hadley v Baxendale applied

Both branches of the rule arising from the case of **Hadley v Baxendale** are based on a test of foresight and probability. In the first branch the test is what would an outsider with no special knowledge of the circumstances regard as the likely consequence of a breach.

In **Hadley v Baxendale** it was held that without inside knowledge the carrier could not be expected to realise that delay on his part would keep the mill idle (in many cases mill owners were likely to have a spare shaft to use in an emergency).

The second branch of the rule starts from the special knowledge (if any) which the parties possessed when they made their contract and asks what with that knowledge, should reasonably have been foreseen as the likely loss resulting from breach.

The rule in **Hadley v Baxendale** has been considered and approved in many cases. One is given here as an example:

Victoria Laundry v Newman Industries [1949]

Facts: a laundry required a new boiler to enlarge its plant. There was delay in delivery of the boiler and as a result the laundry lost:

(a) a normal trading profit from delay in bringing the new plant into use; and
(b) an extra large profit on certain government contracts.

Held: the boiler manufacturer was held liable for the loss of normal profits; under the first branch of the rule, he or anyone else would know that an industrial boiler was essential to the operation of the plant, and, therefore, to earning normal profits from it. He was not liable for the loss of profit on the government contracts, of which he had no information. (If, of course, he had known of them he would have been liable under the second branch of the rule.)

Conclusion If the loss is a normal loss it is recoverable. However where the loss is abnormal it is not recoverable unless the parties knew of it, or ought reasonably to have known of it, at the time the contract is made.

11 MEASURE OF DAMAGES

11.1 General

Definition The measure of damages is the amount which will, so far as money can, put the plaintiff in the position in which he would have been had the contract been performed.

(This is sometimes described as 'damages for loss of bargain'.)

Thus for example if a buyer bought goods for £50 which the seller refused to deliver, the buyer's damages would be the cost to him of acquiring the same goods from someone else. So if he had to pay £60 his damages would be £10 (plus the £50 if he had already paid that to the seller). If a buyer refused to accept goods the seller's loss will be the difference between the contract price and the price he can actually sell for.

If the plaintiff has suffered no actual loss he will be awarded only nominal damages.

Surrey County Council v Bredero Homes Ltd [1993]

Facts: SCC sold some land to BH and in the contract of sale BH covenanted to build no more than 72 houses on the plot. In deliberate breach of contract BH built 77 houses. SCC claimed damages equal to the profit BH had made on the extra houses.

The Court of Appeal **held** that the remedy at common law for breach of contract was the award of damages to compensate the innocent party for his loss: it was not to transfer to him any benefit which the wrongdoer had gained by his breach of contract. Since SCC had not suffered any loss, it followed that the damages recoverable had to be nominal.

Occasionally, the circumstances will demand damages to put the plaintiff in the position he would have been in had there been no contract. These 'reliance damages' can be contrasted with those for 'loss of bargain'.

Reliance damages enable the plaintiff to recover compensation for expenses incurred in performing his part of the contract, in reliance upon it, before the breach. They may be claimed where such losses exceed any likely profit.

Anglia Television v Reed [1972]

Facts: R was engaged to play the leading role in a TV play. The plaintiffs incurred expenses in preparing for filming. R repudiated the contract. Anglia could not find a suitable replacement and had to abandon the project.

Held: Anglia could recover the whole of their wasted expenditure from R.

11.2 Difficulties of evaluation

The court's inability to evaluate the plaintiff's losses with mathematical accuracy is not sufficient reason for refusing to grant any compensation at all, even though the assessment of damages is almost a matter of guesswork.

Chaplin v Hicks [1911]

Facts: Chaplin agreed with Hicks, a theatrical manager, to attend an interview at which twelve girls would be chosen from fifty contestants to work in the theatre. Hick's failure to give Chaplin sufficient notice of the interview prevented her attendance. She claimed damages for loss of her chance of being selected. The defendant contended that Miss Chaplin was entitled to nominal damages only since it was impossible to determine objectively whether she would have been chosen.

Held: although assessment of her loss was problematic, since it could not be determined whether Chaplin would have been chosen, the plaintiff should nonetheless receive some compensation. Damages of £100 were awarded.

However, the plaintiff must provide some justification for his claim and cannot just pick a number.

11.3 Taxation

Sometimes the court will take into account the effect of taxation. This is particularly important in an action for wrongful dismissal where an employee is claiming loss of earnings. His actual loss will not be his gross pay but his net pay after taxation. This is sometimes called the **BTC v Gourlay [1956]** principle. (The amount deducted does not go to the Inland Revenue; it reduces the damages payable by the employer.)

11.4 Mitigation

A duty is imposed upon a plaintiff to take all reasonable steps to mitigate any loss caused to him by the defendant's breach of contract. Compensation will not be awarded for any damage incurred which the plaintiff had a reasonable opportunity to avoid.

Brace v Calder [1895]

Facts: Brace was employed by a partnership for a fixed period of two years, but after only five months the partnership was dissolved thereby prematurely terminating his contract of employment. He was offered identical employment with a reconstituted partnership which was immediately formed to replace the previous one. He refused the offer and sued for wages he would have earned had his job continued for the agreed two year period.

Held: Brace had not mitigated the loss he suffered by his employer's breach of contract, thus he could only recover nominal damages.

If there is an anticipatory breach as in **White & Carter v MacGregor [1961]** it may be that if the innocent party elects to treat the contract as operative he is under no duty to mitigate his loss and may continue with his own performance.

11.5 The available market rule

This special rule applies to contracts for the sale of goods where the breach is either the buyer wrongfully refusing to accept the goods or the seller wrongfully refusing to deliver the goods. By S51 Sale of Goods Act 1979, if an available market exists, the damages are deemed to be the difference between the contract price and the available market price as at the date of breach. An available market exists where goods of that type can be freely bought or sold at prices fixed by supply and demand.

11.6 Activity

S agrees to sell 100 barrels of crude oil to B at £20 per barrel, delivery on 1 May. S refuses to deliver and B buys oil elsewhere at £25 per barrel. The 'spot' price (ie, available market price) for crude on 1 May is £22 per barrel.

What is B's measure of damages?

11.7 Activity solution

£200.

11.8 Date of assessment of damages

In most cases the loss must be assessed as at the date of the breach, and may include a claim for pre-contract expenditure reasonably incurred in anticipation of performance.

Conclusion When calculating the amount of damages to be awarded the court will award an amount which, as far as possible, puts the injured party into the position that he would have been in had the contract been properly performed. Factors include:

- financial loss will be recovered but damages can also be awarded for stress, inconvenience and frustration
- even if the award cannot be mathematically calculated the court will award damages by the process of estimating the loss
- usually losses are assessed as at the date of the breach
- the party who suffered loss is under a duty to mitigate their loss and the damages awarded will reflect this.

12 ACTION FOR THE PRICE

Where the breach of contract is non-payment of the price the seller can sue for the price. This is an action for a liquidated sum - no question of remoteness or quantum arising. It is therefore distinct from a claim for damages. There is also no duty to mitigate: **White & Carter Councils v McGregor (1961)**.

However, under the Sale of Goods Act 1979, the seller will only be able to sue for the price where ownership of the goods has passed to the buyer (as to when ownership/property in goods passes from a seller to a buyer - see Chapter 13), unless it was agreed that the price would be payable on a specific date.

However, if a seller has breached the contract in a sufficiently serious manner, a buyer may be relieved from his obligation to pay the contract price. If the breach is not sufficiently serious to justify non-payment of the contract price, the price must be paid although from it, the buyer may deduct damages.

13 SPECIFIC PERFORMANCE

This is an equitable remedy whereby the court orders the defendant to carry out his obligations under the contract. Like other equitable remedies it is at the discretion of the court to grant it and cannot be obtained as of right (contrast damages which is a common law remedy and is awarded as of right). It therefore follows that it is only given where it is just and equitable to do so. The main principles which determine when specific performance is ordered or refused are:

(a) Where damages are an adequate remedy, specific performance will not be ordered. On a sale of goods (unless they are unique) or an agreement to lend money, damages is an adequate remedy for the extra cost if the plaintiff can obtain similar goods or money elsewhere. By contrast, specific performance will often be ordered on a contract for sale of land: each piece of the earth's surface is unique.

Beswick v Beswick [1968]

Facts: A contract provided for Peter Beswick to transfer property to his nephew and in return, the nephew would make payments to Beswick's wife after his death. The nephew failed to make the payments and Beswick's estate sued the nephew. (Note: the widow could not sue as she was not a party to the contract).

Held: damages were an inadequate remedy as the estate itself had suffered no loss, since the payments were due to be made to the widow in a personal capacity. Therefore, the Court made an order for specific performance, compelling the nephew to carry out his obligations.

(b) Where the court could not adequately supervise the performance of the contract and decide if it was being properly done (in detail) it refuses to order specific performance. Contracts for construction of buildings fall under this head.

Ryan v Mutual Tontine Assoc [1893]

Facts: A lease of a block of flats provided for a porter to be in constant attendance. The tenants sought an order of specific performance in respect of this provision.

Held: as the order would require constant supervision, it was not made.

However, contracts to build or repair property may be enforced where the work is clearly defined, the plaintiff's substantial interest in the work cannot be compensated adequately by damages; **and** the defendant is in possession of the site, thereby preventing a substitute builder being engaged.

(c) Specific performance will not be given where it would cause undue hardship. Thus specific performance will not be ordered of a contract of personal services, such as an employment contract, on the basis that it is contrary to public policy to compel an unwilling party to maintain continuous personal relations with another (also it would require constant supervision).

Lumley v Wagner [1852]

Facts: W contracted to sing only at L's theatre and elsewhere with his consent. She then signed up with another theatre, without L's consent.

Held: this was a contract for personal services and could not be enforced. (However, an **injunction** (below) could be granted preventing performance of the second contract.)

Taylor v Newham London Borough Council [1993]

Facts: The Plaintiff exercised her right to purchase her council house and had agreed a price with the Defendants. The Council prior to completion of the sale sought to evict her on the grounds that she was causing a nuisance to her neighbours. The Plaintiff sought an order of specific performance to enforce completion of the sale and the Council argued that to do so would cause undue hardship to her neighbours.

Held: an order of specific performance was granted as the hardship that might be caused to neighbours was insufficient to justify refusing an order, in circumstances where damages would be an inadequate remedy.

(d) The remedy will only be given on the basis of mutuality, ie, the remedy will only be granted if both parties could, if necessary, seek the protection of the court. For this reason an infant cannot obtain an order for specific performance since the court would not be able to enforce such an order against him.

Therefore, a party who is contractually bound to render personal services cannot obtain an order of specific performance against the other party, as that other party could not obtain such an order against him, as the Court will not make an order of specific performance in respect of a contract of personal services (see paragraph (c) above.

Page One Records v Britton [1968]

Facts: The Plaintiffs, as managers of a pop group (The Troggs), sought an injunction to restrain the group from breaching their contract by engaging another manager.

Held: as the group would have been unable to obtain an order of specific performance to compel the Plaintiffs to perform their personal services as managers, the Plaintiffs could not obtain an injunction against the Defendants, as there was no mutuality between the parties.

Definition An infant, or minor, is a person under eighteen years of age. Infants have only limited power to contract in English law.

(e) Specific performance will not be given to a party who has acted unfairly or improperly. This is expressed by the maxim "He who comes to Equity must come with clean hands".

(f) As will all equitable remedies, a party who wishes for specific performance must act promptly - "Delay defeats Equity".

The Plaintiff must start proceedings within a reasonable time of the Defendant refusing to proceed with the contract. In the case of a contract for the sale of business property with a fluctuating value, a delay of a few months may be sufficient to exclude the remedy. In other cases, a delay of a year will normally exclude it.

14 INJUNCTION

This is also an equitable remedy and is granted on the same principles as specific performance.

Definition An **injunction** is an order of the court which either requires a person to do something (mandatory injunction) or prohibits a person from doing something (prohibitory injunction).

The court will grant an injunction to restrain a party from committing a breach of contract. Although it is said that an injunction will only be granted to enforce a negative stipulation in a contract it may be extended to cases where a negative term may be inferred.

Metropolitan Electric Supply v Ginder [1901]

Facts: the contract obliged the defendant to take all his electricity from the plaintiff; the obligation was in substance not to take electricity from another supplier.

Held: an injunction to that effect was issued.

An injunction will not be granted if it would have the effect of requiring specific performance in circumstances where the latter would be refused. In **Page One Records Ltd v Britton [1968]** (see paragraph 6 (d) of this Chapter) if the injunction had been ordered preventing the Troggs from engaging another manager, the group would in effect have had to employ the Plaintiffs since they could not do without a manager. This would have had the effect of requiring the Plaintiffs to specifically perform a contract for personal services and the injunction was therefore refused.

However, an injunction may be granted in circumstances such as the following:

Warner Brothers Pictures Inc v Nelson [1936]

Facts: the film star, Bette Davis (really Miss Nelson) entered into a contract with the plaintiffs, initially for a term of one year, but giving the plaintiffs the option of extending it, whereby she agreed that she would not undertake other film work without obtaining their written consent and that she would not engage in any other occupation without the plaintiff's consent. The plaintiff sought an injunction to restrain her from doing film work for another company in breach of this agreement.

Held: the injunction would be granted. However, no injunction would be granted to prevent her engaging in 'other occupations' as this would force her to work for the plaintiffs.

An injunction will be granted only where it is 'just and convenient to do so', and, if it is inappropriate, the court can award damages in lieu of the injunction.

15 QUANTUM MERUIT

Quantum meruit means 'as much as it is worth'. It is not a claim for damages under a contract, but an award to compensate a person in some circumstances where a contract either never existed or subsequently ceased to exist or, where the contract has been breached thereby preventing a party from performing under it. The plaintiff can be rewarded for his work or his goods as much as they are worth in the sense of a reasonable value.

Planché v Colburn [1831]

Facts: the plaintiff agreed to write a series of articles for *The Juvenile Library* on costume and ancient armour, to be published by instalments. When the work was partly completed, the defendants abandoned the series.

Held: the plaintiff recovered reasonable remuneration for the work which he had completed, on a *quantum meruit* basis. In such a case, where the defendant unjustifiably prevents completion of the contract the plaintiff can recover either damages (for breach of contract) or on a *quantum meruit*. (This case was previously outlined in the notes on performance of a contract).

Pricket v Badger [1856]

Facts: An agent was employed to sell land at a certain price. He found a purchaser but the owner then refused to sell and revoked the agents authority.

Held: the agent sued on a *quantum meruit* basis for his work up to the date of breach.

Where an innocent party has made a bad bargain, the damages for breach of the contract may well be less than the reasonable remuneration for the work done. However, it is not clear whether the innocent party may, in these circumstances, secure a better settlement by relying on *quantum meruit* rather than damages.

Other applications of *quantum meruit* are:

(a) Where minors or drunken persons are supplied with necessaries, the supplier can recover a reasonable price.

(b) Where the plaintiff has performed services under a void contract.

Craven-Ellis v Cannons Ltd [1936]

Facts: a managing director's contract was unauthorised and void but he nevertheless served under it.

Held: he recovered a reasonable sum for work done for the company.

(c) Where a contract does not fix a precise sum the court will fix a reasonable sum on a *quantum meruit* basis.

In order for the Court to fix a reasonable sum to be paid in respect of a contract for services, the party seeking payment must show that the work was not done gratuitously. The Court will fix a reasonable price where the service was performed in anticipation that further negotiation would lead to the conclusion of a contract so long as the services were requested by the other party.

Way v Latilla [1937]

Facts: W alleged he had made an agreement with L that he, W, should obtain and send to L information relating to gold mines in West Africa. W carried out some work and then L refused to make any payment on the basis that no contract between them had been concluded.

Held: that whilst no contract had been concluded between the parties, it was clearly intended that W should not do the work gratuitously and therefore should be paid a reasonable sum on a *quantum meruit* basis.

(d) Where there is part performance of a contract, voluntarily accepted by the other party.

16 RESCISSION

Rescission of a contract is an equitable remedy, enabling the parties to a voidable contract to treat it as if it had never been made and to recover from one another any money or property which had changed hands before the defect came to light. It is a standard remedy in cases of misrepresentation.

Thus if A parts with his car to B under a contract which is voidable for B's misrepresentation (eg, as to his ability to pay) he can claim it back.

Being equitable in nature the remedy depends on the claimant's having acted equitably himself ('he who comes to equity must have clean hands') and it will not be available if:

(a) The claimant has affirmed the contract eg, by accepting dividends on shares acquired under a voidable contract, or by selling them, or in some other way acting as if the contract was valid and binding:

(b) the property being reclaimed has passed to a third party who took it in good faith and for value (eg, if in the example of the car above, B has sold the car to C who took it in good faith, A cannot recover it) before the original owner took steps to rescind;

(c) third party rights have arisen eg, where property is held by a company whose assets have been frozen during insolvency proceedings;

(d) the claimant delays in acting on his rights.

17 LIMITATION OF ACTIONS

The Limitation Act 1980 provides that any action on a contract is 'barred' if not brought within the requisite period. Normally 'time runs' from the date on which the breach occurred. In the case of **simple contracts** the limitation period is **six years** and in the case of **contracts by deed, twelve years**. If the claim includes damages for personal injuries or death, however, the period is normally reduced to three years (however, the Act provides that the three year period can be extended by the court if the injury does not become apparent within the period).

There are three instances where the limitation period may be extended:

(a) Where the plaintiff is an infant or of unsound mind when the cause of action accrued, time does not begin to run until the disability ceases.

(b) Where the cause of action is concealed by the defendant's fraud, time does not begin to run until such moment as the plaintiff should, with reasonable diligence, have discovered the breach.

(c) Where the defendant makes some acknowledgement in writing of his liability or makes a payment towards it, then time begins to run afresh from the date of such acknowledgement or payment. However, such acknowledgement or part payment made after the limitation period has expired will not start time running again. This rule applies only to claims for liquidated damages.

The Limitation Act 1980 only applies to common law remedies. In equity there is a more flexible doctrine known as **laches** (pronounced 'lay-cheese') which requires the plaintiff to bring his action within a reasonable time depending on all the circumstances.

18 SELF TEST QUESTIONS

18.1 What are the five elements that may need to exist to form a legally binding contract? (1.2)

18.2 How may an offer be terminated? (2.5)

18.3 What is meant by "an invitation to treat"? (3.2)

18.4 What are the three implied terms introduced by SOGA 1979? (7.3-7.5)

18.5 What is the aim of damages? (2.1)

18.6 Where a contract provides a clause which is a genuine attempt at estimating the loss what is this clause know as? (2.2)

18.7 State the rule in **Hadley v Baxendale** (3.2)

18.8 If a person cannot show actual loss as a result of a breach of contract what sort of damages will the court award? (4.1)

18.9 Apart from damages, what other monetary remedy is available for breach of contract? (5)

18.10 What equitable remedy will order the defendant to carry out the terms of the contract? (6)

18.11 Why will specific performance not be given of a contract of employment? (6)

18.12 What is meant by *quantum meruit* and when is this remedy available? (8)

18.13 What is the limitation period in the case of simple contracts? (10)

10 GRANTING CREDIT

PATHFINDER INTRODUCTION

This chapter covers the following performance criteria and knowledge and understanding.

- Data Protection Act and credit control information (Element 14.3)
- Sources of credit status information (Element 14.3)
- External sources of information: banks, credit agencies and official publications (Element 14.3)
- Interpretation and use of credit control information (Element 14.3 & 14.4)
- Understanding that practice in this area will be determined by an organisaiton's credit control policies and procedures (Element 14.3)
- Credit terms are agreed with customers in accordance with the organisation's policies (Element 14.3)
- Internal and external sources of information are identified and used to evaluate the current credit status of customers and potential customers (Element 14.3)
- New accounts are opened for those customers with an established credit status (Element 14.3)
- The reasons for refusing credit are discussed with customers in a tactful manner. (Element 14.3)

Putting the chapter in context – learning objectives.

When a company sells goods it may either demand immediate payment (cash sales basis) or it may permit the payment to be made at a later date (credit sales). The origins of credit sales as a convenience, so that customers who made several purchases during a period could pay for them all together at a later date. The current position is more dependent on trade credit as an interest free source of finance to the purchaser, and a means of creating sales for the supplier.

The benefits from the suppliers point of view are the generation of sales or additional sales. The cost can be considered under three categories:

- use of the money tied up in debtors during the collection period
- cost of administering the collection procedure
- the possibility of non-payment

The benefits and costs should be examined concurrently when a debtor's policy is being decided upon, but due to the complexity of the issues involved, and the existence of various constraints to possible lines of action, such a rigorous theoretical profit maximising approach is seldom used. The company is more likely to specify a certain line of action, and then modify it by means of manipulation of individual variables (eg, increasing the debtors payment period by 30 days).

Credit management is a very important function as it has a significant impact on cash flow. A company can be highly profitable but short of cash! In circumstances where there is some short-term surplus cash this can be invested short-term by employing a treasury management function.

At the end of this chapter you should have learned the following topics:

- Explain the importance of credit management
- Explain the need to establish a credit policy and outline the steps involved and the role of the credit control function.
- List the likely sources of information in assessing the credit worthiness of a new customer from internal and external sources.
- Describe the way in which rejections of credit applications should be dealt with, and the possible reasons for such a rejection.
- Appreciate the impact of the Data Protection Act 1984 on the credit control information gathered and held on computer.

1 IMPORTANCE OF CREDIT MANAGEMENT

1.1 Credit control

Definition The control exercised by a firm over its trade debtors to ensure that customers pay their debts on time and to minimise the risk of bad debts. (*Collins Dictionary of Business*)

Debtors arising from credit sales have to be financed and represents capital tied up. They can be for goods, services, loans etc, and can be for trade or personal purposes.

1.2 Level of trade credit

Of particular concern to us throughout this text is trade credit

Definition Trade credit is credit extended to businesses/organisations.

The optimum level of trade credit extended represents, as always, a balance between two factors:

(a) Profit improvement from sales obtained by allowing credit; and
(b) The cost of allowing credit.

A lenient credit policy may well attract additional custom, but at a disproportionate increase in cost. Why make a sale if there is a strong probability that you will not get paid?

Management will be anxious to do the following:

- Establish a credit policy in relation to normal periods of credit and individual credit limits;
- Devise a means by which prospective customers may be assessed eg, the development of a credit scoring system.
- Develop a system which will control the implementation of credit policy;
- Prescribe reporting procedures which will monitor the efficiency of the system;
- Improve cash flow by collecting debts as quickly as possible.

They will also need to consider policies relating to:

- Legal matters eg, sales to which the Consumer Credit act applied, agreements with customers.
- Settlement discounts
- Procedures for chasing slow payers.
- Monitoring procedures eg, new customers, aged analysis of debtors etc.
- Target markets eg, customers in a specific industrial classification, wholesalers, retailers etc.
- Export credit terms and foreign exchange management eg, invoices in sterling or the local currency, exchange risk etc. This area is extensive and specialist knowledge is required. Extending credit to overseas customers is a whole new ball game. Assistance may have to be sought via bankers, local chambers of trade, trade associations and the ECGD (Export Credits Guarantee Department).

1.3 The role of the credit control function

The credit control function serves the needs of both the finance function and the marketing function. With marketing it is perceived as an important and integral part of the product mix. The credit terms which are offered can win or lose sales/market share. However, the question which still remains is 'Why make a sale if you don't get paid?' Bad debts and late payments do cost money, and debtors do represent capital which is being tied up. Selling on credit does have to be financed, and as a very large proportion of goods and services are traded on credit, their financing is of extreme importance.

It can be exercised as part of the accounts department or as a department in its own right. It is true that in certain companies/organisations it does not command the respect it deserves, and has a very low profile. In view of the amounts involved in credit sales this should not be the case, and a credit control department should be able to prove itself cost effective. It could be thus the responsibility of the Finance Director, Marketing Director, Chief Accountant or Managing Director.

It has been said that sources of finance can be hidden in a balance sheet, and this is most certainly the case for many companies when it comes to the management and control of debtors. Debtors as a percentage of turnover does vary from industry to industry and company to company, and can be a very significant amount. Improvements in credit control can improve cash flow and assist in promoting both success and survival. Those companies who do not give a high priority to credit control risk going out of business eg, incurring significant levels of bad debts.

1.4 The activities of the credit control department/function

The activities of the credit control department extend to much more than collecting the cash from debtors and the prevention of bad debts.

The following are examples of the activities which could be carried out by a credit control department/function:

- Involvement with formulating, reviewing and monitoring the operation of the company's/organisation's credit policy. A policy once introduced cannot remain in force forever as the environment in which it operates changes; the policy should be revised and amended accordingly.

- Vetting new applications for credit. All negotiations should be conducted in a courteous and businesslike manner.

- Providing data to help set up and fine tune credit scoring systems.

- Monitoring and reviewing existing debtors eg, credit limits, signs of problems to come, providing references, looking at average periods of credit given and taken.

- Collecting amounts owing from debtors and chasing slow payers.

- collecting/reviewing information needed to help decide whether or not to write a debt off as bad.

- Involvement with the recording systems eg, sales ledger.

- Meetings to discuss credit control matters (which could be minuted/recorded for reference) eg, to look at and discuss specific cases and new procedures/policies etc, with internal departments/staff and outside bodies eg, agencies.

- Reporting to both staff and management eg, aged list of debtors with a record of action taken to recover amounts from slow payers. Such reports should be presented promptly to the appropriate person.

- The identification of key account customers. Customers who may need special consideration.

- Co-ordination and co-operation with other departments eg, sales/marketing; involving sales personnel in the collection process.

- Legal matters relating to credit control eg, consumer credit, contract, sale of goods etc.

- Matters relating to the credit control and management of exports.

Conclusion Selling on credit brings with it the risk of bad debts. Increasing credit sales increases this risk. It is therefore of paramount importance that the credit control function is given a high priority and provided with sufficient resources to carry out its work efficiently and effectively. Nowadays the volume of trade credit for goods and services runs into millions of pounds and for the majority of companies/trading organisations represents a substantial investment. Sound credit control management can bring about vast improvements in cash flow and avoid/reduce bad debts to an acceptable minimum.

2 THE NEED TO ESTABLISH A CREDIT POLICY

2.1 The credit policy

The period of credit extended should be well publicised, clearly communicated and will be set by reference to the factors below:

- Elasticity of demand for the company's products;
- Credit terms offered by competitors/industry norms
- Vetting and assessing the credit worthiness of prospective customers
- Considered risk of bad debts resulting from extended credit periods;
- Financing costs and the availability of finance;
- Costs of administering the credit system.

Individual credit limits are dependent on an assessment of the creditworthiness of a particular customer: in the first instance, whether the customer would be allowed credit at all; and secondly, the maximum amount that should be allowed.

Assessment involves analysis of the prospective customer's current business situation and credit history, derived from information obtained from all available sources.

Credit policy will, of necessity, be reasonably flexible to reflect changes in economic conditions, actions by competitors and marketing strategy eg, the desire to 'kill off' a new competitor in the market and/or increase market share.

2.2 Example

A study of the debtors of XYZ Co Ltd has shown that it is possible to classify all debtors into certain classes with the following characteristics:

Category	*Average collection period (days)*	*Bad debts %*
A	15	0.5
B	20	2.5
C	30	5.0
D	40	9.5

The average standard profit/cost schedule for the company's range of products is as follows:

	£	£
Selling price		2.50
Less: Material	1.00	
Wages	0.95	
Variable cost	0.30	
Fixed cost	0.05	2.30
Profit		0.20

The company has the opportunity of extending its sales by £1,000,000 per annum, split between categories C and D in the proportions 40:60. The company's short-term borrowing rate is 11½% per annum on a simple interest basis.

Evaluate the effect of the proposed increase in sales by carrying out the steps below.

Step 1 Calculate the additional contribution from the extra sales, split between the different categories of debtor. The profit volume ratio can be very useful when performing this calculation, see 2.3 for definition.

Assume that the contribution per £ of sales will be as shown on the above standard cost card.

Step 2 For each category of debtor work out the bad debts arising from the sales, using the given percentages. Deduct the bad debts from the additional contribution worked out in Step 1.

Step 3 For each category of debtor work out the (absolute) interest cost of allowing credit over the relevant period.

The cost equals

Annual interest rate × Additional debtors, where

Additional debtors =

$$\text{Additional annual sales} \times \frac{\text{Average collection period (days)}}{365}$$

Deduct this cost from the net additional contribution derived in Step 2.

The final result is the net profit or loss from expanding sales.

2.3 The profit volume ratio (PV ratio)

Definition The contribution expressed as a percentage of sales.

Thus, the increase in sales multiplied by the PV ratio will give the additional contribution generated.

2.4 Example solution

	Ref to Steps	£	*Category C* £	£	*Category D* £
Additional contribution	(1)		40,000		60,000
Less Additional costs:					
Bad debts	(2)	20,000		57,000	
Funding debtors	(3)	3,781	23,781	7,561	64,561
Additional profit/(loss)			**16,219**		**(4,561)**

Therefore, total additional profit = £16,219 – £4,561 = £11,658.

NB: It has been assumed that fixed costs will not increase as a result of the sales expansion.

Steps

(1) **Additional contribution** (average per unit = £2.50 – (1.00 + 0.95 + 0.30)
= **£0.25**

$$\text{The profit volume ratio} = \frac{\text{Contribution}}{\text{Sales}} \times 100$$

$$\frac{0.25}{£2.50} \times 100 = 10\%$$

	Category C £	*Category D* £
Additional sales	40% × 1,000,000 = 400,000	60% × 1,000,000 = 600,000
Additional contribution	400,000 × 10% **= 40,000**	600,000 × 10% **= 60,000**

(2) **Bad debts**

Category C	5% × £400,000 =	**£20,000**
Category D	9.5% × £600,000 =	**£57,000**

(3) **Funding debtors**

Additional debtors	$\frac{30}{365} \times 400{,}000$ = 32,876	$\frac{40}{365} \times 600{,}000$ = 65,753
Cost of funding debtors = 11½% × Additional debtors	**= 3,781**	**= 7,561**

It can be seen that total additional profit (£11,658) is halved as a result of the additional financing required (3,781 + 7,561 = £11,342). In fact, the financing cost represents 1.26% of the sales value of Category D, while the bad debts represent 9.5%, a total of 10.76%.

2.5 Activity

The following self assessment should provide a valuable recap and consolidation of the process which was illustrated in 2.2 to 2.4.

An analysis of the debtors of LCBN plc has generated the following classification of debtors:

Category	*Average collection period (days)*	*Bad debts %*
V	15	.75
W	20	2.00
X	25	3.00
Y	30	5.00
Z	60	10.00

The average profit for the company's product mix is as follows (and it is estimated that it will not change in the forthcoming period):

		£	£
Selling price			50
Less:	Materials	12	
	Labour	8	
	Variable overheads	10	
	Fixed overheads	5	35
Profit			15

In the forthcoming period the company has the opportunity increase its sales by £2,500,000. This would be made up of £500,000 to category W, £500,000 to category Y and £1,500,000 to category Z. The company's short-term borrowing rate is 12.5% per annum.

Required

Attempt to calculate the way in which the proposed increases would affect the company's profits, and then compare your attempt with the suggested solution illustrated in 2.6.

2.6 Activity solution

	Working Ref.	*Category* W £	£	*Y* £	£	*Z* £	£
Add. contribution	(i)		200,000		200,000		600,000
Less costs:							
Bad debts	(ii)	10,000		25,000		150,000	
Funding costs	(iii)	3,425	13,425	5,137	30,137	30,822	180,822
Additional profit			**186,575**		169,863		419,178

The increase in total profits if the above went ahead as planned would be £775,616.

It must however, be noted that things may not go according to plan. The sales may be more or less than planned, the selling price may have to be reduced due to competition/other factors, the variable and the fixed costs may increase, and so could the funding costs.

Having pointed out that certain movements in selling prices/costs could change the assessment, the additional profits earned by each category is of such a magnitude that it could quite easily withstand a few knocks.

Workings

(i) **The additional contribution** (average per unit)

	£
Sales	50
Less: Variable costs (£35 - £5)	30
Contribution	**20**

Profit volume ratio:

$$\frac{\text{Contribution}}{\text{Sales}} \times 100 = \frac{20}{50} \times 100 = \mathbf{40\%}$$

	Category		
	W	Y	Z
Additional sales × PV ratio	£	£	£
= additional contribution	**200,000**	**200,000**	**600,000**

(ii) **Bad debts**

	W	Y	Z
	£	£	£
Sales	500,000	500,000	1,500,000
% Bad	× 2%	× 5%	× 10%
=	**£10,000**	**£25,000**	**£150,000**

(iii) **Cost of funding debtors**

	W	Y	Z
Additional debtors	$\frac{20}{365} \times 500{,}000$	$\frac{30}{365} \times 500{,}000$	$\frac{60}{365} \times 1{,}500{,}000$
	= £27,397	= £41,096	= £246,575
× cost of funding	× 12.5%	× 12.5%	× 12.5%
Cost of funding	**£,3425**	**£5,137**	**£30,822**

Conclusion Companies/organisations which sell goods or services on credit need to devise well thought out credit policies. Such a policy would look very carefully at the period of credit eg, looking at what competitors/ the industry in general is offering, the implication for bad debts of extending the credit period etc.

The policy should take account of marketing considerations eg, using trade credit to increase market share, and collection problems which can impact on cash flow and affect profits via the writing off of bad debts.

3 Sources of information to assess credit worthiness

As indicated previously, procedures should be laid down to assess creditworthiness before a new customer is extended credit terms. Sources of available information are as listed below:

- **Trade references**

  The potential customer is asked to give the names of a specified number of existing suppliers who will testify to the firm's credit standing. Note that there is a danger that the firms involved may nominate only suppliers that are paid on time.

- **Bank references**

  Permission is sought to approach the customer's bank to discuss the customer's creditworthiness. Note, however, that banks are often reluctant to give their customers bad references.

- **Visits to customers**

  It may be possible to visit a prospective applicant for credit or an existing debtor on their 'home ground' ie, at their own premises. The purpose of such a visit should help to build up a good working relationship with the (potential) customer concerned. In addition, the visit could also provide a valuable insight into the way in which the business operates and is being managed. The three C's used by some banking organisations could be a useful starting point. An assessment could be made of capacity, capability and character of the company/organisation being visited, as follows:

- Capacity—does the company have the necessary capacity to achieve their objectives, formulate necessary policies in terms of fixed assets, products, personnel etc.?
- Capability—how capable is the company at producing its products or delivering a service eg, in terms of expertise and managerial skills?
- Character—can we trust and work hand in hand with the personnel involved?

In addition it can provide a mutual understanding for the company concerned and its products (or services), and the problems which it has to face.

- **Credit agencies and credit associations**

  These bodies will provide independent assessments of creditworthiness for a fee. Short reports may be obtained from regularly updated registers or special more detailed reports may be commissioned. Dun and Bradstreet are probably the most well-known credit agency in this area. It is important to ensure that such assessments/references are genuine and authenticated eg, by corresponding direct with the provider.

- **Reports from salespersons**

  Salespersons are often the only representatives of the supplying firm that actually meet the potential customer's staff and see the premises. They are therefore in the front line and in a unique position to provide information on customer creditworthiness. They can provide valuable feedback on developments taking place amongst customers in terms of products, expansion plans, laying off staff etc. They can also try to find out why slow payers are paying so slowly and forge stronger links with customers.

- **Information from competitors**

  In 'close-knit' industries competing suppliers often exchange credit information on potential customers.

- **Financial statement analysis, credit scoring**

  Each of these important techniques is discussed fully below:

4 FINANCIAL STATEMENT ANALYSIS

4.1 Introduction

For outsiders, the published financial statements are very often the only, or almost the only, major information available to help them answer basic questions about the company such as:

- How is the business doing?
- How is it placed at present?
- What are its future prospects?

Other than the annual report the following is a list of sources of information about a company's finances which are available:

- Authoritative newspaper articles
- Specialist journals
- Stock Exchange Year Book
- Company reporting services
- Inter-company comparisons

- Status enquiry agencies
- Computer databases

One broad classification of numerical analysis techniques is between **VERTICAL** and **HORIZONTAL** processes, which are as follows:

Definition A vertical analysis involves converting the absolute monetary values in a financial statement into proportions or percentages of, say, total assets or sales. This in turn may reveal matters of significance related to the structure of the finances of the business.

Definition A horizontal analysis involves placing side by side two or more sets of figures (which may in turn be derived from vertical analysis) to carry out comparisons. The sets may be for the same company at different times or for other organisations with features of common interest.

4.2 Key questions

To some degree or other, all interested parties will want to ask questions which are likely to fall into one or other of the following categories and be about:

- **Liquidity** – is the company able to meet its short-term obligations as they fall due from resources immediately available to it? How long on average does it take to pay its debts?
- **Profitability** – is the company making a profit, and if so is it enough? What is its return on capital employed?
- **Efficiency** – is the company making best use of its resources, generating adequate sales from its investment in equipment and people and managing its working capital levels adequately?
- **Stability** – what about the longer term? Is the company generating sufficient resources to repay long-term liabilities and reinvest in required new equipment? What is the structure of its financing? Is it high geared or low geared?
- **Investment return** – what can the investor or lender expect to get out of their investment by way of dividend and capital appreciation?

4.3 Review tools

The answer to questions in the areas above will come from a careful, analytical review of the financial statements and in particular:

- A thorough reading of the annual report including the 'Review of the business' and 'Chairman's statement' etc. This will reveal many qualitative things about the business, its place in its industry, the geographical scope and scale of its operations and its plans and prospects for the immediate and longer-term future. Political, environmental and macro-economic issues may also be raised and some answers suggested by this review.
- Examination of the cash-flow statement. This should reveal where the company's resources have come from and what they have been used for during the year.
- Calculation of significant ratios or relationships between individual figures and amounts in the statements – or in some cases between sub totals of particular categories of asset, liability income or expense.
- Comparisons and identification of trends. Ratios and other financial calculations are rarely very useful when looked at on their own in isolation. We need to carry out comparisons of ratios and

other significant financial figures, for example with previous years (many companies publish five or ten-year summaries with their annual reports) in order to establish positive or adverse trends, or with industry norms – obtained either from "inter-firm" comparisons carried out by third parties or by comparing directly with other businesses of a similar size and in the same industrial sector.

4.4 Common ratios used in credit control

The following liquidity and efficiency ratios are particularly important for the management and control of debtors. All figures used for illustration purposes, are contained in 4.5.

The current ratio

Definition This is the ratio of current assets to current liabilities.

It is used to assess the customer's ability to pay and meet their obligations, and gives an indication of the margin of safety to meet the fluctuations which may arise from time to time in the flow of funds.

This year

$$\frac{\text{Current assets}}{\text{Current liabilities}} \quad \frac{280}{204} = \mathbf{1.37}$$

This simply says that for every £1 owing as current liabilities there is £1.37 of cover provided by the current assets. According to a rough 'rule of thumb' this ought to be around 2 to 1. It does therefore appear to be on the low side. A much better 'yard-stick' against which to measure and compare this and other ratios are the average ratios for the particular industry in which the company trades.

The acid test (or quick ratio)

Definition The ratio of liquid assets (ie, current assets excluding stock) to the current liabilities.

It shows the extent to which liquid resources are available to meet current demands and provides an indication of funds which may be available for investment eg, short-term investments on the money markets.

This year

$$\frac{\text{Liquid assets}}{\text{Current liabilities}} \quad \frac{120}{204} = \mathbf{0.59}$$

The rule of thumb for this ratio is 1 to 1, however companies do tend to work on a slightly lower figure in practice in many industries. Even so the position indicated above appears weak. The company only has 59p of liquid assets per £1 of current liabilities which are outstanding.

Credit management would be most interested in the above ratios in their quest to assess the ability of both new and existing debtors to meet their obligations and to pay up.

Creditors, average payment period

Definition The time taken to pay creditors who have supplied goods and services on credit.

This is calculated as $\dfrac{\text{Average creditors} \times 365}{\text{cost of sales}}$

Average creditors over this year are $\dfrac{130 + 125}{2} = \mathbf{127.5}$

The average time taken to pay creditors is $\therefore \quad \dfrac{127.5 \times 365}{520}$ = **89 days** (to nearest day)

Thus if the average for the industry is, say, 45 days, which is not untypical, this company is taking twice as long to pay. This is of prime importance for credit management as it provides an indication of how long the company concerned (prospective customer) takes on average to pay for the purchases of goods and services which it has bought on credit.

Debtor days

Definition The average number of days which debtors take to pay for the goods and services which have been supplied to them on credit.

It can be computed $\dfrac{\text{Average debtors} \times 365}{\text{Credit sales}}$

which for this year from the figures supplied would be:

Average debtors $= \dfrac{65+120}{2} = \mathbf{92.5}$

Debtor days are $\therefore \quad \dfrac{92.5 \times 365}{752}$ = **45 days** (to the nearest whole day)

Note that where sales are a mixture of cash and credit, only credit sales should be included in the above ratios.

4.5 Balance sheet information

the following balance sheet figures have been used to illustrate the way in which the ratios have been calculated in 3.1.

	Last year		This year	
	£000	£000	£000	£000
Fixed assets:				
Freehold property at cost		320		380
Equipment – cost	240		275	
- depn.	120	120	145	130
Motor vehicles – cost	120		135	
– depn.	60	60	85	50
		500		560
Current assets				
Stock	70		160	
Debtors	65		120	
Cash at bank	125			
	260		280	
Less current liabilities:				
Creditors	130		125	
Bank overdraft			55	
Dividends	20		24	
	150		204	
Net current assets:		110		76
		£610		£636

Capital and reserves:		
Share of capital	200	250
Profit and loss account	300	356
Total shareholders' funds	530	606
Long term loans	80	30
	£610	£636

The credit sales for this year amounted to £752,000, and the cost of sales for this year amounted to £520,000.

4.6 Other ratios

There are many other ratios which could be reviewed to provide a more in-depth appraisal of financial performance, for example profitability ratios, other efficiency ratios and investor ratios etc.

- **Operating performance/profitability**—these ratios tell us whether a business is making profits – and if so whether at an acceptable level.

  - **Return on capital employed** (ROCE)/return on investment (ROI)—this is sometimes referred to as the **primary ratio** and tells us what returns management has made on the total funds entrusted to them, before making any distribution of those returns to the providers of the funds by way of interest and dividend. It is calculated as:

    Definition

    $$\frac{\textbf{Net profit before interest, tax and dividend (PBIT)}}{\textbf{total assets (or total assets less current liabilities)}}$$

    Looked at another way this is the same as PBIT / total long-term capital employed.

  - Gross profit percentage or **gross margin**—this tells us something of a business's ability consistently to control its production costs or recover them in its sales prices. It also tells us about the 'nature' of the business on a scale between 'high volume – low margin' and 'low volume – high margin' in terms of how much activity – represented by sales value – is necessary to make an absolute amount of gross profit. It is calculated as:

    Definition

    $$\frac{\textbf{Gross profit}}{\textbf{sales}} \times \mathbf{100}$$

  - Net profit percentage or **return on sales** – assuming a consistent gross margin, this tells us something about a company's ability to control its other operating costs or overheads. These will bear some relationship to changes in activity/sales levels but would ordinarily be expected to be less variable than the production costs. It is calculated as:

    Definition

    $$\frac{\textbf{Net profit before interest (sometimes called operating profit)}}{\textbf{sales}} \times \mathbf{100}$$

- **Efficiency/activity**—these ratios give us an insight into how efficiently the business is employing those resources invested in fixed assets and working capital.

- **Total asset utilisation.** What sales are being generated by each pound's worth of assets.

Definition $$\frac{\textbf{Sales}}{\textbf{Capital employed}}$$

- **Fixed asset utilisation**. This ratio is about fixed asset capacity. A reducing sales of profit being generated from each pound invested in fixed assets may indicate over-capacity or ailing equipment

Definition $$\frac{\textbf{Sales or profit}}{\textbf{Fixed assets}}$$

- **Stock turnover** – Have they got too much money tied up in inventory? An increasing figure or one much greater than the 'yardstick' industry norm may indicate poor inventory management. We use the **cost of sales** rather than sales in its ratio because stock is stated in the balance sheet at cost rather than at sales value.

Definition $$\frac{\textbf{Cost of sales}}{\textbf{Average stock}}$$

- **Stability (long-term solvency)** These issues relate to the longer-term health of a business and its abilities to withstand stresses and risks introduced by its capital structure and policies relating to long-term growth and development.

  - **Gearing** (or 'leverage' as it is known in the UK) is the proportion of assets financed by borrowing. Basically, the higher the borrowing, the higher the risks to the business, since the payment of interest, and the repayment of loans are non-discretionary and form a 'first call' on the profits and cash of the business – even when times are tough!

Definition $$\frac{\textbf{Borrowing (long - term or long - term plus overdraft, or all liabilities)}}{\textbf{net assets}}$$

Note that, depending on which 'borrowing' figure is used, the 'net assets' will require appropriate adjustment.

  - **Interest cover** – is a measure of the extent to which the company can settle its 'first call' obligation to pay interest out of its current profits. Anything much below two is alarming and is unlikely to be sustainable in the longer-term.

  -

Definition $$\frac{\textbf{net profit before interest}}{\textbf{interest}}$$

  - **Asset replacement policies** – this covers a number of things from capital commitments to discretionary revenue expenditures on research and development, brand promotion and maintenance, training etc. It is tempting, in hard times, to cut back or abandon expenditure in these areas, which are traditionally written-off in arriving at reported profits, and therefore adversely affect EPS.

- **Investor ratios**
  Investors will obviously be interested in the operating efficiency of the company but will wish to see this related to their investment.

- **Earnings per share (EPS)** – All London stock Exchange listed companies show the EPS for the previous and current years in the published financial statements. This is an important ratio because:

  (i) it serves as a good indicators of the directors' profitable use of assets
  (ii) it is used in determining the price/earnings ratio (see below)

It is currently calculated as net profit left after deducting cost of loan capital (interest), tax and preference dividends but before extraordinary items – the **earnings attributable to ordinary shareholders (EATOS)** – divided by the weighted average ordinary shares in issue during the year

Definition
$$\frac{\textbf{EATOS}}{\textbf{Number of ordinary shares}}$$

- **Price/earnings ratio (P/E)** – Market price of share as multiples of EPS (See above). This shows how long it would take to recover the share price out of the earnings of the company, at current levels.

Definition
$$\frac{\textbf{Market price per ordinary share}}{\textbf{EPS}}$$

The theory is that investors are concerned about future levels of returns and the market price reflects the market's anticipation and estimation of those future returns. at any time, therefore, the P/E ratio is an indication of how highly the market 'rates' a particular company in terms of the number of times current earnings it is prepared to pay for a marginal share in its future prosperity.

- **Dividend cover** – This is also known as the payout ratio. It provides a guideline to the company's ability to maintain the dividend payment. It also measure the proportion of earnings retained by the company and the probability of the company being able to maintain current levels of dividend payments should earnings decline in future years. it is determined by the following:

Definition
$$\frac{\textbf{EATOS}}{\textbf{Year's dividend on ordinary shares}}$$

An additional ratio sometimes used is:

- **Return on shareholders equity** – This is a measure of the return earned by the company on the total shareholders' funds invested (compare with the ROCE, which is the return on total capital employed both equity and borrowings), and is calculated as:

Definition
$$\frac{\textbf{EATOS}}{\textbf{Ordinary shareholders' funds (ordinary share capital plus reserves)}}$$

Review of the above ratios will reveal that many of them are – not unexpectedly – linked to each other through a subdivided, hierarchical structure sometimes referred to as **the pyramid of ratios**. So for example the **primary ratio** of **ROCE** is seen to break down into the two **secondary ratios** of **asset utilisation** and **return on sales.**

4.7 Limitations of ratio analysis

It must be noted however, that ratios such as those in 4.4 and 4.6 only show the position as the date of the balance sheet. It should also be noted that the published accounts do have limitations caused by the application of the concepts, the accounting policies followed, methods of valuation adopted and creative accounting etc, for example:

- Figures are based on 'one-off' annual accounts at one point in time, which may be susceptible to 'window dressing' or seasonal abnormalities, and therefore do not show a representative position.
- Various sophistications such as allowance for taxes, adjustment for VAT included in balances and ascertainment of actual purchases/expenses made on credit are difficult to handle.
- Comparison between similar/same industry companies may be obscured because of the application of different accounting policies.
- There is a danger that ratios will be used in isolation or as the only evidence in analysis, rather than as one part of a jigsaw which is used in conjunction with other data.
- You should remember that ratio analysis of annual accounts is carried out by the 'outsider looking in' and the detailed information is inevitably limited. It enables a broad overall picture to be developed and suggests the appropriate questions to ask.

5 CREDIT SCORING

5.1 Introduction

Definition Credit scoring is a technique which enables companies to apply a systematic approach to the granting of credit.

It can be applied in all circumstances where credit is under consideration, but is more applicable where sales are direct to the public, and the use of the previously discussed evaluations are either not possible or are too expensive. In the areas of hire purchase and personal loans, the companies/institutions involved have been able to streamline their processing of applications via credit scoring systems based on the information extracted from the application forms.

5.2 Example

A sample of past customers would identify the factors associated with bad debts. Age, sex, marital status, family size, occupation etc, may be significant factors.

The company may allocate a points score to potential customers as follows:

Factor	*Points score*
Aged over 40	15
Married with fewer than three children	20
Home owner	20
At same address for over three years	15
At existing job for over two years	20
Car owner	10
Total	100

Past records may show that there had been no records of payment difficulties with customers with a score of 80 or over, bad debts of 10% for scores between 35 and 80, and bad debts of 25% where customers had a score of less than 35. A 'cut-off' point of 35 would probably be established, and credit refused to any potential customer with a score of less than 35.

It may be considered worthwhile to carry out some further form of credit evaluation for potential customers with scores between 35 and 80, in order to reduce the bad debts below 10%. The costs of the further analysis would have to be compared with the financial benefits from the reduction in bad debts.

The factors which are considered most likely to influence creditworthiness are of course a matter of judgement, as are the respective weights which should be attached to each factor.

Conclusion You should have observed, that there are a number of internal and external sources of information which can be used to assist the credit control function/department in the performance of their duties, and which are as follows:

Internal sources:

- information from sales staff/reports prepared by them eg, including the views of other customers.
- experiences from earlier (or current) contacts eg, how well the customer concerned settled their accounts with the company/organisation.
- Financial statement analysis eg, key ratios and directors' reports etc.
- credit scoring eg, rating scales which provide scores which reflect the various attributes which are perceived as a necessary quality.

External sources

- trade references
- bank references
- visits to customers' place/places of business
- credit agencies
- other customers, competitors and suppliers eg, references/testimonials.

6 REJECTING AN APPLICATION FOR CREDIT

6.1 Dealing with rejections

Companies/organisations cannot and should not provide credit to all applicants. If they did, their level of bad debts could be so high that they themselves may go out of business.

Procedures for dealing with rejections should be established. For example, would-be customers could be informed in person, by phone, fax or letter. Whichever method is adopted the tone should be clear, concise, tactful and polite. It could also include some indication if and when and under what circumstances it would be possible to provide credit in the future. Alternatives could also be suggested so as not to close the door completely eg, offering to supply on COD (cash on delivery terms) or by getting the customer to agree to pay by direct debit. In such situations, the way in which the customer performed could be monitored, and after a time credit granted and credit limits/terms etc, agreed with the customer.

With credit scoring systems it would not be possible to disclose all of the reasons, and in certain cases a concise and polite rejection may be the best course of action.

6.2 Reasons for rejecting an application for credit

These may include one or more of the following:

- a poor (reject) score ascertained via the use of a credit scoring system.

- a poor track record of financial performance via an analysis of the applicant's accounts eg, downward trends in profits and liquidity, poor investor ratios.

- no track record because the applicant is a new business.

- a company which is highly geared ie, has a large amount of interest to pay for loans and/or debentures.

- a company which has put up a significant proportion (in value terms) of its assets as security for loans and debentures eg, 'mortgaged up to the hilt'.

- information from third parties eg, banks, credit rating agencies, existing customers, suppliers etc.

- not being part of the required customer portfolio eg, individuals wanting to deal with a wholesale which only supplies other businesses/organisations.

Conclusion In conclusion, suffice it to say that all dealings should be conducted in a businesslike, courteous and polite manner. This could well result in being able to do business at some future date eg, when the new company has become established and can successfully pay its way.

7 OTHER CONTROL ISSUES

7.1 Preventing credit limits from being exceeded

Control of credit limits should be directed at the order processing stage ie, the customer's sales ledger account will be adapted to reflect orders in the pipeline as well as invoiced sales. Thus, when a new order is received, checks will be made with the customers' account in sales ledger before delivery/fulfilment of the order is authorised. In cases where the amount outstanding would exceed the credit limit if the order went ahead, the credit control department could request full or part payment as the circumstances dictate.

7.2 Prompt invoicing

The customer's period of credit will commence from the date of receipt of invoice, so it is essential to minimise the time-lag between despatch of the goods or delivery of the service and invoicing eg, by streamlining authorisation and administrative procedures. This should be of particular interest to small/medium sized business who do tend to be less well organised when it comes to sending out invoices with the minimum of delay.

7.3 Knowing customer's 'pass for payment' systems

Most firms/organisations in the private or public sectors do operate a 'pass for payment' system.

Definition A system in which several checks are made before an invoice is authorised to be paid.

The checks involved could include:

- comparing invoice details with the original order
- checking with the delivery note/goods received notes to ensure the goods have in fact been received
- checking the calculations of VAT, discounts, denomination of quantity etc.
- where appropriate, compare with estimates/tenders received etc.
- ensuring that the goods have been received by the stores or that the service to be paid for has been performed to the satisfaction of internally appointed inspectors.

These systems do take time and invoices may be processed in batches at certain times of the month. It could well happen that if an invoice arrives as little as one day later it could miss out on being included in the next batch to be processed. Thus, it could pay to find out about customers' payment systems and then ensure that invoices arrive by appropriate deadlines, so that they could be processed in the earliest possible batch. This should help to reduce the lead times which customers take to process invoices and pass them for payment.

The information needed to operate this kind of approach may not always be easy to obtain, and in certain cases would be restricted to key customer accounts. However, where the company/organisation has established a good working relationship with its customers' accounts departments, it may be quite possible to obtain sufficient information of the type necessary to be in a position to target various key customers ie, to prioritise sending the invoices/statements out to them.

8 THE DATA PROTECTION ACT 1984

8.1 Introduction

The Data Protection Act 1984 was introduced into UK law for two major reasons:

(a) to counteract the threat to privacy caused by the increased ability of computers to hold, transfer and process personal data

(b) to enable the UK to meet its obligations to ratify the Council of Europe Data Protection Convention. When fully operational this convention will enable the countries who have signed it to refuse to allow data to be transferred to other countries which do not have equivalent data protection laws.

As part of the system of establishing creditworthiness of customers, a business may gather and hold information on computer. It is important that you are aware of the effect of the Data Protection Act 1984 on this information.

8.2 The scope of the Act

The Act applies to personal data of data subjects which is automatically processed by, or on behalf of, data users.

For the purposes of the Act, data is information recorded in a form in which it can be processed by equipment operating automatically. The implication is that data held in a computer system falls within the scope of the Act. The Act however, carefully avoids the use of the word 'computer'. Records kept entirely manually are excluded.

Personal data is data relating to a living person who can be identified from the data itself. The Act would apply even if the data referred only to codes which could then be related to individuals on a different file. However, data concerning deceased persons or companies is not within the scope of the Act.

A data user is a person who 'holds' data. Data is 'held' when all of the following conditions apply:

(a) the data forms part of the data processed or intended to be processed by, or on behalf of, that person

(b) the person controls the contents and use of the data

(c) the data is in the form in which is has been, or is intended to be, processed.

The implication is that a data user does not have to own their own computer, eg it could be processed by a computer bureau. Alternatively physical custody of a floppy disc does not make that person a user if he has not, and does not, intend to process it.

8.3 The Data Protection Register

A register of data users and bureaux compiled by the Data Protection Register.

The register lists names and addresses of all users and bureaux together with general details of the nature of the personal data held and the purposes for which it is held. One or more addresses will be provided to which data subjects may write to request access to the data which relates to them.

8.4 The data protection principles

The Act establishes eight general principles or standards to be observed by data users and bureaux. Failure to comply with these principles can result in seizure of data and unlimited fines. The Secretary of State has the power to amend the principles.

THE DATA PROTECTION PRINCIPLES

Personal data held by users

(1) The information to be contained in personal data shall be obtained, and personal data shall be processed, fairly and lawfully.

(2) Personal data held shall be held only for one or more specified and lawful purposes.

(3) Personal data held for any purpose or purposes shall not be used or disclosed in any manner incompatible with that purpose or those purposes.

(4) Personal data held for any purpose or purposes shall be adequate, relevant and not excessive in relation to that purpose or those purposes.

(5) Personal data shall be accurate and, where necessary, kept up to date.

(6) Personal data held for any purpose or purposes shall not be kept for longer than is necessary for that purpose or those purposes.

(7) An individual shall be entitled:

- (a) at reasonable intervals and without undue delay or expense:
  - (i) to be informed by any data user whether he holds personal days of which that individual is the subject; and
  - (ii) to access to any such data held by a data user; and
- (b) where appropriate, to have such data corrected or erased.

Personal data held by data users or in respect of which services are provided by persons carrying on computer bureaux

(8) Appropriate security measures shall be taken against unauthorised access to, or alteration, disclosure or destruction of, personal data and against accidental loss or destruction of personal data.

One of the main duties of the Registrar is to encourage data users and computer bureaux to comply with these principles. The registrar will investigate complaints that these principles have been contravened and may issue the following:

(a) **an enforcement notice** requiring the recipient to comply with the principles within a set time

(b) **a de-registration notice** threatening to remove the recipient from the register

(c) **a transfer prohibition notice** forbidding the transfer of specified data out of the UK.

If a user or bureaux is de-registered that user may no longer process personal data which could effectively put them out of business. The user or bureau may appeal to a Data Protection Tribunal against these notices.

8.5 Access to data

Individuals are entitled to ask data users whether they are the subject of personal data, and if so, be supplied with copies of that data. A reasonable fee (eg £15) may be charged by the user.

A response should normally be made within forty days of the request of the individual.

If the individual has correctly requested the data and has not been supplied with it, he or she may apply to the courts to order the data user to comply with the Act. If the data is inaccurate the individual may claim compensation and the Registrar may order the removal or amendment of the offending data.

8.6 Exclusions from the Act

Certain data is excluded from the Act either through the definitions used in the Act or by way of specific exclusions. It should be noted that many of the exclusions mentioned below are conditional.

The main exemptions are:

(a) records which are kept entirely manually

(b) data which does not identify a living individual

(c) intentions rather then opinions, of the data user, eg 'Mr X is not credit worthy' is a matter of opinion and would be subject to the Act. 'We will not give credit to Mr X' is a statement of intention and does not count as personal data

(d) preparing the text of a document, eg if the name of an author is mentioned in a text using a word processor that is not personal data but if the name of the author were held for other purposes it may be personal data.

(e) data processed wholly outside the UK and not for use within the UK

(f) payroll and accounts data. Registration is not required by a business just because they use a computer to process their payroll and accounts. However, the information must not be used for other purposes, eg the payroll records should not be used for personal reasons

(g) back-up data

(h) club records

(i) distribution lists

(j) domestic records

(k) national security matters

(l) criminal and taxation records.

Finally, you might note that access to examination marks is restricted until 40 days after the announcement of the results.

8.7 Likely changes to the Data Protection Act

One of the main reasons for the Data Protection Act having been implemented was to harmonise UK laws with those of the European Community. It seems likely, therefore, that future changes to the Act will be the result of pan European initiatives.

UK laws may, in future, be affected by a draft directive issued by the European Commission. This seeks to widen the scope of data protection legislation across Europe and to harmonise the laws in different countries.

8.8 Increased controls over data

As data is becoming more easily disseminated on a worldwide basis, it is important to regulate to protect individual freedom. Although the sophisticated controls needed to protect people's privacy are expensive, failure to improve these controls may be disastrous.

Two enhancements suggested in the draft directive are the coverage of non-computer based data and the giving to individuals of more control over data referring to them.

8.9 Harmonisation of data protection

There are two basic ways of harmonising data protection across Europe. The first is to impose a common law across Europe, and the second is to set minimum standards and to allow individual countries to enact their own statutes.

9 CHAPTER SUMMARY

Debtors represent capital tied up and have to be financed. It is therefore important to formulate a debtors policy eg, including screening, credit terms etc.

The purpose of credit control is to ensure that:

- There is an adequate inflow of cash.
- Debtors meet their obligations.
- Bad debts are kept to a minimum.

Probability of non-payment

From the vetting procedure an estimate may be made of the likelihood of the customer paying up eventually.

Sources of information about prospective debtors are:

- Credit Ratings and Reports by Dun & Bradstreet.
- Company history (inspection of our own sales ledger).
- Trade references (liable to abuse).
- Visits to prospective customers at their place of business.
- Bank references (unwilling to condemn).
- Financial statement analysis (out of date by the time it is available).
- Salesperson's reports (salespeople are not financial analysis).

Rejecting an application for credit

Procedures must also be drawn up to deal with rejections. The communications by whatever means used should be polite and helpful, and where possible give reasons for the rejection and make suggestions of ways in which credit would be possible in the future.

Reasons for rejecting an application for credit

There are many reasons why a firm may not wish to extend credit to a new applicant. The reasons could for example be due to a poor credit rating score, a poor or no track record of sound finance performance, high gearing, being 'mortgaged up to the hilt' etc.

Data Protection Act 1984

It is important that businesses are aware of the provisions of the Data Protection Act 1984 as they gather and hold credit control information on their computers.

10 SELF TEST QUESTIONS

10.1 Define, in your own words what is meant by the term credit control. (1.1)

10.2 Describe the role of the credit control function. (1.3)

10.3 List the activities which could be carried out by the credit control function/department, in the performance of its duties. (1.4)

10.4 Which factors affect the length of the credit period which is given? (2.1)

10.5 Explain briefly how each of the following can be used to assess creditworthiness: (3)

(a) trade references
(b) visits to customers
(c) reports from salespersons
(d) credit scoring.

10.6 Explain the significance of the following ratios in assessing the credit worthiness of a potential customer: (4.4)

(a) The current ratio
(b) The acid test
(c) Creditors' average payment period
(d) Debtor days

10.7 How can credit control help to prevent credit limits being exceeded? (7.1)

10.8 Explain what is meant by a 'pass for payment system. (7.3)

11 MONITORING AND CONTROL

PATHFINDER INTRODUCTION

This chapter covers the following performance criteria and knowledge and understanding.

- Legal and administrative procedures for the collection of debts (Element 14.4)
- The effect of bankruptcy and insolvency on organisations (Element 14.4)
- Interpretation and use of credit control information (Elements 14.3 & 14.4)
- Methods of collection (Element 14.3)
- Debt insurance (Element 14.4)
- Methods of analysing information on debtors: age analysis of debtors; average periods of credit given and received; incidence of bad and doubtful debts (Element 14.4)
- Evaluation of different collection methods (Element 14.4)
- Information relating to the current state of debtors' accounts is regularly monitored and appropriate action taken (Element 14.4)
- Information regarding significant outstanding accounts and potential bad debts is promptly sent to relevant individuals within the organisation (Element 14.4)
- Discussions and negotiations with debtors are conducted courteously and achieve the desired outcome (Element 14.4)
- Debt recovery methods used are appropriate to the circumstances of individual cases and are in accordance with the organisation's procedures (Element 14.4)
- Recommendations to write off bad and doubtful debts are based on a realistic analysis of all known factors (Element 14.4)

Putting the chapter in context – learning objectives.

In this chapter we build on and expand on the information described in chapter 10. We look at the costs involved in managing the credit function and the need to monitor both the credit system and the debtors. The area of settlement discounts is reviewed and the importance of the aged debtor analysis is considered. We then turn to the methods of recovery of debts, and include a summary of the effects of insolvency and bankrutpcy in businesses. Finally, we take a look at the role of audit in the management and control of debtors. We also provide valuable consolidation and recapitulation self-assessments which integrate with what has been learned in earlier chapters.

At the end of this chapter you should have learned the following topics:

- appreciate the costs involved in managing the credit control function and possible benefits
- calculate the effective annual rate of interest to illustrate why giving settlement discounts can be expensive
- prepare and make use of an Aged Debt Analysis
- understand how the Debtors Control Account is put together
- discuss the various methods of debt recovery and in what circumstances each becomes appropriate
- have a basic understanding of the effects of bankruptcy and liquidation on individuals / organisations
- describe how auditing can assist the management and control of debtors.

1 COSTS AND BENEFITS OF A CREDIT SYSTEM

1.1 Introduction

As we have seen, the extending of credit to customers is common in most industries, and if a business tries to operate without offering credit, or imposing much more restrictive terms, it is likely to lose sales to more generous competitors. However, the costs of financing and administering a credit control system should not be underestimated; if these are likely to outweigh the benefits (in terms of additional sales) then, in theory, credit should not be offered.

1.2 How do we determine the cost?

- **Financing of debtors**

  Is the money in the company available for use?
  If yes – what is the opportunity cost of investing in debtors? (interest lost)
  If not – where can we borrow it? (is it possible?), how much will it cost? (interest charge)
  How long will the debt be outstanding? (combination of industry average and customer variables)
  Can we modify this period in any way? (discounts, security, factoring, etc).

- **Administration costs may include:**

  - Vetting applicants for credit sales.
  - Recording credit sales by customer at point of sale.
  - Credit control checks on customers at point of sale.
  - Processing credit sales for individual customer records.
  - Sending invoices to customers.
  - Chasing up late paying customers.
  - Dealing with queries.
  - Recording receipt of cash and processing on individual customer records.
  - Use of office space, equipment (including computers) and employees for the above tasks.

  Note that the more unreliable the customer, the more expensive the administration of their account!

1.3 What are the benefits?

These are generally taken to be the contribution generated by the additional sales made as a result of offering credit to customers. This is, in practice, very difficult to estimate. However, the following example illustrates the quantification of the benefit derived from the generation of an additional £60,000 sales per period, where the additional variable costs include those brought about by the credit function (ie, will include some of those listed in 1.2 above):

	Existing System £	*Proposed Change* £	*New Total* £
Variable costs	500,000	+50,000	550,000
Fixed costs	200,000		200,000
Total costs	700,000	50,000	750,000
Profit	200,000	10,000	210,000
Sales value	900,000	60,000	960,000
Average profit as % of sales	22.2%	16.7%	21.9%

£10,000 is the marginal profit of the proposed change. It is this figure which must be compared with the relevant additional fixed costs in order to assess the viability of the scheme.

1.4 Monitoring the credit system

Management will require regular information to facilitate corrective action and the measurement of the impact of credit allowed on the investment in working capital. The credit system as a whole will have to be monitored to ensure that it keeps up with changes in the environment. Thus, periodic reviews will be necessary and amendments made to the credit policies/systems accordingly.

Typical reports will include the following:

- Aged analysis of outstanding debts.
- Ratios, compared with the previous period or target, to indicate trends in credit levels and the incidence of overdue and bad debts.
- Statistical data to identify causes of default and the incidence of bad debts among different classes of customer and types of trade.

Conclusion The costs of administering the credit system, can as indicated in 1.2 be quite substantial. A system once introduced has to be reviewed from time to time and be flexible enough to change to meet changes in the environment. However, the cost of running such a system or the cost of changes to the system should not exceed the benefits that arise from the system or changes to the system.

2 SETTLEMENT DISCOUNTS

Definition A discount allowed, if the invoice is paid by a specified date eg, 2½% if paid by the end of the month.

2.1 The offer of a settlement discount

A company may offer settlement discounts to its customers, that is, it allows debtors to pay less than their full debt if they pay sooner than the end of their credit period. The company must ensure that offering the discount is financially sensible, with the benefit of receiving the cash early exceeding the cost of the discount; this has already been considered in the context of taking credit from suppliers (Chapter 7).

General terms in the UK are for payment to be due at the end of the month following the month of delivery of goods. This will give rise to an average credit period of 45 days. (½ month of delivery + following month). In practice trade credit is outstanding for longer periods eg, 70 - 80 days.

2.2 Effective annual rate of interest

Cash (settlement) discounts may be offered in order to speed up payment eg, customers are permitted to deduct a 2½% 'prompt payment discount' if they pay the invoice within 7 days. For those customers who would otherwise have paid on the date (say 45 days from invoice date) this will be a substantial *effective annual interest rate* of around 25% which is computed as follows:

$$\frac{2\frac{1}{2}}{97\frac{1}{2}} \times \frac{365}{(45-7)} = 24.6\% \text{ pa}$$

For the customer who was going to pay one month late, the discount is far less of an inducement, as the effective annual interest rate is reduced to 14%, is computed as follows:

$$\frac{2\frac{1}{2}}{97\frac{1}{2}} \times \frac{365}{(75-7)} = 13.8\% \text{ pa}$$

Definition From the two illustrations above, it should be apparent that the formula for computing the effective annual rate of interest is as follows:

$$\frac{\text{Rate of discount}}{(100 - \text{rate of discount})} \times \frac{365 \text{ days}}{(\text{Normal credit period - number of days in which the invoice has to be paid})} \times 100$$

2.3 Activity

To reinforce the point, that a small percentage discount can have a high effective annual rate of interest, compute the effective annual rate of interest from the following information:

Terms 3% discount if payment is made within 14 days from the date of the invoice.

The normal period of credit is 60 days.

2.4 Activity solution

$$\frac{3}{100-3} \times \frac{365}{60-14} \times 100 = \frac{3}{97} \times \frac{365}{46} \times 100 = \mathbf{24.5\%}$$

2.6 Why give settlement discounts?

Prompt payment discounts are therefore more of an inducement to the already prompt payer, rather than the reluctant one, and are not a device to be used indiscriminately. As illustrated above it should be observed that a small percentage discount can have a high effective annual rate.

Some sectors of the economy have tried a late payment surcharge on delinquent accounts, but this is not popular and not always highly successful.

2.7 Activity

The following activity has been designed to help with the problems of computing which credit policy to select and a review of cash discounts and sources used to assess the credit worthiness of customers.

Creative plc produces a new type of mini-lawn mower. It has an annual turnover of £1,980,000. The costs of each lawnmower are as set out below:

	£	£
Selling price		115
Variable costs	69	
Fixed cost apportionment	19	88
Net profit		27

Creative plc plans to expand sales by offering customers an extended credit period. The average credit period is currently 30 days, but three other credit periods are being considered:

	Option		
	1	*2*	*3*
Average credit period (days)	40	50	55
Expected annual sales increase	£96,000	£144,000	£150,000
Expected additional annual bad debts	£3,000	£7,000	£9,000

At the same time, Creative plc is re-evaluating its payment policy towards trade creditors. Suppliers offer a 2% discount if paid within 10 days, otherwise the full invoice price is to be paid within 30 days, although the company currently pays after 40 days. Creative plc is considering paying on the 10th day.

The cost of capital is currently 15 % pa.

You are required to calculate:

(a) Which credit policy should be offered to Creative plc's customers

(b) Whether cash discounts should be taken, assuming that Creative plc would otherwise continue to take 40 days to pay its suppliers.

(c) Discuss three sources of information which may be used in assessing the credit worthiness of customers.

When you have attempted the above, compare your attempt with the suggested solution which is given below

2.8 Activity solution

(a) Evaluation of credit policies

(All (000s)	*1*	*2*	*3*
New debtors:			
1,980 + 96 × 40/365	227.5		
1,980 + 144 × 50/365		291	
1,980 + 150 × 55/365			321
Less			
Current debtors			
1,980 × 30/365	163	163	163
Increase in debtors	64.5	128	158
Cost of additional debtors (15%)	9.7	19.2	23.7
Plus			
Cost of bad debts	3.0	7.0	9.0
	(12.7)	(26.2)	(32.7)
Increase in contribution:			
40% (W) additional sales			
40% × 96,000	38.4		
40% × 144,000		57.6	
40% × 150,000			60.00
Additional profit	**25.7**	**31.4**	**27.3**

(b) Implicit annual interest cost of cash discounts: (40 days)

Payment after 10 days $\frac{2}{98} \times \frac{365}{(40-10)}$ = **24.8%**

As the annual cost of foregoing cash discounts of 24.8% is well above the 15% cost of capital, the company should pay on the 10th day following the invoice date and claim the discounts.

(c) Sources of information in assessing credit worthiness:

- Financial accounts
- Other credit managers
- Credit agencies
- Trade references
- Bank references
- Interviews and visits

WORKING

(W)

Contribution = Sales	115
Less variable cost	69
	46 (P.V. ratio 40%)

2.9 Trade discounts

Cash discounts (settlement discounts) for prompt payment should not be confused with trade discounts.

Definition Trade discounts are the discounts that have already been calculated and taken into account in arriving at the invoice figure. They could have been given as quantity discounts to encourage customers to buy in bulk.

3 THE ANALYSIS OF DEBTORS - AGED DEBT ANALYSIS

3.1 Introduction

When customers are allowed a period of credit, an organisation must ensure that it has some control over the actual credit period that is taken. This is often done by means of an aged debt analysis.

Definition An analysis of debtors broken down into categories according to how long the debt/s are outstanding (see the illustrations which follow).

3.2 Purpose of an aged debt analysis

The purpose of an aged debt analysis is to analyse the debts owed by each customer in terms of the time that each debt has been outstanding. This will give the organisation an indication of the time that is taken by each debtor to pay debts, and also of any problem debts that there might be, ie, any potential bad debts.

3.3 Layout

An aged debt analysis will most probably be set out in the following manner:

Credit customer	*Total owing* £	*Outstanding for:-* *Less than (<)30 days* £	*30 - 60 days* £	*60 - 90 days* £	*More than (>)90 days* £
T Grainger plc	551.86	279.30	272.56	-	-
C N Lawson Ltd	713.59	-	-	279.03	434.56
Burdon & Co Ltd	518.47	219.50	248.30	50.67	-

This indicates the amount of each total debt that relates to each period of time.

Most organisations would normally hope for the majority of their debts to be clustered in the 'less than 30 days' category and only a few debts outstanding for more than that period.

3.4 Interpreting and using an aged debt analysis

Aged debt analyses are produced for the management of an organisation in order to provide them with information about the payment patterns of debtors.

3.5 Example

The following aged debt analysis uses the layout illustrated earlier

Credit customer	*Total owing* £	*Outstanding for:* *<30 days* £	*30 - 60 days* £	*60 - 90 days* £	*>90 days* £
T Grainger plc	551.86	279.30	272.56	-	-
C N Lawson Ltd	713.59	-	-	279.03	434.56
Burdon & Co Ltd	518.47	219.50	248.30	50.67	-

This could possibly be interpreted in the following manner:

T Grainger plc would appear to pay their debts reasonably promptly as nothing has been owing for more than 60 days.

Alternatively T Grainger plc may be a new customer and the only sales that have been made to them have been made in the last 60 days.

C N Lawson's debts show a potentially rather worrying position. Most of the debt has been owing for more than 90 days and the remainder for 60 - 90 days. As there are no more recent amounts owing this implies that sales to this customer have stopped. This might be a policy decision due to the poor payment record or a decision by C N Lawson due to some sort of dispute or maybe C N Lawson has simply disappeared.

Burdon & Co Ltd's debts show perhaps the most common position for a debtor who tends to pay after about 60 days. Only a small amount of the debt has been outstanding for longer than this period.

3.6 Stated credit terms

When analysing and interpreting an aged debtor analysis it is important to bear in mind the stated credit terms of the organisation concerned.

If the credit terms are 'net 30 days' then if the majority of debts have been due for more than 30 days then this is potentially a worry. However, if the stated credit terms were payment within 60 days then such a picture would not be of concern.

The offer of cash or settlement discounts may also affect the aged debt analysis in that a greater proportion of debtors would pay within the period qualifying them for a discount.

4 PREPARATION OF AN AGED DEBTOR ANALYSIS

4.1 Introduction

In practice, if the accounting system is computerised, then this will be performed by the computer system. However you should be aware of how to prepare an analysis in a manual system.

4.2 Debtors ledger accounts

The base document for preparation of an aged debtor analysis will be the individual debtor accounts in the debtors (sales) ledger. Each individual account should show the date of outstanding invoices and the dates of payments received. From this the aged debt analysis can be performed.

4.3 Example

Given below is the debtors ledger account for T K Glade as at 30 June 20X7.

T K Glade

		£			£
14 March	Inv 20391	48.39	30 April	Cash	64.90
29 March	Inv 20405	64.90	22 May	Cash	51.51
7 April	Inv 20436	13.28	31 May	Cash	17.38
15 April	Inv 20487	51.51	15 June	Credit note	19.30
25 April	Inv 20511	17.38	28 June	Cash	80.00
3 May	Inv 20552	72.45			
27 May	Inv 20599	80.00			
6 June	Inv 20683	19.30			
15 June	Inv 20697	12.57			
20 June	Inv 20724	62.39	30 June	Bal c/d	209.08
		442.17			442.17

Prepare an aged debtor analysis for T K Glade.

4.4 Solution

Step 1 Match each of the cash receipts and credit notes to the related invoice.

T K Glade

		£			£
14 March	Inv 20391	48.39	30 April	Cash	64.90✓
29 March	Inv 20405	64.90✓	22 May	Cash	51.51✓
7 April	Inv 20436	13.28	31 May	Cash	17.38✓
15 April	Inv 20487	51.51✓	15 June	Credit note	19.30✓
25 April	Inv 20511	17.38✓	28 June	Cash	80.00✓
3 May	Inv 20552	72.45			
27 May	Inv 20599	80.00✓			
6 June	Inv 20683	19.30✓			
15 June	Inv 20697	12.57			
20 June	Inv 20724	62.39	30 June	Bal c/d	209.08
		442.17			442.17

Step 2 Analyse the remaining invoices according to their date.

		£
> 90 days	14 March	48.39
60 - 90	7 April	13.28
30 - 60	3 May	72.45
< 30 days	15 June	12.57
	20 June	62.39
		209.08

Step 3 Prepare the aged analysis report.

Credit customer	*Total owing*			*Outstanding for:*	
		<30 days	*30 - 60 days*	*60 - 90 days*	*>90 days*
	£	£	£	£	£
T K Glade	209.08	74.96	72.45	13.28	48.39

4.5 Activity

Given below are two debtors ledger accounts as at 31 March 20X4. Prepare an aged debt analysis on the following proforma.

Credit customer	*Total owing days*			*Outstanding for:*	
		<30 days	*30 - 60 days*	*60 - 90 days*	*>90*
	£	£	£	£	£

Gilde & Co

		£			£
20 Dec	Inv 2946	118.38	30 Jan	Credit note	172.48
28 Dec	Inv 2983	72.03	15 Feb	Cash	228.36
17 Jan	Inv 3029	228.36	28 Feb	Cash	72.03
25 Jan	Inv 3046	172.48	12 Mar	Cash	48.30
2 Feb	Inv 3103	48.30	14 Mar	Credit note	49.20
11 Feb	Inv 3135	69.02			
26 Feb	Inv 3157	159.27			
12 Mar	Inv 3204	49.20			
15 Mar	Inv 3221	49.20			
28 Mar	Inv 3252	169.39	31 Mar	Bal c/d	565.26
		1,135.63			1,135.63

Brandreth Ltd

		£			£
3 Jan	Inv 2999	378.29	12 Jan	Cash	363.16
12 Jan	Inv 3012	115.29	12 Jan	Discount	15.13
26 Jan	Inv 3047	39.20	25 Feb	Cash	398.59
13 Feb	Inv 3140	415.20	25 Feb	Discount	16.61
18 Feb	Inv 3145	415.20	28 Feb	Credit note	162.41
25 Feb	Inv 3156	162.41	28 Feb	Cash	115.29
4 Mar	Inv 3178	441.79	4 Mar	Credit note	39.20
18 Mar	Inv 3229	150.39	16 Mar	Cash	424.12
20 Mar	Inv 3237	66.20	16 Mar	Discount	17.67
27 Mar	Inv 3250	551.29	30 Mar	Cash	415.20
			31 Mar	Bal c/d	767.88
		2,735.26			2,735.26

4.6 Activity solution

Step 1 Match each of the cash receipts and credit notes to the related invoice.

Gilde & Co

		£			£
20 Dec	Inv 2946	118.38	30 Jan	Credit note	172.48✓
28 Dec	Inv 2983	72.03✓	15 Feb	Cash	228.36✓
17 Jan	Inv 3029	228.36✓	28 Feb	Cash	72.03✓
25 Jan	Inv 3046	172.48✓	12 Mar	Cash	48.30✓
2 Feb	Inv 3103	48.30✓	14 Mar	Credit note	49.20✓
11 Feb	Inv 3135	69.02			
26 Feb	Inv 3157	159.27			
12 Mar	Inv 3204	49.20✓			
15 Mar	Inv 3221	49.20			
28 Mar	Inv 3252	169.39	31 Mar	Bal c/d	565.26
		1,135.63			1,135.63

Brandreth Ltd

		£			£	
3 Jan	Inv 2999	378.29✓	12 Jan	Cash	363.16 }	✓
12 Jan	Inv 3012	115.29✓	12 Jan	Discount	15.13 }	✓
26 Jan	Inv 3047	39.20✓	25 Feb	Cash	398.59 }	✓
13 Feb	Inv 3140	415.20✓	25 Feb	Discount	16.61 }	✓
18 Feb	Inv 3145	415.20✓	28 Feb	Credit note	162.41	✓
25 Feb	Inv 3156	162.41✓	28 Feb	Cash	115.29	✓
4 Mar	Inv 3178	441.79✓	4 Mar	Credit note	39.20	✓
18 Mar	Inv 3229	150.39	16 Mar	Cash	424.12 }	✓
20 Mar	Inv 3237	66.20	16 Mar	Discount	17.67 }	✓
27 Mar	Inv 3250	551.29	30 Mar	Cash	415.20	✓
			31 Mar	Bal c/d	767.88	
		2,735.26			2,735.26	

(Tutorial note: Brandreth Ltd is rather more complicated to analyse as cash discounts are being taken. However, as most of the cash payments have a discount shown on the same date, it should be reasonably clear that the cash payment and the discount should together be equal to the invoice value.*)*

Step 2 Analyse the remaining invoices according to their date.

Gilde & Co

		£
> 90 days	20 December	118.38
60 - 90 days		-
30 - 60 days	11 February	69.02
	26 February	159.27
		228.29
< 30 days	15 March	49.20
	28 March	169.39
		218.59

Brandreth Ltd

< 30 days	18 March	150.39
	20 March	66.20
	27 March	551.29
		767.88

Step 3 Prepare the aged analysis report.

Credit customer	*Total owing*	*Outstanding for:* *<30 days*	*30 - 60 days*	*60 - 90 days*	*>90 days*
	£	£	£	£	£
Gilde & Co	565.26	218.59	228.29	-	118.38
Brandreth Ltd	767.88	767.88	-	-	-
	1,333.14	986.47	228.29	-	118.38

In practice most of the debtors which are outstanding will have settled their accounts up to a particular date eg, up to the date of the last but one statement or last but two statements. Thus, only the invoices from these dates will be outstanding.

4.7 Control accounts

Definition Control accounts (also called total accounts) are used in accountancy as an arithmetic check on the accuracy and completeness of the balances in a ledger/s.

There can for example be control accounts for debtors, for creditors, for cash, for cost ledgers. These can be sub-divided further with each sub-division having its own control account.

Of particular concern in the management and control of debtors is the sales ledger control account (or several sales ledger control accounts if the sales ledger is sub-divided). As mentioned above it provides an arithmetic proof that the balances in the sales ledger/s are correct, in total. It provides an indication that all the postings to the accounts have been made correctly in terms of debits and credits (ie, increases and decreases) to the individual accounts. What it will not show is if an amount is posted to the wrong individual account. For example a sale to J.R. Cheslett & Co Ltd for £2,000 on credit could have been posted to the account of J. Chesterton & Sons Ltd in error. It would however pick up errors where debits had been posted as credits, and vice-versa.

It should be noted that control accounts are not necessarily part of the double entry book keeping system.

4.8 The sales ledger control account

Definition The account which checks, in total, the balances which appear in the sales ledger/ledgers.

A sales ledger control account could be constructed as follows: *(numbers have been invented for illustration purposes).*

Sales Ledger Control Account	£	£
Opening balances of debtors brought forward from last month		184,250
Add Credit sales for this month		420,750
		605,000
Less Cash received from debtors	162,000	
Discounts allowed to debtors	12,000	
Goods returned by debtors	20,000	(194,000)
Balance of debtors at this month end		**£411,000**

The £411,000 should agree with the total of the list of debtors extracted from their individual accounts which are kept in the sales ledger.

If the figures did not agree, investigations would have to take place to detect errors. This can apply to both handwritten and computerised systems. However because of the way in which computer systems are set up eg, cash received postings being dealt with as one batch and programmed to be deducted from the balance outstanding, errors tend to be less frequent.

Conclusion The preparation of an aged debtor analysis should be done at frequent intervals eg, monthly. It highlights problem customers, and in effect directs the energy and effort of the credit control function to the accounts that really need their attention. It provides a focus and forces them into action. Making good use of the aged analysis can provide an early warning of problems ahead, improve cash flow and reduce bad debts eg, by talking to a customer before a minor problem becomes a major problem via granting a temporary increase in the credit period.

5 COLLECTION OF OVERDUE DEBTS

5.1 Introduction

The longer a debt is allowed to run, the higher the probability of eventual default. Thus, a systematic progression of follow-up procedures is required, bearing in mind the risk of offending a valued customer to such an extent that their business is lost.

This usually involves the installation of a sound credit control and reminder system. The cost of not collecting debts within the credit period allowed could be argued to be either one of the following:

- The same as the cost which the selling business has to pay on any bank overdraft which it is using; or
- The rate of return which could be earned by the business with funds released by its debtors - ie, the 'opportunity cost'.

Definition An opportunity cost represents the advantage that has to be given up, in this particular case as a result of selling on credit and having to wait for payment.

5.2 Techniques for 'chasing' overdue debts include the following:

- **Reminder letters**

  These are often regarded as being a relatively poor way of obtaining payment, as many customers simply ignore them. Sending reminders by fax is usually more productive than simply using the normal postal service.

  A system of reminder letters could be along the following lines, in which a series of letters could be used. The first letter being polite, courteous and to the point and the final letter using much stronger language. The first letter could be sent through the post or by fax and could also be computer generated.

  A typical first letter could be drafted, as follows:

Leswik & Co PLC
4 Westcroft Court
Somewhere South
HONTINGTUM

The Accounts Dept
Messrs Rob Yu Ltd
2 Hardup Row
Debt Dodgers Hide
NOWHERE

1st April 20X1

Dear Sir or Madam

We would like to point out that our invoice number XLC0171212 dated 19th Ja nuary, 20X1 for £12,100 has now been outstanding for over two months and we would be pleased if you would settle it within the next fourteen days.

If there are any problems concerning this invoice, will you please contact Billy Nile in our accounts department.

Yours faithfully,
Can Yu Paye
Credit Controller

Activity

It is now 4th June 20X1, and after sending another reminder Messrs Rob Yu Ltd have still not paid the above invoice. They have not contacted the accounts department, as suggested.

Required

Draft a final letter, and then see how it compares with our suggested solution

Activity solution

Leswik & Co PLC
4 Westcroft Court
Somewhere South
HONTINGTUM

Final letter

5th June, 20X1

The Accounts Dept
Messrs Rob Yu Ltd
2 Hardup Row
Debt Dodgers Hide
NOWHERE

Dear Sir or Madam,

Our invoice number XLC0171212 dated 19th January, 20X1 for £12,100 is still outstanding despite repeated reminders.

If this amount is not received within the next seven days, it is with regret that we will have to put this matter in the hands of our solicitors.

Yours faithfully,

A.N. Other
Credit Control Officer

- **Telephone calls**

These are more expensive than reminder letters but where large sums are involved they can be an efficient way of speeding payment. You will also find out why the debtors have not paid, and it could even be your fault eg, they could be waiting for a credit note because they agreed to accept materials of a quality which was lower than that which was ordered. The impact of using this method should not be underestimated. It is quite cost effective and can produce results.

Some computerised systems, in addition to producing aged lists of debtors, (see next chapter) also print out the telephone number of debts over a certain age. This is rather like saying to the credit control department/accounts department, 'ring them up as soon as you can, and find out the reasons why they have not paid'. In such cases it may be possible to at least get a payment on account and sort out how and when the balance will be forthcoming.

In addition to cash flow problems and acceptance of a different quality, it could well be the case that the goods were returned in whole or part, or the invoice was wrongly priced, or the invoice had gone to the wrong customer.

- **Relationships**

  It can work to your advantage if you establish a good working relationship with your customer's accounts department. This may ensure that any payment problems are quickly resolved. If a bond of mutual trust can be built up and you know the people in the customer's accounts department, when you have cash flow problems it may be possible to get them to pay you a little quicker. If they, on the other hand, have problems they may talk to you and you may be able to help them.

- **Charging interest on overdue accounts**

  Some companies do use and this find that it does speed up their payments. However, it can pose a problem where interest is charged but when the payment is received it is for the amount excluding the interest.

- **Withholding supplies**

  Putting customers on the 'stop list' for further orders or spare parts can encourage rapid settlement of debts. However, this type of action can force those customers into taking their business elsewhere. It can damage goodwill and destroy the supplier–customer relationship.

- **Debt collection agencies and trade associations**

  These offer debt collection services on a fixed fee basis or on 'no collection no charge' terms. The quality of service provided varies considerably and care should be taken in selecting an agent. Using a bad agent could seriously damage goodwill, and the word may get around and be off-putting for both existing and prospective customers.

- **Contra**

  You buy goods or services on credit from your debtors (ie, customers) and off-set what you owe them against what they owe you!

- **Insure against bad debts**

  Get someone else to carry the risk, particularly if non-payment would cause serious cash flow problems. This can be expensive, but it is sometimes foolish not to.

- **Legal action**

  This is often seen as a last resort. A solicitor's letter often prompts payment and many cases do not go to court. Court action is usually not cost effective but it can discourage other customers from delaying payment.

5.3 Statements for credit sales customers

Definition A statement will include details of the balance outstanding which has been brought forward from the last statement, plus details of invoices for goods supplied on credit, less the credit notes, discounts and cash received, to compute the balance outstanding at the end of the period. Many companies do use them, and send them out at the end of each month.

Many customers wait until they receive a statement before they pay and use them, in part, as a double check on the amount owing. The statement may also have a remittance advice attached. This gives details of the balance outstanding and should be detatched by the customer and sent back to the company concerned together with the payment.

The use of statements has been found to be valuable aid to credit control. In fact, some customers will not pay unless they do receive a statement! Several years ago in the UK there was a move to discontinue the use of statements by a number of companies. This move did not meet with the approval of credit customers, and so today the use of statements continues to be an integral and important part of credit control systems used throughout the UK. However, it should be noted that if the frequency in sending out statements was increased, this could well lead to the earlier settlement of accounts by quite a number of customers. However, the benefits of such actions would have to be weighed up against the costs involved.

Conclusion You should, by now have acquired a good working knowledge of the ways in which you can chase/recover debts/overdue debts. The recovery method which is adopted should be appropriate to the circumstances of the individual case. For example legal action is considered to be the last resort, possibly because it can be expensive and also it is sure to damage goodwill.

From personal experience I have observed that polite contacts via letter or telephone can have the desired effect, but so can strong language! I have also observed credit control stickers 'pay up or else!' attached to reminders, going straight into the waste paper basket! Thus, it can be seen that selecting the most appropriate method is by no means an easy task, and that it should envelop with experience and by getting to know your customers.

6 THE EFFECT OF BANKRUPTCY AND INSOLVENCY ON ORGANISATIONS

6.1 Introduction

For this unit you are required to have an elementary understanding of the effect of bankruptcy and insolvency. If a potential bad debt is so significant to the cash flow (and thus, possibly its own survival) of a business, its management may have to take action that may result in the insolvency (if a company) or the bankruptcy (if an individual, sole trader or partnership) of the debtor in order to realise some part of the debt. It is important for all concerned to appreciate the effects of such an action.

6.2 The liquidation of a company

The liquidation of a company may be by a compulsory liquidation, a members' voluntary liquidation or a creditors' voluntary liquidation. Alternatively an administration order may be brought which protects a company against a petition for winding up and gives it breathing space for an administrator to sort out its financial affairs.

Definition Winding up, or liquidation, is concerned with bringing the business and existence of the company to an end, although dissolution, as such, follows the completion of winding up. It is the company law equivalent of bankruptcy in the case of sole traders and partners, although the parallels are by no means precise.

There are several reasons why winding up may be sought eg, the company may simply wish to cease trading, a minority shareholder may resort to winding up as a remedy against the majority, or a creditor, secured or unsecured, may wish to protect his position, to ensure that the company does not disable itself from repaying him. A creditor may wish to apply for an administration order instead in which case the company cannot be wound up while the administration order is in effect.

6.3 Methods of dissolution

A company is a creation of the law. It can only be dissolved and its name removed from the register of companies when the proper legal procedure has been completed. A company cannot generally be dissolved until its assets have been realised and then applied in payment of its debts (in the correct order) and any surplus distributed among its members according to their entitlement to participate in a return of capital. That is the process of liquidation or winding up.

Liquidation begins either by court order (**compulsory liquidation**) or by the members of the company passing a resolution to wind up (**voluntary liquidation**). Voluntary liquidation is of two types (members' and creditors' voluntary winding-up).

Conclusion The choice of method of dissolution may be shown in diagrammatic form as follows:

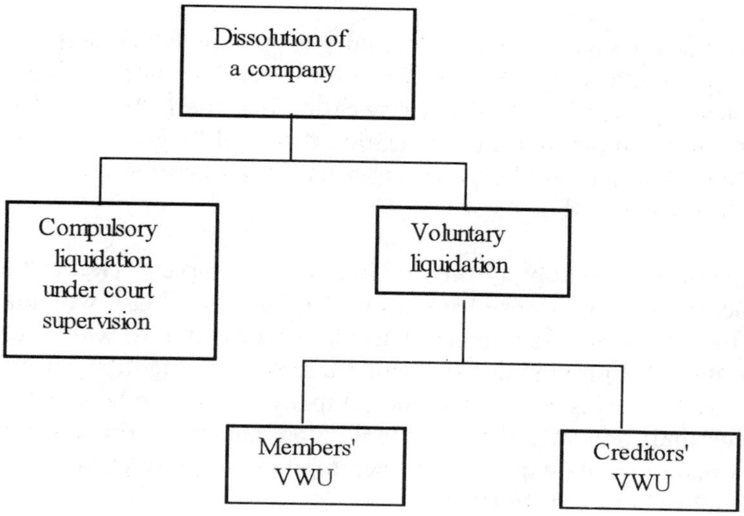

6.4 Compulsory liquidation

To commence a compulsory liquidation a **petition** is presented to the court ie, the Chancery Division of the High Court or, if the company's issued and paid up share capital does not exceed £120,000, the petition may be presented to the County Court within whose district the company has its registered office.

The two most significant grounds for such a petition are:

- the company is unable to pay its debts; and/or
- the court is of the opinion that it is just and equitable that the company should be wound up.

It is the former we are concerned with here.

A company is deemed to be unable to pay its debts if any one of three circumstances is shown to exist:

(a) the petitioner has delivered to the company at its registered office a written demand for payment of a debt owing to him exceeding £750 and within the ensuing three weeks the company has neither paid the debt nor given security for its payment;

(b) judgement has been obtained against the company for debt and execution ie, the attempt to obtain payment out of the company's assets remains unsatisfied;

(c) the court is satisfied after taking account of contingent and prospective as well as immediate liabilities that the company is unable to pay its debts.

Where the petition is based on an unsatisfied demand for payment the court will not make an order if the company denies liability and appears to have a reasonable defence to the claim.

When the matter is before the court the company and other interested parties, such as creditors other than the petitioner, are entitled to be heard. A secured creditor or an assignee of the debt may present a petition, so may a contingent or prospective creditor. If some creditors oppose the petition the court is likely to prefer the views of the creditors to whom in aggregate the largest amount is owing - but much depends on the particular facts.

A petition may be presented by various parties, including the company itself, its directors or its shareholders; however for this Unit we shall generally assume it is presented by a (trade) creditor.

6.5 Procedure for a compulsory liquidation

A compulsory liquidation is commenced by presenting a petition which sets out the grounds on which the petitioner (eg, a creditor) seeks to obtain an order of the court winding up the company. His petition must be accompanied by an affidavit swearing that the facts set out in the petition are true. When the court issues the petition a court hearing date will be given. The petitioner must be able to prove at the court hearing that the grounds set out in his petition are true and convince the court that a winding up order should be made.

The petitioner will have to serve a copy of the petition on the company. He must also advertise the petition to enable other interested parties to be aware that he is seeking a winding up order and to attend the hearing if they so wish. As the advertisement of a petition to wind a company up could damage its reputation the rules provide that he cannot advertise the petition for seven days after he has served it on the company. This is to enable the company to apply to have the petition struck out if there are in fact no grounds on which the court could grant an order. The advertisement must also be at least seven days before the date of the court hearing to give those persons who wish to attend the hearing sufficient notice to be able to attend.

Thus there will be a period of time between the issue of the petition and the court hearing at which the court may or may not make the order. The company is in a position where it may be wound up but this is not certain until the hearing. Thus certain rules apply to this 'interim' period.

(a) the company or any creditor or member may apply for a stay of any execution of a judgement against the company and of any legal proceedings in which it is either plaintiff or defendant; and

(b) a standstill on any disposition of assets or transfer of shares (unless approved by the court) from the date of commencement of the liquidation (if an order is made).

(c) Any distress or execution put into force during this period is void, if an order is later made.

6.6 Effect of an order for compulsory liquidation

If an order is made it is retrospective in effect to the date on which the petition was presented which becomes the **date of commencement** of liquidation (unless the company has already gone into voluntary liquidation at an earlier date).

The Official Receiver (an official of the Department of Trade) becomes provisional liquidator and remains in office until someone else is appointed liquidator. (It is important not to confuse this person with a receiver appointed under a fixed charge just because the word 'Receiver' appears in his title).

Among the **legal consequences** of an order for compulsory winding up are:

(a) the company must cease business except as necessary to wind up;

(b) the directors' powers are assumed by the liquidator;

(c) all floating charges crystallise;

(d) all invoices, letters, orders must show the company is being wound up;

(e) no legal proceedings may be started or commenced with out leave of the court;

(f) the effective dismissal of the directors and employees;

(g) The Official Receiver **may require** officers of the company (present or within the previous year) or any persons employed by the company (present or within the previous year) and any persons who have taken part in the formation of the company at any time within the previous year to submit to him a **statement of affairs** within twenty-one days of the date of receipt of notice requiring the statement to be supplied. Anyone who fails without reasonable excuse to comply is liable to a fine. The Official Receiver may release anyone from the duty or extend the period for compliance.

Definition The statement must be in the prescribed form, verified by affidavit of the person making it, and include:

- details of the company's assets, debts and liabilities;
- names and addresses of the creditors;
- details of securities held by creditors; and
- any other information required by the rules.

(h) Under S132 IA86 the Official Receiver is under a duty to investigate:

- if the company has failed, the causes of the failure; and
- generally, the promotion, formation, business dealings and affairs of the company;

and make a report to the court if he thinks fit.

(i) The Official Receiver or liquidator **may** apply to the court for public examination of any person being an officer, liquidator, administrator, receiver or manager **or** anyone who has been concerned in the management, formation or promotion of the company. The purpose is to obtain information about what has happened and the whereabouts of any remaining assets.

A person so summoned who fails to attend the public examination is guilty of contempt of court and the court may issue a warrant for his arrest and seizure of any books, records, money or goods in his possession if there is no reasonable excuse for his failure to attend.

(j) The Official Receiver **may** summon meetings of the members and creditors to choose a liquidator.

If meetings are called the creditors and members may nominate a person to be liquidator and if different people are nominated the creditors' nominee will generally take office. The liquidator must be a qualified insolvency practitioner.

(k) The Official Receiver as liquidator may apply to the Registrar of Companies for early dissolution of the company where it appears to him that there are insufficient assets to cover the costs of winding up **and** the company's affairs do not require further investigation.

(l) At the conclusion of the liquidation the liquidator must call a meeting and report.

Conclusion The stages of compulsory liquidation can be shown as follows:

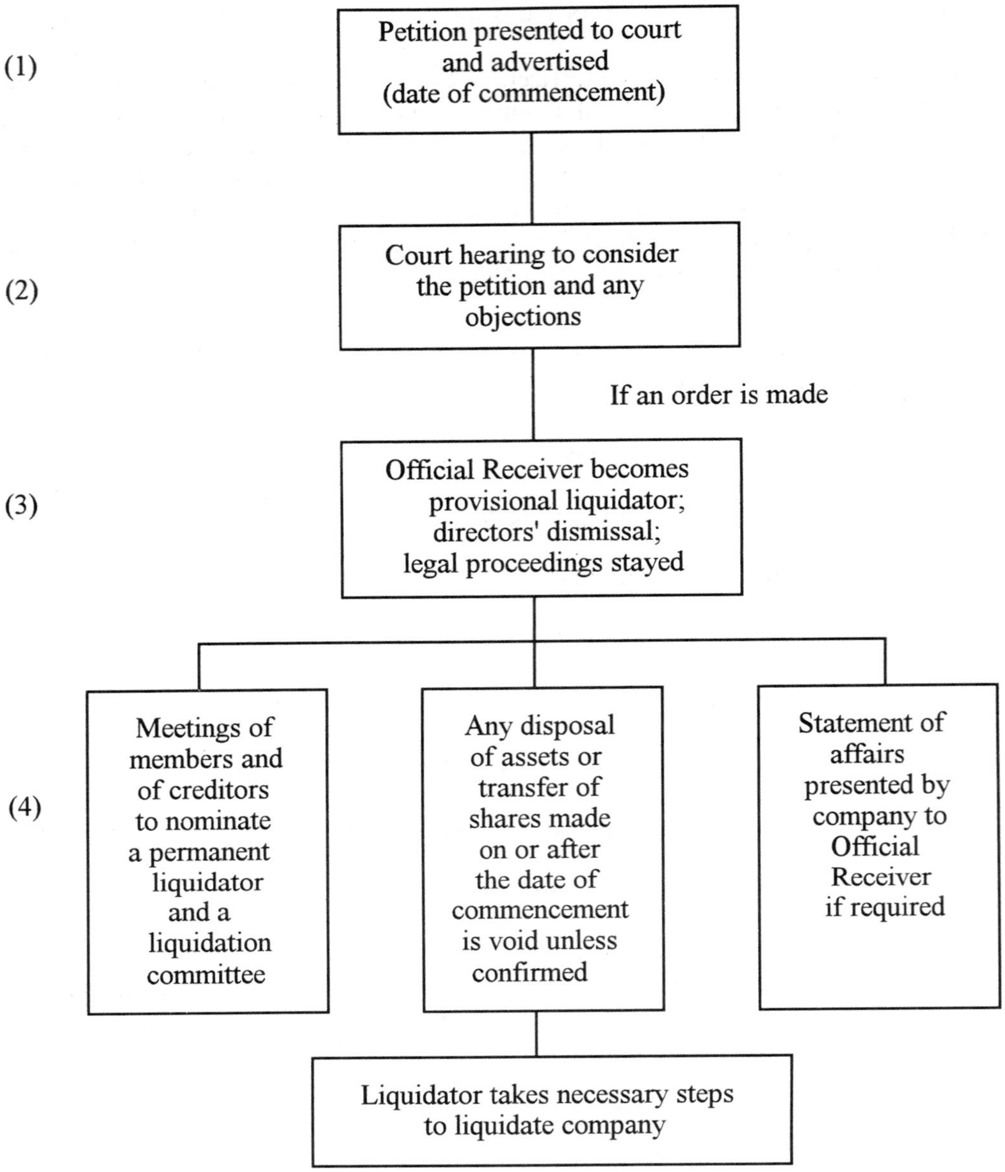

6.7 Voluntary liquidation

Definition A voluntary liquidation is effected and has its **commencement** from the **passing in general meeting** of the company of a **resolution** for voluntary winding up. The resolution may be of any of three types.

(a) **An ordinary resolution** is passed when **the articles provide** that the company is to be wound up when a specified purpose has been achieved or a specified period has elapsed. In practice articles do not usually contain such provisions.

(b) An **extraordinary resolution** may be passed stating that **by reason of** the company's **liabilities** it cannot carry on its business and should be wound up. This type of resolution requires only fourteen days notice because in a situation of insolvency the decision to wind up may have become urgent. This then becomes a **creditors' voluntary winding-up** because the company is technically insolvent.

(c) A **special resolution** specifies no grounds for winding up and is used in any other case such as a solvent liquidation. This then becomes a **member's voluntary winding-up** because the company is technically solvent.

It is the second of these that is particularly relevant here.

6.8 Creditors' voluntary winding up

The choice between a **members' voluntary winding up** in which the creditors take no part since they may expect to be paid their debts in full and a **creditors' voluntary winding up**, which is effectively controlled by the creditors, depends on whether or not the directors are prepared to assume the responsibility of making a **statutory declaration of solvency.** In this, they must declare that having made full enquiry (a statement of assets and liabilities is attached) they are of the opinion that the company will be able to pay its debts in full within a specified period not exceeding twelve months.

If the directors do **not** make a **statutory declaration** the liquidation proceeds as a **creditors' voluntary liquidation**:

(a) A creditors' meeting must be held within fourteen days of the winding up resolution. A statement of affairs, verified by affidavit by at least some of the directors, must be laid before the creditors' meeting over which one of the directors must preside.

(b) The members may have appointed a liquidator at the meeting which decided to wind up the company. If so he is entitled to act until the creditors' meeting, but with limited powers. Except in emergency (eg, in respect of perishable goods) he cannot exercise most of his powers without the court's consent, plus they have power to call a creditors' meeting).

The creditors may nominate the liquidator and if this person is different from the person selected by the members the creditors' nominee becomes liquidator. However, any director, member or creditor may apply to the court for the appointment of the members' nominee.

The liquidator must be a qualified insolvency practitioner.

A liquidator may be removed either by the general meeting or by the creditors' meeting. However, special rules apply if the liquidator was appointed by the court.

(c) The creditors may, if they think fit, appoint a 'liquidation committee' of not more than five people. The members may also appoint five people to act as members of the committee. However, if the creditors object to the people selected by the members they cannot act unless given leave by the court.

The purpose of the liquidation committee is to have a body which represents both members and creditors to keep a check on the liquidator and to which the liquidator can turn for guidance.

(d) If no liquidator is appointed the directors cannot exercise their powers except in the specified circumstances.

(e) On appointment of a liquidator the directors' powers cease except so far as the liquidation committee (or the creditors if there is no committee) sanction.

(f) The liquidator must call separate meetings of both members **and** creditors every year.

(g) The liquidator must also call meetings of members and creditors when the company's affairs are fully wound up and send accounts to the Registrar who publishes notice in the London Gazette.

Conclusion The commencement of creditors' voluntary liquidation can be summarised as follows:

Creditors' VWU

1. General meeting of members to:
   (a) resolve to wind up
   (b) nominate a liquidator
   (c) appoint members (up to five) for liquidation committee

2. Creditors' meeting to:
   (a) appoint a liquidator
   (b) appoint creditors (up to five) for liquidation committee
   (c) consider directors' financial statement

Law provides that payments of debts should be made *pari passu* (ie, equally within each class) after allowing for secured creditors' rights and subject to the duty to pay all creditors before distributions are made to shareholders, whose rights will be set out in the articles.

6.9 Activity

James is a creditor of XYZ Ltd, a company with an issued share capital of £100,000. He wishes to present a petition for the compulsory liquidation of XYZ Ltd. To which court would this petition be presented?

6.10 Activity solution

The County Court within whose district XYZ Ltd has its registered office.

6.11 Control and realisation of assets

The liquidator is under a duty to take control of the company's assets, including its business undertaking if it is still trading, and to convert those assets into money with which to pay the liquidation expenses, discharge the company's debts and, if any surplus then remains, to distribute it to members in accordance with their entitlement.

The assets of the company do not vest in the liquidator unless the court by order vests specific property in him. They are, however, under his control. The company's contracts existing at the commencement of the liquidation remain in force unless by provisions of the contracts they are terminated on liquidation. Any new contracts which the liquidator may make are the company's contracts and he has no personal liability on them.

6.12 Liquidators' powers

Law gives liquidators extensive powers, which include the following:

(a) Exercisable **with** sanction of members **or** liquidation committee:

- Pay any class of creditor in full;

- Enter into a compromise or arrangement with creditors;
- Compromise claims to which the company is entitled.

(b) Exercisable without sanction in voluntary liquidation and court's sanction in compulsory liquidation:

- Bring or defend legal proceedings. In a compulsory winding up leave of the court is required to commence or proceed with a legal action. If liquidation is voluntary the court may order a stay;
- Carry on the company's business.

(c) Exercisable without sanction in any winding up:

- Sell the company's property;
- Execute documents;
- Borrow on the security of the company's assets;
- Do all such things as may be necessary for the winding up of the company's affairs;
- Make a call on unpaid or partly paid shares if the assets of the company are insufficient to meet liabilities.

In addition, the liquidator has the power to apply to court to set aside or to avoid certain transactions by the company which will result in more assets being available to pay the company's debts.

In addition, the liquidator may ask the court to make an order that particular people contribute to the company's assets if they have been:

(a) fraudulently trading; or
(b) wrongfully trading.

The following items are not available to a liquidator:

(a) Money held on deposit for mail order customers.
(b) Money given to the company for a specific purpose and held on a resulting trust.
(c) Property over which the vendor has reserved title pending payment.

6.13 Activity

Andrew is a creditor of ABC Ltd, being owed £800. Andrew delivered a written demand for the £800 to ABC Ltd's registered office a month ago. There has been no response from ABC Ltd. What is Andrew entitled to do?

6.14 Activity solution

He may petition the court for the compulsory liquidation of ABC Ltd on the grounds of the company being unable to pay its debts.

6.15 Proof of debts

The liquidator must establish which claims against the company are valid. The creditors therefore must produce sufficient evidence to the liquidator to **prove** that their debts are payable by the company. The insolvency rules made under the Insolvency Act 1986 set out the procedure to be followed in proving debts. Basically this procedure consists of setting out the details of the debt allegedly owed which in a compulsory liquidation must be done in writing and signed by the creditor or his agent. The rules allow a liquidator in a voluntary liquidation to require a creditor to produce the same details in written form.

Proving a debt against a company is much the same as proving any debt. Thus, normal rules of enforceability such as whether the debt is statute-barred are applicable. In addition it is possible to set off certain debts owed to the company by a person against those owed by the company to that person.

6.16 Application of assets

The assets of the company are applied in the following order:

(a) Costs of winding up;

(b) Some categories of creditor may have a priority claim to be paid out of **particular assets** eg, a secured creditor (in this context it means a creditor with a fixed charge);

(c) Preferential creditors (examples are some part of the debt owed to the Inland Revenue or Customs and Excise);

Definition Preferential debts are unsecured debts which must be paid in priority to other unsecured debts.

Broadly they fall into two categories ie,:

(i) taxes and other sums due to public authorities; and

(ii) wages and other money sums due to employees.

In both cases there are limits on the amounts due to these creditors which are preferential.

(d) Creditors having floating charges;

(e) Ordinary unsecured creditors;

Ordinary debts include among others any sums owing for taxes or wages which are not preferential or exceed the limit of preference. Ordinary debts rank equally by value for participation in assets remaining after preferential debts have been paid in full.

(f) Deferred debts;

Definition Debts owing to members of the company as members (but not as loan creditors for money lent) are **deferred debts** which are paid only after ordinary debts have been paid in full but before share capital is repaid.

The important case here is dividends declared but unpaid at the commencement of winding up.

(g) Distribution of any remaining assets to members according to their rights under the articles.

6.17 The alternative to winding up - administration orders

This is another new procedure to enable an attempt to be made to rescue a company in financial difficulty by placing its affairs in the hands of an administrator. While the order is in force the leave of the court is needed before any winding-up proceedings can be taken or any process, charge, hire-purchase or other agreement can be enforced. Thus, the idea is that the granting of an administration order will 'buy time' for the company and give a procedure similar to that of receivership used by secured creditors to secure the company in financial difficulties.

An application may be made to court for an order by petition presented by the company, the directors, or a creditor (or creditors), or any combination of them.

Once the petition has been presented:

(a) **No** resolution may be passed to wind up the company. However, a petition may be presented for a compulsory winding up or an administrative receiver may be appointed.

(b) A **moratorium** is imposed on the company's debts until such time as the court decides to make the order or dismiss the petition. This means that creditors may not:

- Take any steps to enforce any security over the company's property.
- Repossess goods under a hire-purchase agreement, leasing agreement, retention of title or conditional sale agreement.
- Commence legal proceedings or levy executions or distress.

However, these actions may be taken with the court's permission.

6.18 Consequences of administration order

If the court makes an order:

(a) The prohibitions against enforcing securities, repossessing goods etc. continue.

(b) Every invoice, order or letter issued must contain the administrator's name and a statement that the company is being managed by him.

(c) Any petition for winding up the company is dismissed.

(d) Any administrative receiver must vacate office. In addition, any receiver must also vacate office if the administrator requires him to do so.

Thus, the holders of a floating charge may feel less protected by an administration order than by appointing their own administrative receiver. However, there are other reasons why they may prefer an administration order, in particular the wide powers of an administrator.

(e) A qualified insolvency practitioner is appointed to administer the affairs of the company. The administrator is given the same wide powers as an administrative receiver (see above) to manage the business and property of the company, including the power to bring and defend legal proceedings, sell assets, borrow money, insure and appoint agents. In case of difficulty the administrator may apply to the court for directions.

In addition, the administrator has the following powers:

(a) property subject to a floating charge may be disposed of as if unencumbered;

(b) property subject to a fixed charge and property held under a hire-purchase agreement, conditional sale agreement or lease may be disposed of providing the court is satisfied that the disposal is likely to promote the administration. The court must order that the proceeds of sale be used to discharge the liability of the secured creditors or the owners of the goods.

6.19 Carrying out the order

(a) Once the order has been made the administrator must send notice to the company forthwith, to all creditors within twenty-eight days, and to the Registrar of Companies within fourteen days. (He may be fined for default.)

(b) He must also require a statement of affairs from officers (current and past) employees or independent contractors (current or in the past year) or persons who have taken part in the company's formation within the year before the order. This statement must show the company's assets, debts and liabilities, creditors' names and addresses and details of securities held by them, and be provided within twenty-one days of the date on which it was required, unless the administrator extends the time period.

(c) The administrator must, within three months of the order, send a statement of his proposals to the Registrar and to all creditors. In addition he must send a copy of his proposals to all members, or he may publish a notice giving members an address from which they can obtain copies instead of sending copies to members.

(d) A copy of the proposal must be presented to a meeting of creditors at which they shall decide whether to approve them. They may only make modifications to the proposals with the administrators consent.

(e) The administrator must report the results of the meeting to the Registrar and to the court. If the meeting did not approve the proposals the court may dismiss the order or make such provisions as it thinks fit.

If the proposals are approved the administrator must carry out the proposals as stated. If he wishes to make any 'substantial' revisions he must call a further meeting of creditors and obtain their approval.

(g) Any creditor or member may apply to the court on the ground that the company's affairs, business and property are being managed in a manner which is unfairly prejudicial to the interests of its creditors or members generally, or of some part of its creditors or members (including at least himself) and that any actual or proposed act or omission of the administrator is or would be so prejudicial. The court may make such order as it thinks fit. In particular:

- regulate the future management by the administrator of the company;
- require the administrator to do or not to do specified acts of which the applicant has complained;
- require meetings of creditors or members to be called; and
- discharge the order. However, if the application is made more than twenty eight days after the proposal is approved the court cannot prejudice or prevent the implementation of the proposals.

The administrator may apply to the court for discharge at any time. He must make such an application when it appears that the purpose of the order has been achieved or is incapable of being achieved.

Conclusion The purpose of an administration order is to place the company in the hands of an administrator for a period in order to attempt to allow the company to recover rather that winding it up.

6.20 Activity

A company finds itself in the position of being unable to pay its debts. Why might an administration order be more appropriate than a winding up order?

6.21 Activity solution

An administrative order effectively gives a company a breathing space in which to attempt to put its affairs in order. Therefore an administrative order might be more appropriate than a winding up order if it is possible that the company or any part of it may survive as a going concern.

7 PERSONAL BANKRUPTCY

7.1 Introduction

Bankruptcy, or personal insolvency, is covered by the Insolvency Act 1986. The legislation provides a procedure which must be followed if an individual is to enter bankruptcy.

7.2 Who can petition?

The three main categories of person who can petition for bankruptcy are

(i) a creditor, or group of creditors, owed more than £750;
(ii) the Director of Public Prosecutions, if a criminal bankruptcy order has been made against an individual;
(iii) the debtor himself.

In any situation, the petition is presented either in the High Court or certain County Courts (not all County Courts have bankruptcy jurisdiction)

7.3 Creditor's Petition

The creditor(s) must prove that the debtor is unable to pay the sum owed. This is usually demonstrated by the creditor issuing a formal written demand for the amount due, which then remains unpaid for three weeks. The statutory demand is normally served personally on the debtor by the creditor.

At least 14 days must elapse between the service of the petition and the Court hearing, although the time may be shortened, for example if the debtor has absconded.

7.4 Debtor's Petition

A debtor's petition must contain a statement by the debtor that he is unable to pay his debts and a request that a bankruptcy order be made against him. The petition must be accompanied by a statement of affairs, setting out the debtor's assets and his various types of liability. The Court may demand further investigation of the debtor's financial affairs by an insolvency practitioner before proceeding with the hearing.

Once a bankruptcy petition has been presented, regardless of by whom, the Court can prevent anyone from taking further legal action against the debtor.

7.5 The Bankruptcy Order

The order must state the date of presentation of the petition and the date and time of the making of the order. It will instruct the bankrupt to meet the Official Receiver to whom a copy of the order will also be sent.

7.6 Statement of Affairs and Public Examination

In the absence of a trustee in bankruptcy, the Official Receiver will always act. In all cases at the outset the Official Receiver has a duty to investigate the bankrupt's affairs. The bankrupt has a duty to produce a statement of affairs. The Official Receiver may, and on the application of at least half in value of the creditors must, conduct a public examination of the bankrupt's affairs. Where a public examination is held, the bankrupt is on oath to answer any questions put to him by the Official Receiver or the creditors (or the Director of Public Prosecutions in the case of a criminal bankruptcy).

7.7 Reports to Creditors

The Official Receiver must, at least once after the making of the order, send a report on the bankrupt's affairs to the creditors.

7.8 The Trustee in Bankruptcy

Where there are assets likely to be realised for the benefit of creditors, a trustee other than the Official Receiver will be appointed. The trustee must be a licensed insolvency practitioner, and may be appointed by the creditors, the Court or the D.T.I.

The duties of the trustee are to realise the assets of the bankrupt, distribute dividends to creditors, and keep then informed as to progress (via a creditors' committee). The trustee has considerable powers to investigate the affairs of the bankrupt and obtain possession of his assets to this effect, including the right to claim such part of the bankrupt's income as exceeds the amount necessary for meeting the reasonable and domestic needs of the bankrupt and his family. The trustee also receives claims from creditors, who may, as in corporate insolvency, be secured, preferential or unsecured.

7.9 Closure of the Bankruptcy

When all assets have been realised and all creditors' claims agreed the bankruptcy can move towards closure. At this point, the trustee produces draft final accounts and convenes a meeting of creditors, at which he is released from office.

7.10 Discharge of the Bankrupt

The Insolvency Act 1986 provides for automatic discharge of the bankrupt after three years, although this may be suspended by the court.

8 THE ROLE OF AUDIT IN THE MANAGEMENT AND CONTROL OF DEBTORS

8.1 An introduction to auditing

'An Auditor is a watchdog, not a blood hound' (Kingston Cotton Mills case: 1896)

'An AAT student is a terrier not a greyhound!'

8.2 Various classes of audit

Statutory, eg, Limited companies, Building societies etc.
Private firms (by letters of appointment)
Trust accounts
Partnerships (partnership agreement)
Internal audit (employees of the company/firm)

8.3 The objectives of an audit

Verify and report upon the financial state of an organisation
(True and fair view)

Detect errors and fraud **Prevent errors and fraud**

Errors and fraud can take place in relation to debtors eg, undisclosed debtors, cash from debtors being misappropriated, fraudulent credit notes, fictitious bad debts etc.

A knowledge of basic documents is very important, ie, invoices, statements, credit notes, goods received notes, orders, contracts, remittance advice notes etc.

8.4 An outline of the work of an auditor (VEREC or Verec)

Verify the *existence, ownership* and *basis of valuation* of the assets eg, fixed assets and current assets, such as debtors, and ensure that the liabilities are fully and accurately disclosed, eg, see whether or not the provision for bad debts is fair and reasonable.

Examine (VOUCH) vouchers and any other evidence that may be required to prove that the entries in the books of account are complete and authentic. In the case of debtors this would include orders received, copy invoices, credit notes, remittance advices etc.

Report to the owners/shareholders whether the balance sheet shows a true and fair view of the affairs, and the profit and loss account a true and fair view of the profit or loss for the financial period under review. Debtors could be circularised in whole or part to confirm their balances.

Enquire as to the *authority* for transactions and see that all benefits which should have been accounted for have in fact been received. For example the authority to issue credit notes or receive and account for the cash received from debtors, or to write-off a debt as bad. The aim being to see that bad debts are only written off on the basis of realistic appraisal of all known factors.

Check the arithmetical accuracy of the books of account eg, via control accounts mentioned earlier on in this chapter.

8.5 Internal control and internal check

In order to achieve its objectives, auditing depends to a great extent on assessing the adequacy of the system of internal control, which incorporates those of internal check and internal audit.

Internal control

Definition 'not only internal check and internal audit but the whole system of controls, financial or otherwise, established by the management in order to carry on the business of the company in an orderly manner, safeguard its assets and secure as far as possible the accuracy and reliability of its records.'

Internal check

Definition 'the checks on day-to-day transactions which operate continuously as part of the routine system whereby the work of one person is proved independently or is complementary to the work of another, the object being the prevention or early detection of errors or fraud.'

Internal audit

Definition 'a view of operations and records, sometimes continuous undertaken within a business by specially assigned staff'.

The auditor would look at the systems which have been set up to account for and control debtors. Such systems should ensure that fraud can only take place via collusion and the abuse of delegated authority.

8.6 Auditing in depth

Used by the auditor, in order to assess the efficiency of the system of internal control.

It involves tracing a transaction through its various stages from origin to conclusion, examining at each stage and observing the incidence of internal check and the delegated authority.

8.7 Errors and fraud

Errors may be classified as follows:

- **Errors of omission**—transaction wholly or partly unrecorded
- **Errors of commission**—transaction wholly or partly incorrectly recorded.
- **Clerical errors**—eg, posting to the wrong account.
- **Errors of principle**—wrong accounting treatment
- **Compensating errors**—one which is counter-balanced by another.

Examples of fraud

- 'Teeming and lading' one account set off against another.
- Fictitious returns, allowances and bad debts etc.
- Collusion, eg, between cashier and ledger clerk in manipulating accounts.

Manipulation to disclose a false position:

- Suppression of invoices
- Fictitious purchases and sales
- Window dressing/creative accounting.

8.8 Authority

One of the keywords relating to auditing is 'authority'. Authority is particularly important in the areas of internal control, internal check and internal audit. The use of delegated authority to various personnel limits what they can and cannot do eg, signing cheques, counter-signing cheques, placing contracts or orders etc. The delegated authority relating to the management and control of debtors could include:

Cash from debtors

- receiving cash from debtors sent to the company/organisation, or via sales persons.
- paying the cash into the bank
- writing up the cash book and sales ledger
- having the keys or duplicate keys to the safe

Vetting

- vetting applicants for credit
- checking orders/credit limits and giving the go-ahead for the supply of the goods or service.

Documentation

- preparation of and the issue of invoices and credit notes
- issue of delivery notes/despatch notes/goods returned notes
- the safe custody of unused stocks of documents eg, invoices, credit notes etc.

Others

- writing OFF bad debts
- awarding cash discounts

Conclusion The audit function does not have a role to play in the control and management of working capital ie, debtors (as described) but also stock and cash. The auditor can be external or internal. Either way, they both have a part to play eg, ensuring that systems of internal control are working to their satisfaction. Debtors do tend to involve a hefty investment and this is why it is so important to ensure that errors and fraud are avoided. Audit tends to keep staff on their toes and acts as a moral deterrent.

What has been covered within this section on auditing applies also to the management of cash and the management of stocks. it is however, outside the scope of this text to go into greater detail.

9 CHAPTER SUMMARY

9.1 The costs of administering the credit control function include:

Vetting applicants; recording systems eg, at point of sale, sales ledger work, cash from debtors etc; chasing slow payers.

The additional relevant costs of any proposed change in the volume of credit sales should be compared with the marginal profit which results from the proposed change.

9.2 Settlement discounts

Cash discounts for prompt payment are used to speed up payments from debtors. There are, however a number of points which should be noted relating to their use, which are as follows:

- Why give settlement discounts when the debtor would pay up anyway within a reasonable time?
- What happens to customer goodwill if settlement discounts are offered to certain customers and not others?
- A small percentage settlement discount does tend to have a high effective annual rate of interest (see 5.2).

9.3 Aged list of debtors

Within the credit control department it is common to prepare a list, showing the age of the debtors which are outstanding. This eliminates the averaging effect of the ratio method.

Example:

Aged Debtors List of Les Co Ltd as at 31.12.20X4

	Total Current	*1 month Overdue*	*2 month overdue*	*3 months and more overdue*
	£000	£000	£000	£000
Customers				
Area 1				
Area 2				
Area 3				
TOTAL				
%				

Debtors which are more than 3 months overdue would be separately listed, with details of what action has been taken to collect them.

This is one of the internal sources of credit control information, and regarded as a very important one. It is widely used and can be prepared by any business large or small. It can be prepared by hand or by computer.

The individual sales ledger accounts also provide a valuable source of relevant information eg, how the customer has conducted the accounts, changes in payment patterns, keeping within the credit limits set etc.

9.4 Control accounts

Another useful internal aid which can be used for credit control purposes is the construction of sales ledger control accounts (also called total accounts). Although not necessarily part of the double entry bookkeeping system, this provides an arithmetic proof on the accuracy of the sales ledger balances. The control account/s should agree with the total/s of the list/s of outstanding balances contained in the sales ledger/s. They will not, however, show whether or not a transaction has been posted to the correct account within the ledger.

9.5 Collection of overdue debts

Obtaining payment from debtors could be assisted by:

- setting credit limits.
- well published payment terms printed on contracts/invoices/statements.
- timely presentation of invoices, statements and credit notes.
- reminder letters.
- phone calls and personal visits, to find out the reasons for non-payment.
- aged analysis of debts/ratio analysis.
- debt collection agencies, but this could damage goodwill.
- legal proceedings (own legal department or solicitor).
- cash discounts for prompt payment.

9.6 Bankruptcy and Insolvency

It is important that you are aware of the broad effects of these.

9.7 The role of audit

Debtors do represent a significant investment. Auditors have to ensure that they are fully and accurately disclosed and ensure that systems of internal control and internal check are working to their satisfaction in order to avoid / prevent errors and fraud.

Auditors need to: (V-E-R-E-C)

Verify the existence, ownership and basis of valuation of the debtors and see that the provision for bad debts is fair and reasonable.

Examine vouchers eg, copy invoices, credit notes, delivery notes, orders, contracts etc, to ensure that transactions are genuine.

Report whether the accounts give a true and fair view.

Enquire in order to confirm or allay suspicions eg, who has the authority to issue credit notes?

Check the arithmetic accuracy of the books.

In looking at systems of internal control and internal check the auditor needs to ensure that the delegated authority is being adhere to. This should help to ensure that fraud can only take place via collusion.

10 SELF TEST QUESTIONS

10.1 What administrative costs are likely to be incurred in managing the credit control function? (1.1)

10.2 How can the credit system be monitored? (1.2)

10.3 What is the purpose of producing an aged analysis of debts? (2.2)

10.4 Describe briefly what an aged analysis of debts would look like. (2.3)

10.5 Which figures are used to construct a sales ledger control account? (4.7)

10.6 Which errors will not be disclosed by a sales ledger control account? (4.7)

10.8 Calculate the effective annual rate of interest where customers are given 2½% discount for settlement within 7 days, where the normal period of credit is 45 days. (5.2)

10.9 How can the work performed by an auditor help to manage and control debtors? (8.4)

AAT

AT FOULKS LYNCH

HOTLINES

Telephone: 0181 844 0667
Enquiries: 0181 831 9990
Fax: 0181 831 9991

AT FOULKS LYNCH LTD

Number 4, The Griffin Centre
Staines Road, Feltham
Middlesex TW14 0HS

Intended Examination Date: Dec 99 ☐ June 2000 ☐		Textbooks	Workbooks	Distance Learning UK MAINLAND ONLY
Foundation		* Combined textbook and workbook		
Unit 1	Cash Transactions	£9.95 ☐	£9.95 ☐	£85 ☐
Unit 2	Credit Transactions	£9.95 ☐	£9.95 ☐	£85 ☐
Unit 3	Payroll FA98	£9.95 ☐	£9.95 ☐	£85 ☐
Unit 19	Data Processing	£9.95 ☐*		£85 ☐
Units 21 - 25	The Business Background	£9.95 ☐*		£40 ☐
Foundation Level Distance Learning Course				£360 ☐
Intermediate				
Unit 4	Financial Records & Preparing Accounts	£9.95 ☐	£9.95 ☐	£95 ☐
Unit 5	Recording Cost Information	£9.95 ☐	£9.95 ☐	£95 ☐
Unit 6	Preparing Reports and Returns	£9.95 ☐	£9.95 ☐	£95 ☐
Unit 20	Using Information Technology	£9.95 ☐*		£95 ☐
Unit 22	Health and Safety	£3.95 ☐*	** When any other AAT DLC is purchased	Option-FOC** ☐
Intermediate Level Distance Learning Course				£380 ☐
Technician	*Notes:* Units 7, 8 and 9 are compulsory. Students choose 1 out of Units 10, 11, 12, 13 (only 10 available) Students choose 3 out of Units 14, 15, 16, 17, 18			
Units 7, 8 & 15	Cost Management, Resource Allocation and Evaluating Activities	£9.95 ☐	£9.95 ☐	Please contact us regarding availability
Unit 9	Managing Accounting Systems	£9.95 ☐	£9.95 ☐	
Unit 10	Drafting Financial Statements	£9.95 ☐	£9.95 ☐	
Unit 14	Cash Management and Credit Control	£9.95 ☐	£9.95 ☐	
Unit 16	Implementing Auditing Procedures	£9.95 ☐	£9.95 ☐	
Units 17 & 18	Business and Personal Taxation	£9.95 ☐	£9.95 ☐	
Technician Level Distance Learning Course (See notes above)				
P & P + Delivery	UK Mainland	£2.00/book	£2.00/book	Post Free
	NI, ROI & EU Countries	£5.00/book	£5.00/book	UK Mainland Only
	Rest of world standard air service	£10.00/book	£10.00/book	
	Rest of world courier service (tel number essential)	£22.00/book	£22.00/book	

SINGLE ITEM SUPPLEMENT: If you only order 1 item, INCREASE postage costs by £2.50 for UK, NI & EU Countries or by £15.00 for Rest of World Service

TOTAL				
	Sub Total £			
	Less 23% tax relief for Distance Learning paid for by student only £			
	Post & Packing £			
	Total £			

Payments in Sterling in London | **Order Total** £

DELIVERY DETAILS

☐ Mr ☐ Miss ☐ Mrs ☐ Ms Other

Initials Surname

Address

Postcode

Telephone Deliver to home ☐

Company name

Address

Postcode

Telephone Fax

Monthly report to go to employer ☐ Deliver to work ☐

PAYMENT

1 I enclose Cheque/PO/Bankers Draft for £___________
Please make cheques payable to AT Foulks Lynch Ltd.

2 Charge Mastercard/Visa/Switch A/C No:

Valid from: Expiry Date:

Issue No: (Switch only)

Signature Date

DECLARATION

I agree to pay as indicated on this form and understand that AT Foulks Lynch Terms and Conditions apply (available on request). I understand that AT Foulks Lynch Ltd are not liable for non-delivery if the rest of world standard air service is used.

Signature Date

Please Allow:	
UK mainland	- 5-10 w/days
NI, ROI & EU Countries	- 1-3 weeks
Rest of world standard air service	- 6 weeks
Rest of world courier service	- 10 w/days

Notes: All delivery times subject to stock availability. Signature required on receipt (except rest of world standard air service). Please give both addresses for Distance Learning students where possible.

Form effective from June 99 *All details correct at time of printing* *Source: AATTXTJ99*